Culture and Difference

Critical Studies in Education and Culture Series

Media Education and the (Re)Production of Culture
David Sholle and Stan Denski

Critical Pedagogy: An Introduction
Barry Kanpol

Coming Out in College: The Struggle for a Queer Identity
Robert A. Rhoads

Education and the Postmodern Condition
Michael Peters, editor

Critical Multiculturalism: Uncommon Voices in a Common Struggle
Barry Kanpol and Peter McLaren, editors

Beyond Liberation and Excellence: Reconstructing the Public Discourse on
Education
David E. Purpel and Svi Shapiro

Schooling in a "Total Institution": Critical Perspectives on Prison Education
Howard S. Davidson, editor

Simulation, Spectacle, and the Ironies of Education Reform
Guy Senese with Ralph Page

Repositioning Feminism and Education: Perspectives on Educating for Social
Change
*Janice Jipson, Petra Munro, Susan Victor, Karen Froude Jones, and
Gretchen Freed-Rowland*

Culture, Politics, and Irish School Dropouts: Constructing Political Identities
G. Honor Fagan

Anti-Racism, Feminism, and Critical Approaches to Education
Roxana Ng, Pat Staton, and Joyce Scane

Beyond Comfort Zones in Multiculturalism: Confronting the Politics of Privilege
Sandra Jackson and José Solís, editors

CULTURE and DIFFERENCE

Critical Perspectives on the Bicultural Experience in the United States

EDITED BY
ANTONIA DARDER

Critical Studies in Education and Culture Series
Edited by Henry A. Giroux and Paulo Freire

BERGIN & GARVEY
Westport, Connecticut • London

Library of Congress Cataloging-in-Publication Data

Culture and difference : critical perspectives on the bicultural
    experience in the United States / edited by Antonia Darder.
        p.   cm.—(Critical studies in education and cultural series,
    ISSN 1064–8615)
    Includes bibliographical references and index.
        ISBN 0–89789–384–0 (alk. paper).—ISBN 0–89789–457–X (pbk. :
    alk. paper)
        1. Biculturalism—United States.   2. Pluralism (Social sciences)—
    United States.   3. United States—Race relations.   4. United
    States—Ethnic relations.   I. Darder, Antonia.   II. Series.
    E184.A1C85   1995
    306.4'46'0973—dc20   95–11211

British Library Cataloguing in Publication Data is available.

Library of Congress Catalog Card Number: 95–11211
ISBN: 0–89789–384–0
        0–89789–457–X (pbk.)
ISSN: 1064–8615

First published in 1995

Bergin & Garvey, 88 Post Road West, Westport, CT 06881
An imprint of Greenwood Publishing Group, Inc.

Printed in the United States of America

∞™

The paper used in this book complies with the
Permanent Paper Standard issued by the National
Information Standards Organization (Z39.48–1984).

10   9   8   7   6   5   4   3   2   1

In memory of Cesar Chavez,
whose life, with all its wisdom and frailties, continues to
exemplify the transgressions of a powerfully courageous
and spiritually committed human being.

Contents

Foreword

Henry A. Giroux

Increasingly, the fractured realities that constitute diverse cultural traditions and experiences have called into question the meaning of national identity, what it means to be an American, and how as educators we address the formation of new publics of difference as a defining principle of democratic society. For many of us, the tropes of border and borderland suggest a sense of flux, movement, and in-betweenness in which it becomes increasingly difficult for any singular notion of ethnicity, class, gender, or culture to "inhabit any claim to identity in [a] (post)modern world" (Bhabha, 1994, p. 15). Many conservatives and liberals see in the emerging claims to difference a threat to national identity and what it means to be an American. Difference in this context becomes transgressive because it infringes on the norms of the monocultural status quo and in doing so unsettles and calls into question the institutions, histories, languages, and social relationships that produce the process of "othering." What must be clear here is cultural differences that cannot be managed, assimilated, or incorporated as fashion and spectacle become dangerous because they offer the possibilities through language, social movements, and radical cultural work to challenge borders that are racist, sexist, hierarchical, and oppressive.

When cultural differences are not linked to primordial identities, they function as sites of complexity and dialogue, as identities formed in transit. It is precisely within such an in-between space that "social differences are at once a vision and a construction that takes you 'beyond' yourself in order to return, in a spirit of revision and reconstruction, to the political conditions of the present" (Bhabha, 1994, p. 16). What is significent about the relationship between politics and difference in this formulation is that questions of identity and community, inclusion and exclusion, voice and representations, exceed monolithically fixed categories of experience, identity, and voice. Experience and the politics of representation exist in an unsettling tension within critical discourses of differences. That is, while language always constructs and mediates the multiple experiences of identity by both historicizing it and revealing its partiality and incompleteness, its limits are realized in the material nature of experience as it marks the body through the specificity of place, space, and history. The cultural meanings that construct our identities are central to but do not fully register how specific experiences are felt, taken up, endured, registered, and lived out. As John Fiske (1994) reminds us:

> There is a material experience of homelessness that is of a different order from the cultural meanings of homelessness . . . but the boundary between the two cannot be drawn sharply. Material conditions are inescapably saturated with culture and, equally, cultural conditions are inescapably experienced as material (p. 13).

It is in the attempt to bring into theoretical and political balance questions concerning the construction of identity, the importance of the specificity of experience, and the essential need to understand cultural differences with structures of power within the existing social order that Antonia Darder's *Culture and Difference* makes a major contribution to the pedagogy and politics of cultural difference and identity.

For Darder and her co-authors, the politics of biculturalism must address not merely how cultural identities are constructed differently, but also how they are produced, sustained, and transformed within the structures of power at work in a deeply hierarchical and exploitive society. Within this discourse, there is a call to move beyond the mere celebration of ethnicity in order to provide the conditions for students and others to understand and negotiate differences, especially in relation to unequal structures of power.

In addition, as a strategy of engagement, the politics of biculturalism refuses to venerate theories of hybridity in which the specificity of experience, the corporeal nature of particular communities, and the particularities of langauge and belonging are erased in a relativistic notion of identity. Identity may be open but it cannot be understood exclusively through discursive constructions that erase how cultural differences are marked traces of history, place, and shifting, but specifically felt experience. But the call to recognize the importance of experience as a register of identity is not meant by Darder and her co-authors to reassert the theoretical trappings of essentialism. In fact, anti-essentialism only becomes meaningful in this discourse in positing a view of cultural experience that is nuanced, anti-assimilationist, and lived out through a self-conscious presentation and recognition of its strengths and partiality while simultaneously acknowledging that cultural and political authority cannot rest on claims to transhistorical and allegedly transparent personal testimonies.

Finally, *Culture and Difference* reinvents the transgressive politics of cultural difference by developing an energized and active idea of the public.

References to the broader context of political and social life are always at work in defining the multiple issues taken up in this book. Pedagogy and politics intersect in addressing multiple sites of learning where cultural differences point to the possibilities of deepening and expanding democratic public life. Issues regarding how we engage, negotiate, and construct differences are consistently addressed through a language in which values, ethics, and social responsibility are reworked to rewrite the related notions of belonging, social justice, and democratric community. In many ways, Darder and her co-contributors have provided new maps of meaning for educators, students, and others to address the complexities and possibilities at work in living with cultural differences through new ethical and pedagogical frameworks. Within this critical perspective, the pluralization of identities and cultural differences are defended not through a nostalgic or essentialist appeal to personal testimony or authentic places of origin but in reference to how difference and uncertainty can be addressed and affirmed within a new language of cultural and political community.

REFERENCES

Bhabha, Homi K. (1994). "Beyond the Pale: Art in the Age of Multicultural Translation." *Kunst and Museum Journal*, 5(4), p. 15.

Fiske, John. (1994). *Power Plays, Power Works*. London: Verso Press.

Acknowledgments

They say that writing is a lonely task, done in isolation and in the solitary corners of our existence. This is what makes it so painful for so many of us who are most happy when we are in the company of others—when we feel the essence of life being exchanged through human touch, the shine of smiling eyes, the sound of belly laughs. What keeps many of us going is a deep, burning commitment to struggle in the intellectual and political domain, so that a place for such freedom of life can exist. What allows us to return to the writing are the moments that we share with the people we love and who love us unconditionally . . . warts and all . . . all with whom we walk and make our paths.

At this moment, I would like to fully acknowledge the support, appreciation, and caring that I receive from my community of cultural workers, my friends, and my family. A special thanks to all my colleagues at CGS for their patience and good will, which successfully got me through the tenure process. To all the contributors to this book, whose work and life represent beautiful examples of "organic intellectuals." To Henry Giroux and Lynn Flint at Bergin & Garvey for making a place for this book. To Teresa Wilborn for all her assistance and patience in the preparation of this manuscript. To Peter McLaren for his kind support of my scholarship. To my comrade and political soulmate, Rudy Torres, for his very unique contribution to my critical understanding of the world and his assistance in the completion of this book. To my students, David, Gina, Alexandro, Marta, Garrett, Sue, Daniel, Rene, Lalo, Barbara, Patricia, Evangelina, Veronica, Caron, Denise, Tryphenia, Lawson, Paul, and the rest, who always challenge me to walk my talk—thank you! To Ernie Salcedo, David Diaz, Serafin Espinoza, Nicholas Rodriguez, Makungu Akinyela, Arturo Lemus, Edmundo Norte, Javier Pacheco, Eugene Pickett, Jr.,

Jeff Furman, Bill Gallegos, Phaizon Wood, Rafael Rivera, Jim Hight, and Jose La Luz, for their enduring friendship and support. To Maria Elena Gaitan, Adel Sartin, Connie Hurston, Lourdes Arguelles, Patricia Jimenez, Patty Watson, Sally Peña, Jai Lee Wong, Daryl Smith, Angela Paige, Melinda Garcia, Kim Recendiz, and Patti Capauldi, who keep both their minds and heart channels ever open to me, no matter what. To my wonderful sister, Mirna, who shares her tenacity for life with me. To my children, Gabriel, Christy, and Kelly Flores, for the never-ending love and generosity they extend to their *Mami*. And to my mother, Carmen Francisca Rodriguez, for her *arroz con pollo, pasteles, y corazon Puertorriqueño*.

Culture and Difference

Culture and Difference

Introduction

The Politics of Biculturalism: Culture and Difference in the Formation of *Warriors for Gringostroika* and *The New Mestizas*

Antonia Darder

There is a whisper within you that reminds me of who I am. . . .
—Guillermo Gomez-Peña (1993)

The dormant areas of consciousness are being activated, awakened.
—Gloria Anzaldúa (1987)

The yearning to remember who we are is a subject that is rarely discussed in the realms of traditional academic discourse. It is not easily measured or observed by the standard quantification of scientific inquiry, or is it easily detected in the qualitative dimensions of focus groups and ethnographic research methods. It is a deeply-rooted quality, obscured by layers upon layers of human efforts to survive the impact of historical amnesia induced by the dominant policies and practices of advanced capitalism and postmodern culture.

For these reasons, efforts to articulate a conclusive politics of biculturalism is a highly complex and messy endeavor. Yet it is significant to note that even the naming of such a phenomenon clearly is linked to an experience of listening to "the whisper within" and giving voice to an unspoken, yet ever-present memory of difference—"dormant areas of consciousness" that must be awakened. This view is readily supported by the fact that despite countless studies and writings about people of color by white researchers, none name or engage the experience of two-worldness or double consciousness. It was not until scholars of color, such as Du Bois (1903), Fanon (1952), Valentine (1971), Ramirez & Castañeda (1974), Solis (1980), Rashid (1981), Redhorse (1981), de Anda (1984), Buriel (1984), and others began to posit specific theoretical frameworks grounded in their own community histories and cultural knowledge that notions of biculturalism began to appear in the discourse of the social sciences and historical studies. These scholars of color during the last thirty years have made significant contributions to an understanding of biculturalism. As a consequence, there has been a slowly, but consistently, emerging body of work that has attempted to give voice to a variety of explanations of bicultural processes and identities. These efforts, to a greater or lesser degree, have discussed the societal and psychological impact of living between two world views. In more recent years, a new wave of critical scholars of color (Darder, 1991; Akinyela, 1992; Millán, 1993; and Romay, 1993) in different disciplines have also begun to address the notion of biculturalism in their work.

TOWARD A CRITICAL THEORY OF BICULTURALISM

> The story never stops beginning or ending. It appears headless and bottomless for it is built on differences (p. 2).
>
> —Trinh Minh-ha (1989)

Within a critical theoretical tradition, biculturalism must be understood as a contested terrain of difference. It is upon this highly complex and ambiguous ground that subordinate groups create both a private and public space in which to forge battle with the faces of oppression, while flying high their banners of cultural self-determination. Biculturalism as a critical perspective acknowledges openly and engages forthrightly the significance of power relations in structuring and prescribing societal definitions of truth, rules of normalcy, and notions of legitimacy which often defy and denigrate the cultural existence and lived experiences of subordinate groups.

The story of where, when, and how biculturation processes and identities begin, move, and end is generally a difficult one to recount, given the historical and contextual dimensions which shape the particular survival requirements of different groups at any given moment in their histories. This is to say that each subordinate group grapples with the effects of cultural imperialism according to the manner in which geographical, political, social, and economic forces shape and influence the efforts of members of a group to resist, oppose, negotiate, or even accept passive or voluntary assimilation into the dominant group.

Further, given the wide-reaching effects of advanced capitalism and a deeply rooted tradition of cultural oppression and domination in the United States, African Americans, Chicanos, Puerto Ricans, Native Americans, Asians, and other subordinate cultural groups for the most part exist in a hybridized state. This is to say that their histories of forced interaction with the dominant culture have required consistent forms of adaptional behaviors which have, in many instances, eroded, restructured, and reconstructed the language system, cultural beliefs, and social traditions of these groups.

Michael Omi and Howard Winant (1983a) argue that throughout most of the history of the United States, the discourses of subordinate cultures received very little political legitimacy. "However democratic the United States may have been in other respects, with respect to racial [and cultural] minorities it may be characterized as having been to varying degrees despotic for much of its history" (p. 55). Given a collective history of social marginalization, exploitation, cultural invasion, powerlessness, and systematic violence,[1] all subordinate cultures in this country currently experience an advanced state of hybridization. Understanding this phenomenon requires that we acknowledge the deep historical consequences of being driven out of the dominant political space and relegated to a subordinate position. Black, indigenous, and mestizo communities across the United States evolved over the last four hundred years through their efforts to survive conditions of oppression, develop alternative structures, and resist annihilation of cultural knowledge and traditions.[2]

It cannot be denied that patterns of cultural, economic, and political oppression have been repeated in the international arena wherever European colonizers and their descendants have appropriated the land and resources of indigenous populations. Usurping the people's natural resources, destroying their economic and agricultural self-sufficiency, placing the children in foreign educational environments, devaluing the language community, and interfering with the generational transmission of spiritual knowledge are all common strategies of cultural imperialism. As such, every subordinate cultural group in the United States, to one extent or another, has been required to contend with the destructive impact of all or some of these strategies. Most insidious are the established relationships of domination and dependency which, despite ongoing and persistent group efforts to resist cultural oppression, further complicate the struggle to affirm the cultural integrity and self-determination of subordinate cultural groups.

RETHINKING ETHNICITY AND THE FORMATION OF IDENTITY

> We will not remain the same. Either we re-make ourselves or we will be remade by others (p. 24).
>
> —Gonzalo Santos (1992)

In many respects, biculturalism entails an ongoing process of identity recovery, construction, and reconstruction driven by collective efforts of subordinate cultural groups to build community solidarity, engage tensions surrounding nationality differences, revitalize the boundaries of subordinate cultures, and redefine the meaning of cultural identity within the current social context (Nagel, 1994). Further, this phenomenon is influenced by the persistent efforts of those who have been historically marginalized to establish a sense of place from which to struggle against relations of domination. Along the same lines, Stuart Hall (1990a) argues that a notion of ethnicity is required in order to truly engage the relationship between identity and difference.

There is no way, it seems to me, in which people of the world can act, can speak, can create, can come in from the margins and talk, can begin to reflect on their own experience unless they come from some place, they come from some history, they inherit certain cultural traditions. What we've learned about the theory of enunciation is that there's no enunciation without positionality. You have to position yourself some-where in order to say anything at all . . . the relation that peoples of the world now have to their own past is, of course, part of the discovery of their own ethnicity. They need to honor the hidden histories from which they come. They need to understand the languages which they've been taught not to speak. They need to understand and revalue the traditions and inheritances of cultural expression and creativity. And in that sense, the past is not only a position from which to speak, but it is also an abso-lutely necessary resource in what one has to say (p. 19).

Hall's use of the term *ethnicity* provides us with a framework upon which to rethink the analytical value of ethnicity with respect to biculturalism, par-ticularly as it relates to identity formation. This requires a dialectical reading of ethnicity[3] that, first of all, retrieves the category from the political oppor-tunism and academic domain of neo-conservatives, and secondly, challenges the failure of critical scholars to conceptualize the liberatory dimensions of this category in more fully class-specific terms. Thus, a critical definition of ethnicity is one that engages, in both concept and articulation, a politics of difference and class specificity within the context of a changing economy and postmodern world.

ON ESSENTIALISM

I can voice my ideas without hesitation or fear because I am speaking, finally, about myself (p. 189).

—June Jordon (1992)

In conventional critical debates about culture, there is generally a tremen-dous uneasiness when there is any effort made to seriously explore notions of cultural consciousness and the merits of knowledge that is rooted in the lived cultural experience of marginalized communities.[4] Often this uneasiness seems to stem most directly from an overarching commitment to protect Western assumptions of individualism, objectivity, and universal truth which decep-tively conceal institutionalized structures of entitlement and privilege embed-ded in critiques of identity politics that, intentionally or unintentionally, function as "the new chic way to silence . . . marginal groups" (hooks, 1994, p. 83). And though it is true that cultural groups are not entities that exist apart from individuals, neither are they just arbitrary classifications of individuals by attributes which are external to or accidental to their cultural identities.

Group meanings partially constitute people's identities in terms of the cultural forms, social situations, and history that group members know as theirs, because their meanings have been either forced upon them or forged by them or both. Groups are real not as substances, but as forms of social relations. . . . A person's sense of history, affinity, and separateness, even the person's mode of reasoning, evaluation, and expressing feelings, are constituted partly by her or his group affinities (Young, 1990, pp. 44–45).

Along with the traditional academic anxiety over obliterating the individual as subject are the overzealous denouncements of essentialism whenever scholars of color attempt to grapple with those actual experiences of cultural identity rooted in social and material conditions of racialized relations— experiences that, more often than not, reinforce a strong sense of cultural consciousness and solidarity among members of subordinate cultural communities. There is an expectation that they abdicate the power of their experience, without concern for the fact that "only the powerful can insist on a neat separation between the thought and reality . . . a separation that serves them well" (Sampson, 1993, p. 1227).

It is not surprising then to note that often critiques of essentialism embody the mistaken dichotomous notion that inquiry focused on subordinate life experiences automatically precludes recognition of in-group differences and cultural change, and amounts to nothing more than the act of reducing culture to a theory of reifying collectivity. As a consequence, scholars of color whose research engages cultural questions in their own communities are often marginalized by the "enlightened" mainstream of their disciplines, while those who are deemed more "open-minded" by Eurocentric standards are permitted to play freely in the arena of intellectual thought.

At this point, it is imperative to stress that I am not suggesting that subjective interpretations of lived experience alone can suffice in the struggle to overcome and transform structural conditions of domination, whether in theory or practice. And further, it cannot be denied that claims to exclusive "authority" derived solely from lived experience can be misused to silence and undermine the possibility of dialogue. Yet, despite these possible dangers, we must find the manner to incorporate in our intellectual work those ways of knowing that are rooted in experience. Hooks (1994) addresses eloquently this idea in the following passage from her essay *Essentialism and Experience.*

Though opposed to any essentialist practice that constructs identity in a monolithic, exclusionary way, I do not want to relinquish the power of experience as a standpoint on which to base analysis or formulate theory. For example, I am disturbed when all the courses in black history or literature at some colleges and universities are solely taught by white people, not because I think that they cannot know these realities but that they know them differently. Truthfully, if I had been given the opportunity to study African American critical thought from a progressive black professor instead of the progressive white woman with whom I studied . . . I would have chosen the black person. Although I learned a great deal from this white woman professor, I sincerely believe that I would have learned even more from a progressive black professor, because this individual would have brought to the class that unique mixture of experiential and analytical ways of knowing—this is, a privileged standpoint. It cannot be acquired through books or even distanced observation and study of a particular reality. To me this privileged standpoint does not emerge from "the authority of experience" but rather from the passion of experience, the passion of remembrance (p. 90).

CULTURAL CONSCIOUSNESS AND DECOLONIZATION

> Whereas the colonized usually has only a choice between retraction of his being and a frenzied attempt at identification with the colonizer, the [decolonized] has brought into existence a new, positive, efficient personality, whose richness is provided . . . by his certainty that he embodies a decisive moment of [cultural] consciousness (p. 103).
>
> —Frantz Fanon (1964)

It is impossible to arrive at an emancipatory politics of biculturalism without questions of cultural consciousness and knowledge derived from lived experience receiving a rightful place within critical discourses on culture and difference. Likewise, the reality of subordinate groups cannot be sufficiently grasped without a foundational understanding of culture as an epistemological process that is shaped by a complex dialectical relationship of social systems of beliefs and practices which constantly moves members between the dynamic tension of cultural preservation and cultural change. This is to say that no culture (particularly within the Western postmodern context of advanced capitalism) exists as a fixed, static, or absolute entity, since culture, and hence cultural identity, is a relationally constituted phenomenon, activated and produced through constant social negotiation between others and one's own integration in the daily life and history of the community (Epstein, 1987). "It is something that happens over time, that is never absolutely stable, that is subject to the play of history and the play of difference" (Hall, 1990a, p. 15).

Nevertheless, forms of cultural consciousness, grounded in collective memories of historical events, language, social traditions, and community life, exist. This collective experience of affinity that emerges from such forms of cultural knowledge is often echoed in historical discursive accounts of African Americans, Latinos, Native Americans, and Asian Americans in this country. For example, it is not unusual for a person who identifies ethnically with the Latin

American cultural experience to readily discuss the differences in affinity experienced when immersed within a Spanish-speaking versus an English-speaking context. This experience of affinity is a powerful connecting and perpetuating force in the lives of members of subordinate cultural groups—a force so strong that it continues to play a significant role in supporting a politics of identity, resistance, self-determination, and cultural nationalism among members of historically disenfranchised cultural communities worldwide.

In light of this, it is no wonder that all strategies of colonial oppression, to one extent or another, function to interfere with cultural community beliefs and practices that foster cultural integrity and cohesion among colonized subjects (Fanon, 1964). This process of cultural subjugation continues within the current so-called post-colonial era. This is readily evident in a multitude of economic, political, legal, educational, and religious institutional policies and practices in the United States aimed at furthering the assimilation process of subordinate groups. More specifically, we see it at work today in the forging of trade agreements that solidify the labor market's exploitation of workers of color, English-only initiatives to interfere with the advancement of bilingualism, covert and overt educational strategies that support cultural domination, laws to prevent particular religious activities of groups who exist outside Judeo-Christian traditions, the current inflammatory politics of immigration control as evidenced in California's passage of Proposition 187, and the worldwide commodification of subordinate cultural forms as multinational profit ventures.

There can be no question that biculturalism in the United States has evolved from a set of conscious and unconscious adaptational strategies to preserve significant dimensions of cultural knowledge and collective identity, adapt to changing material conditions, and resist institutional forms of psychological and physical violence (Young, 1991). In many respects, the bicultural process reflects what Frantz Fanon (1963) describes as a process of decolonization where "the meeting of two forces, opposed to each other by their very nature, which in fact owe their originality to the sort of substantiation which results from and is nourished by [the political and economic context of domination]." Biculturalism can then best be understood as incorporating the complex multilayered realities that shape a people's cultural and material struggle for survival. It is a phenomenon that "is born of violent struggle, consciousness raising, and the reconstruction of identities" (West, 1993, p. 15), and one that is most intensely felt within those subordinate cultural contexts that most greatly differ from the established social beliefs, expectations, and norms of the dominant group. As such, subordinate communities continue to be stigmatized by both external and internalized perceptions of inferiority and deficit, whereby their members are, for the most part, viewed as inadequately prepared or socially unfit to enter mainstream American life.

GROWING POVERTY AND THE EVASION OF CLASS

> [P]olitical [economic] questions are disguised as cultural ones, and as such be-
> come insoluble (p. 149).
>
> —Antonio Gramsci (1971)

At this juncture, it must be stressed that the dominant culture and its fabrication of the American middle-class mainstream is clearly driven by the
political economy of advanced capitalism, with its overwhelming emphasis on
the interests of the marketplace and its "tendency to homogenize rather than
diversify human experience" (Wood, 1994, p. 28). Even more important is the
recognition that postmodern mechanisms of cultural domination in the United
States and abroad are most directly linked to the domination of multinational
firms and new international divisions of labor. The impact of these rapidly
changing and deepening economic and class relations serves to perpetuate the
embroilment of subordinate cultural communities in a fierce struggle for economic survival with fewer and fewer possibilities of self-sufficiency. And despite the growing number of professionals of color and the glossy image
portrayal of their success, the majority of American institutions, with their
accompanying resources, continue to be overwhelmingly controlled by a cadre
of elite white males who are, slowly but steadily, being joined by their female
counterparts. The consequences have resulted in an actual decrease in the
proportional wealth and resources of communities of color over the last thirty
years (Children's Defense Fund, 1994).[5] This widening economic gap is directly linked to what Xavier Gorostiaga (1993) characterizes as the "dominant
fact of our age—growing poverty" (p. 4). In his analysis of a 1992 United
Nations report, he explains:

[T]hroughout the world the last decade has been characterized by the rise of inequality
between the rich and the poor. . . . In 1989 the richest fifth controlled 82.7 percent of
the revenue; 81.2 percent of the world trade; 94.6 percent of commercial loans; 80.6
percent of internal savings and 80.5 percent of investment. If in terms of distribution
the panorama is untenable, it is equally so regarding resources: The rich countries
possess approximately one-fifth of the world population but consume seventy percent
of world energy, seventy-five percent of the metals, eighty-five percent of the timber,
and sixty percent of the food. Such a pattern of development . . . is only viable in the
degree to which the extreme inequality is maintained, as otherwise the world resources
would be exhausted. Therefore, *inequality is not a distortion of the system. It is a
systematic prerequisite for growth and permanence of the present system* (p. 4, author's
emphasis).

It is the tendency to ignore or overlook this "systematic prerequisite" of
capitalism in discussions of culture, difference, and identity politics in the
United States that motivates Ellen Meiksins Wood (1994) to question why

"having recognized the complexities, diversities, and multiple oppressions in the so-called postmodern world, we can't also recognize that capitalism is not only dominant but massively present in every aspect of our lives and in all our 'identities' " (p. 28). Wood's critique rightfully challenges class-blind notions of cultural identity and argues that identity politics decontextualized from material conditions only limit and narrow the impact of such discourse upon the deep structures of economic inequality. Further, the absence of class discourse in the politics of marginalized communities in no way lessens the exigencies of class struggle. In fact, "since the discourse of justice is intimately tied to class, ethnicity, race, and gender, the absence of one of its most salient components—class" (Aronowitz, 1992, p. 59) foredooms the transcultural solidarity required to effectively address the plight of economically dispossessed people, not only in this country but around the world. Stanley Aronowitz (1992), in his writings on working-class identity,[6] sheds light on this issue.

The American evasion of class is not universal. We have no trouble speaking of ourselves as a "middle class" society or, indeed, endowing the economically and politically powerful with the rights and privileges of rule. American ideology identifies the middle class with power and, in its global reach, has attempted to incorporate manual workers into this family. The anomaly of the large and growing working poor, some of whom are hungry, others homeless and, indeed, the increasing insecurity suffered not only by industrial workers but also professional and clerical employees in the service sector, make some uneasy but have, until recently, failed to faze the ongoing celebration. Or, to be more accurate, class issues are given other names: crime, especially drugs; teenage pregnancy and suicide; homelessness and hunger; chronic "regional" unemployment that is grasped as an exception to an otherwise healthy national economy (p. 71).

THE MEDIA AND IDEOLOGICAL DISTORTIONS OF DIFFERENCE

> Mass media in the United States exploit . . . representations of race and racialized contact in various ways daily: angry black folks doing violence, somebody— usually a young black man—dying (p. 173).
>
> —bell hooks (1990)

It is impossible to fully grasp the social formation of ideological distortions about class, "race," and gender in the postmodern world if we ignore the overwhelming impact of today's accelerated media and communications technology. Through its captivating influence on "mental production" and its false presentation of democratic cultural differentiation, the media increasingly gives shape to new forms of postmodern repression while sustaining common-sense approval for its capitalist representations. Within the structured relationships between the media and the ideas it extends forth to the public, its ideological function is deceptively concealed. Hall and his colleagues (1978) explain this relationship in terms of Marx's basic proposal that "the ruling ideas of any age are the ideas of its ruling class."

> [The] dominance of the "ruling idea" operates primarily because, in addition to its ownership and control of the means of production, this class also owns and controls the means of "mental production." In producing their definition of social reality and the place of "ordinary people" within it, they construct a particular image of society which represents particular class interests of all members of society; this class's definition of the social world provides the basic rationale for those institutions which protect and reproduce their "way of life." This control of mental resources ensures that theirs are the most powerful and "universal" of the available definitions of the social world. Their universality ensures that they are shared to some degree by the subordinate classes [and cultures] of the society (p. 59).

The media, with its highly centralized and almost monolithic structure, provides an essential link between the ruling ideology of the dominant culture and the society at large (Winston, 1982). In a society such as the United States where most of the people do not have any direct access to nor power over the bulk of decisions that affect their lives, the media plays a powerful legitimating role in the social production of mass consensus. And although it may be argued that the power of the media is not absolute, in that there frequently exist counter-ideologies and definitions which challenge its legitimacy by way of dissident voices,

> many emergent counter-definers however have no access to the defining process at all . . . [for] if they do not play within the rules of the game, counter-spokesmen [sic] run the risk of being defined out of the debate (because they have broken the rules of reasonable opposition). . . . Groups which have not secured even this limited measure of access are regularly and systematically stigmatized, in their absence, as "extreme," their actions systematically deauthenticated by being labelled as "irrational" (Hall et al., 1978, p. 64).

OPPOSITIONAL CONSCIOUSNESS

> This means locating the structural causes of unnecessary forms of social misery, depicting the plight and predicaments of demoralized and depoliticized citizens caught in market-driven cycles of therapeutic release . . . and projecting alternative visions, analyses, and actions that proceed from particularities and arrive at moral and political connectedness (p. 35).
> —Cornel West (1992)

It is against such a backdrop of societal contradictions and mainstream cultural complexities that subordinate cultural groups must endeavor to rethink past strategies for cultural survival that now prove ineffective and to discover new ground upon which to carry out political projects of resistance and negotiation. This also includes the need to forge a new consciousness of opposition, in light of assimilationist postmodern rhetoric and right-wing conservative backlash.[7]

In the face of wide social and economic inequalities, biculturalism as a political construct must move beyond simple notions of individual psychological theories of identity, liberal paradigms of pluralism, and unproblematic notions of two distinct cultural world views interacting. Instead a genealogy of biculturalism must be theoretically grounded in the historical intricacies of social formations that emerge from the collision between dominant/subordinate cultural, political, and economic relations of power which function to determine the limits and boundaries of institutional life in this country. Given the hegemonic nature of American institutions, marginalized communities must develop the ability to negotiate and navigate through the current social complexities and co-opting nature of postmodern conditions of cultural domination. This requires a mode of oppositional consciousness that depends on the ability to read actual situations of power and to choose and adopt tactics of resistance that are best suited to push against the different forms of power configurations that shape actual experiences of injustice and inequality. Chela Sandoval (1991), in her work on U.S. Third World feminism and oppositional consciousness, describes this as a "differential mode of oppositional consciousness" which provides members of subordinate groups with

enough strength to confidently commit to a well-defined structure of identity . . . enough flexibility to self-consciously transform that identity according to the requisites of another oppositional ideological tactic, if readings of power's formation require it; enough grace to recognize alliances with others committed to egalitarian social relations and race, gender, and class justice, when their readings of power call for alternative oppositional stands (p. 15).

In historical struggles against cultural oppression, bicultural communities have oftentimes joined together, albeit not always smoothly or easily, to oppose practices of social injustice directed against those groups in the United States who have been perceived consistently as unentitled to a rightful place within the mainstream. These coalitions and movement organizations have generally been primarily founded upon bicultural affinities of struggle rooted in the shared historical opposition of African Americans, Latinos, Asians, and Native Americans to cultural, class, and gender subordination. As the "nature" of postmodern social oppression presents itself in a more highly sophisticated, differentiated, and confusing manner, there is a greater necessity for members of subordinate groups to incorporate a differential mode of oppositional consciousness in order to build expanding alliances of struggle. Such alliances can serve as vehicles by which to more effectively identify and challenge actual relations of power at work and to select more effective modes of intervention that are directed toward actualizing an alternative vision of both institutional and community life.

RACIALIZATION AND NOTIONS OF DIFFERENCE

[W]here cultural difference is represented as natural and immutable, then it has all the qualities signified by the notion of biological difference, with the result that the distinction between racism and nationalism seems to have been dissolved (p. 100).

—Robert Miles (1993)

As discussed earlier, expressions of bicultural affinity among members of subordinate cultural groups are generally linked to experiences of difference and the role that difference plays in the social construction of both dominant and subordinate attitudes, beliefs, and practices in the United States. This is particularly at play when both dominant and subordinate groups struggle to challenge racism and the problematic inherent in notions of "race relations;" for the manner in which these notions are commonly used, more often than not, implies "an acceptance of the existence of biological differences between human beings, differences which express the existence of distinct, self-producing groups" (Miles, 1993, p. 2). Robert Miles (1993), in his most recent book, *Racism After Race Relations*, challenges this racialization of groups by arguing that all forms of racism "are always mediated by and through other structures and social relations, the most important of which are class relations and the political reality of the nation state" (pp. 12–13). Therefore as relations of economic domination intensify worldwide, subordinate cultural groups must not fall into the trap of defining cultural differences as a "race problem" or a "race struggle." Instead what must be confronted is

the problem of racism, a problem which requires us to map and explain a particular instance of exclusion, simultaneously in its specificity and in its articulation with a multiplicity of other forms of exclusion. Hence, we can now confront the fundamental issues concerning the character and consequences of inequality reproduced by and in contemporary capitalist social formations, freed from a paradigm which finds an explanation for that inequality within the alleged "nature" of supposedly discrete populations rather than within historical and so humanly constituted social relations (Miles, 1993, p. 23).

From this vantage point, we must also understand notions of "race identity and difference" as politically formed rather than embedded in the color of the skin or a given nature (Hall, 1990a, 1990b). In other words, to identify as Black or Chicano is not so much a question of color as it is a question of cultural, historical, and political differences. Hence, to conceptualize accurately the social construction of bicultural identity formation requires an understanding of the process of racialization. In other words, the theoretical foundation of a politics of biculturalism challenges the "common sense" discourse of "race" and problematizes its utility as an analytical category. This summons a bold analytical transition from the politics of "race" to recognizing the centrality of racism and racialization in the interpretation of exclusionary practices.

LIFE ON THE BORDER

> The prohibited and forbidden are its inhabitants. Los atravesados live here: The squint-eyed, the perverse, the queer, the troublesome, the mongrel, the mulatto, the half-breed; in short, those who cross over, pass over, or go through the confines of the "normal" (p. 3).
>
> —Gloria Anzaldúa (1987)

The transcultural dimensions of biculturalism must then be situated within a continually changing process of cultural identity formation, as much as within complex human negotiations for social and material survival. The place where these processes and negotiations evolve and shift, construct and reconstruct, is what Homi Bhabha (1990) terms "the third space." It is also in his discussions of the third space that Bhabha engages the "process of hybridity." Hybridity here does not represent a relativist notion of culture, but instead challenges the global structures of domination which shape the lives of subordinate groups and creates a space for new formations of cultural identity to take hold. "This process of hybridity gives rise to something different, something new and unrecognizable, a new area of negotiation of meaning and representation" (p. 211).

It is then this "process of hybridity" that constitutes one of the central characteristic of border existence where the border itself becomes a political terrain of struggle and self-determination. Lawrence Grossberg (1993) expounds on the nature of this "in-between" place by engaging the work of Gloria Anzaldúa, *Borderlands/La Frontera: The New Mestiza.*

Here the subaltern are different from the identities on either side of the border, but they are not simply the fragments of both. The subaltern exists as different from either alternative in the place between colonizer and the (imagined) precolonial subject or, in Gloria Anzaldúa's borderland, between the Mexican and the American: "A borderland is a vague and undetermined place created by the emotional residue of an unnatural boundary. . . . People who inhabit both realities . . . are forced to live in the interface between the two." . . . Anzaldua describes the third space as "a shock culture, a border culture, a third culture, a closed country" (p. 97).

In the safety of the "third space," notions of bicultural identity are constructed, deconstructed, and reconstructed anew, all while negotiating the

tension of ongoing interactions with social and material conditions of subordination. This suggests "a form of border crossing which signals forms of transgression in which existing borders forged in domination can be challenged
and redefined" (Giroux, 1992, p. 28). In short it is a "transborder" experience
of identity that "is involved in constantly struggling to emerge from the bottom-up" (Santos, 1992, p. 16).

In many respects at its very core, this "bottom-up" act of challenging and
redefining reflects an effective strategy of cultural survival that Trinh Minh-
ha (1992) terms "displacing."

Displacing is a way of surviving. It is an impossible truthful story of living in-between
regimens of truth. The responsibility involved in this motley in-between living is a
highly creative one; the displacer proceeds by increasingly introducing difference into
repetition. By questioning over and over again what is taken for granted as self-evident,
by reminding oneself and the others of the unchangeability of change itself. Disturbing
thereby one's own thinking habits, dissipating what has become familiar and cliched,
and participating in the changing of received values—the transformation (without master) of the selves through one's self. . . . Strategies of displacement defy the world of
compartmentalization and the system of dependence it engenders, while filling the
shifting space of creation with a passion named wonder (pp. 332–333).

The meaning and complexity of this culture of hybridity, transgressing nature, and bottom-up displacement that shapes and enlivens a critical politics
of biculturalism is fiercely echoed in the border culture manifesto of Guillermo
Gomez-Peña's *Warrior for Gringostroika*.

Border culture means boycott, complot, ilegalidad, clandestinidad, contrabando, trans-
gresión, desobediencia, binacional; en otros [sic] palabras, to smuggle dangerous poetry
and utopian visions from one culture to another, desde alla, hasta aca. But it also means
to maintain one's dignity outside the law. But it also means hybrid art forms for new
content-in-gestation . . . to be fluid in English, Spanish, Spanlish, and Ingeñol, 'cause
Spanglish is the language of border diplomacy. . . . But is [sic] also means transcultural
friendships and collaborations among races, sexes, and generations. But it also means
to practice creative appropriation, expropriation, and subversion of dominant cultural
forms . . . a multiplicity of voices away from the center . . . to return and depart once
again . . . a new terminology for new hybrid identities (p. 43).

BICULTURAL RE-PRESENTATIONS AND A SOLIDARITY OF DIFFERENCE

The incidious colonial tendencies we have internalized—and that express themselves in sadistic competition for money and attention, political cannibalism, and

moral distrust—must be overcome. We must realize that we are not each other's enemies and that the true enemy is currently enjoying our divisiveness (p. 62).
—Guillermo Gomez-Peña (1993)

The bicultural re-presentations of Gomez-Peña and Anzaldúa, as the *warrior of gringostroika* and the *new mestiza,* unmistakably emerge from the passion of experience, the power of reflection, and the courage to act. From these examples, we can glimpse at the face of revolutionary commitment—a grounded commitment to struggle against any and all forms of theory or practice that imprison our minds and incarcerate our hearts. Collectively these bicultural re-presentations call forth not only themes of opposition to dominant structures and cultural forms that impede the humanity and liberation of subordinate subjects, but also signal new ways of perceiving our dialectical capacities to transform the social and material conditions of our communities. It is through their vibrant discourses of simultaneous deconstruction and reconstruction, undoing and redoing, embracing and releasing, that we find the hidden seeds of self-determination and catch glimpses of the possibilities awaiting us, possibilities that are given birth through our courage to transgress the antiquated "sacred cows" of profit and privilege, and that join us together in a solidarity of difference—a solidarity that is ever mindful of the manner in which

Institutionalized rejection of difference is an absolute necessity in a profit economy which needs outsiders as surplus people. As members of such an economy, we have all been programmed to respond to the human differences between us with fear and loathing and to handle that difference in one of three ways: ignore it, and if that is not possible, copy it if we think it is dominant, or destroy it if we think it is subordinate. But we have no patterns for relating across human difference as equals. As a result, those differences have been misnamed and misused in the service of separation and confusion (Lorde, 1992, pp. 281–282).

Audre Lorde's words strongly reflect one of the most important questions we must openly acknowledge and consistently address in our efforts to establish a solidarity of difference. How do we move across a multiplicity of subjectivities rooted in both material conditions and diverse orientations that historically shape our world views? For example, so often we hear people, even within bicultural communities, bemoan the "loss of community." Yet, if the truth be told, a return to the good old days of such an imagined community actually would require returning to a simpler, unproblematic vision of community—a vision that, in fact, was often theorized in monolithic and solely essentialist terms and enacted through exclusionary practices that precluded the full participation of women, poor and working class people, gays, lesbians, and those perceived as "racially" inferior.

As critical beings we must consistently recognize the dangers of falling into the hidden traps of both absolutely exclusionary (assimilationist) and relativistically inclusive (liberal pluralist) theories and practices. A solidarity of difference instead challenges us to actively struggle across human differences within the ever-present dialectical tension of inclusionary/exclusionary personal and institutional realities and needs. For the purpose is not to obscure or obliterate differences or diminish and destroy cultural self-determination in the search for "common values"; rather, our greatest challenge is to negotiate the on-going construction and reconstruction of relations of power and material conditions that both affirm and challenge our partialities in the interest of cultural and economic democracy, social justice, human rights, and revolutionary love.

CONCLUSION

The theoretical foundation for a politics of biculturalism posited upon these pages represents, above all, one effort to articulate a dialectical reading of issues that are central to extending our political understanding of culture and difference and the impact of these forces upon the identity formation of members from subordinate communities. In so doing, this has entailed (1) a reexamination of notions of identity and ethnicity; (2) the reclamation of the power of experience in the construction of cultural knowledge; (3) the reconsideration of colonization, decolonization, and the development of cultural consciousness; (4) the reinstitution of class relations and material conditions as central to identity formation; (5) the distorting impact of the media on social perceptions of difference; (6) a move away from race-based specificity to a clear focus on racism and racialization; (7) an engagement with transcultural notions of border existence; and (8) the necessity for a solidarity of difference as a significant strategy of struggle against the forces of domination that shape our world.

Further, this introduction is meant to serve as a critical lens by which to consider the essays found in this book. The following chapters provide an array of critical perspectives related to different communities of color in the United States. This is to say that they do not represent a uniform or all-inclusive perspective; nor do they arise from one specific field of study. Instead these essays provide a range of topics which constitute significant concerns or issues within bicultural communities, but that seldom find expression within traditional or conventional pedagogical literatures. In addition, most of these scholars represent emerging or seldom recognized voices— voices that can ultimately help to broaden the critical discourse of biculturalism across academic disciplines and within the context of a rapidly changing economy and society. Most importantly, this work embodies a recognition that critical bicultural scholars must engage actively and persistently with the political challenges faced by our communities—not through simplistic platitudes of hope, but rather the committed intellectual discipline and critical practice required to boldly imagine and bring into existence a world that up to now has existed only in our dreams.

NOTES

1. See Iris Marion Young's (1991) text *Justice and the Politics of Difference* for an excellent critical analysis of the sociopolitical contexts that shape the histories of subordinate cultural groups in the United States.

2. Although there no longer exist cultural groups in the United States untouched by the dominant artifacts, structures, and economic relations of power, the beginning stages of this hybridization process can be observed in indigenous cultures that exist in remote regions of the world. One such example is the culture of the Q'eros in Peru. The Q'eros are the remaining community of people in the Peruvian highlands who are the direct descendants of the Inca. To flee the violent rampage of the conquistadors in the 1500s and to protect their way of life, the Q'eros fled into the Andes, living virtually in isolation for five hundred years. It is only recently that the Q'eros have begun to have some contact with the West. Government projects to assimilate the Q'eros into the mainstream of Peruvian life have taken the form of setting up farm collectives and Spanish language educational programs for the children. As the Q'eros begin to have greater contact with the West, it is expected that a way of life conserved for hundreds of years will undergo dramatic reconstruction, if not be lost altogether. This is already evident in those members of Q'eros who have moved into the cities, only to face harsh conditions of poverty and very few opportunities for a better life amidst the Peruvian mainstream (Cohen, 1993).

3. For a more extensive and thought-provoking discussion of ethnicity, see "Ethnicity: Identity and Difference" and "Cultural Identity and Diaspora" by Stuart Hall (1990a, 1990b); and Stanley Aronowitz's (1992) *The Politics of Identity*.

4. See chapter 6, "Essentialism and Experience," in *Teaching to Transgress* by bell hooks (1994) for an incisive discussion and critique of Diana Fuss's *Essentially speaking: Feminism, nature, and difference*, particularly with respect to the manner in which Fuss problematizes student voices that she characterizes as speaking from the "authority of experience."

5. According to the Children's Defense Fund yearbook, *The State of America's Children*: In 1992, more children lived in poverty than in any year since 1965; the share of family income received by the poorest one-fifth of families shrank to 4.4 percent in 1992, while the share going to the richest one-fifth reached 44.6 percent. In *Who We Are: A Portrait of America*, among other income inequities Roberts (1993) shows that despite an increase in total Black families who earn more than $50,000 (from 7 percent to 15 percent), the total number of Black families earning under $5,000 has risen from 8 percent in 1967 to 12 percent in 1990. Edward Luttwak (1993) bemoans the "Third-Worldization" of America in his book *The Endangered American Dream*. He writes: "America's slide toward Third World conditions is even now being prepared by the sheer force of demography: the proportion of poor Americans is increasing, the concentration of wealth in the hands of the richest one percent is also increasing, and the proportion of Americans in between who have enough wealth and income to claim genuine middle-class status is therefore in decline" (p. 153). Luttwak also provides the following figures: between 1979 and 1990, the number of workers below the poverty

line nearly doubled, from 7.8 million to 14.4 million; the combined net worth of the richest one percent was greater than the total net worth of the bottom 89.9 percent of all American families, at $5.2 trillion.

6. For an eloquent discussion of the history of working-class identity see *The Politics of Identity: Class, Culture, Social Movements*, a text by Stanley Aronowitz (1992).

7. Michel Omi and Howard Winant (1983b) in their essay "By the Rivers of Babylon: Race in the United States (Part II), provide an informative and useful discussion of the New Right's "programmatic attempts to limit the political gains of the minority movement (and its successors) by reinterpreting their meanings." In their work, the authors outline several of the major currents in the rearticulation process which have fueled the right-wing conservative backlash in the United States.

REFERENCES

Akinyela, M. (1992). "Critical Africentricity and the politics of culture." *Wazo Weusi (Think Black)* (Fall). Fresno, CA: California State University.

Anzaldúa, G. (1987). *Borderlands/La frontera: The new Mestiza*. San Francisco, CA: Aunt Lute.

Aronowitz, S. (1992). *The politics of identity: Class, culture, social movements*. New York, NY: Routledge.

Bhabha, H. (1990). "The third space," in J. Rutherford (ed.), *Identity, community, culture difference*. London, England: Lawrence and Wishart.

Buriel, R. (1984). "Integration with traditional Mexican-American culture and socio-cultural adjustment," in J. Martinez (ed.), *Chicano Psychology* (2d ed.). New York, NY: Academic Press.

Children's Defense Fund. (1994). *The state of America's children yearbook*. Washington, DC.

Cohen, J. (1993). *Q'eros: The shape of survival*. New York, NY: Mystic Fire Video.

Darder, A. (1991). *Culture and power in the classroom: A theory for a critical bicultural pedagogy*. New York, NY: Bergin & Garvey.

de Anda, D. (1984). "Bicultural socialization: Factors affecting the minority experience," in *Social Work*, 2, pp. 101–107.

Du Bois, W.E.B. (1903). *The souls of black folk*. Chicago, IL: A.C. McClurg.

Epstein, S. (1987). "Gay politics, ethnic identity: The limits of social constructionism." *Socialist Review*, 17 (May–August), pp. 9–54.

Fanon, F. (1964). *Toward the African revolution*. New York, NY: Grove.

———. (1963). *Wretched of the Earth*. New York, NY: Grove.

———. (1952). *Black skin, white masks*. New York, NY: Grove.

Giroux, H. (1992). *Border crossings*. New York, NY: Routledge.

Gomez-Peña, G. (1993). *Warrior for Gringostroika*. Saint Paul, MN: Graywolf Press.

Gorostiaga, X. (1993). "Is the answer in the South?" Paper presented at the international seminar on *First world ethics and third world economics: Christian responsibility in a world of plenty and poverty*, Sigtunn, Sweden.

Gramsci, A. (1971). *Selections from prison notebooks*. New York, NY: International Publishers.

Grossberg, L. (1993). "Cultural studies and/in New Worlds," in C. McCarthy, & W. Crichlow (eds.), *Race, identity, and representation in education*. New York, NY: Routledge.

Hall, S. (1990a). "Ethnicity: Identity and difference." *Radical America, 13*(4), pp. 9–20.

———. (1990b). "Cultural identity and diaspora," in J. Rutherford (ed)., *Identity, community, culture, difference.* London, England: Lawrence & Wishart.

Hall, S., et al. (1978). *Policing the crisis.* London, England: McMillan Press.

hooks, b. (1994). *Teaching to transgress.* New York, NY: Routledge.

———. (1990). *Yearnings.* Boston, MA: South End Press.

Jordon, J. (1992). *Technical difficulties.* New York, NY: Vintage Books.

Lorde, A. (1992). "Age, race, class and sex: Women redefining difference," in R. Ferguson et al. (eds.), *Out there: Marginalization and contemporary culture.* New York, NY: The New Museum of Contemporary Art.

Luttwak, E. (1993). *The endangered American dream.* New York, NY: Simon & Schuster.

Miles, J. (1993). *Racism after race relations.* London, England: Routledge.

Millán, D. (1993). "The Chicano collective bicultural consciousness: Identity and the politics of race," in A. Darder (ed.), *Bicultural studies in education: The struggle for educational justice.* Claremont, CA: Institute for Education in Transformation/Claremont Graduate School.

Minh-ha, T. (1992). "Cotton and iron," in R. Ferguson et al. (eds.), *Out there: Marginalization and contemporary culture.* New York, NY: The New Museum of Contemporary Art.

———. (1989). *Woman native other.* Indianapolis, IN: Indiana University Press.

Nagel, J. (1994). "Constructing ethnicity: Creating and recreating ethnic identity and culture." *Social Problems, 41*(1) (February), pp. 152–176.

Omi, M. & H. Winant. (1983a). "By the rivers of Babylon: Race in the United States" (Part I). *Socialist Review, 13*(5), pp. 31–65.

———. (1983b). "By the rivers of Babylon: Race in the United States" (Part II). *Socialist Review, 13*(6), pp. 35–68.

Ramirez, M. & A. Castañeda. (1974). *Cultural democracy: Bicognitive development and education.* New York, NY: Longman.

Rashid, H. (1981). "Early childhood education as a cultural transition for African American children." *Educational Research Quarterly 6*(3), pp. 55–63.

Redhorse, J., et al. (1981). "Family behavior of urban American Indians," in R. Dana (ed.), *Human services for cultural minorities.* Baltimore, MD: University Park Press.

Roberts, S. (1993). *Who we are: A portrait of America.* New York, NY: Random House.

Romay, E. (1993). "Policy implications for the United States through Mexican immigration bilingual teachers' experiences of bilingual-bicultural education: A participatory research process." Ph.D. dissertation, The University of San Francisco.

Sampson, E. (1993). "Identity politics: Challenges to psychology's understanding." *American Psychologist, 48*(12) (December), pp. 1219–1230.

Sandoval, C. (1991). "U.S. third world feminism: The theory and method of oppositional consciousness in postmodern world." *Genders* (Spring), pp. 1–24.

Santos, G. (1992). "Somos RUNAFRIBES? The future of Latino ethnicity in the Americas." *National Association of Chicano Studies Annual Conference Proceedings.*

Solis, A. (1980). "Theory of biculturality." *Calmeccac de Atzlan en Los, 2*, pp. 36–41.

Valentine, C. (1971). "Deficit, difference, and bicultural models of Afro-American be-
    havior." *Harvard Educational Review, 42*, pp. 137–157.
West, C. (1993). *Race matters*. Boston, MA: Beacon Press.
———. (1992). "The new politics of difference," in R. Ferguson et al. (eds.), *Out there:
    Marginalization and contemporary culture*. New York, NY: The New Museum
    of Contemporary Art.
Winston, M. (1982). "Racial consciousness and the evolution of mass communications
    in the United States." *Daedalus, 8*, pp. 171–182.
Wood, E. M. (1994). "Identity crisis," *In These Times* (June 13), pp. 28–29.
Young, I. M. (1990). *Justice and the politics of difference*. Princeton, NJ: Princeton
    University Press.

Rethinking Afrocentricity: The Foundation of a Theory of Critical Africentricity

Makungu M. Akinyela

Over ninety years ago, W.E.B. Du Bois (1989) wrote prophetically that the "problem of the 20th century" would be the problem of the color line. The question of color, race, ethnicity, and tribe, while appearing to be subsumed after the Bolshevik revolution under the class struggle, has, as Du Bois so clearly envisioned, emerged in recent years as the premier defining and motivating force of the century.

That struggle has taken many forms. Whether it was Du Bois' own Niagara Movement; Garvey's U.N.I.A.; Cesaire's Negritude; N'Krumah's Pan-Africanism; the religious nationalism of the Nation of Islam; the Soul Force of the civil rights movement; the cultural and revolutionary black nationalism of the 1960s; or Steve Biko's Black Consciousness in South Africa, the "problem of the 20th century" has remained at the center of historical development and change in the world. All of these trends attest to the long history in the African diaspora of African centered, hence *Africentric,*[1] social, political, and cultural discourse. They all have been attempts to place the experiences and ideas of descendants of African peoples at the center of discourse. And in the last part of the century, one of the main forms taken in this historical struggle has been the development of the Afrocentric idea (Asante, 1987) as a theoretical construct in itself.

In malls and storefronts across the United States, shops specializing in Afrocentric clothing, books, art, and other commodities are flourishing. The "X" worn on caps, shirts, and buttons by millions of U.S.-born Africans[2] has in many ways taken on a life of its own beyond identification with Malcolm X and has come to symbolize simply the wearer's attempts to establish links with an Afrocentric identity. New Afrikan teachers and administrators have come together for several "Immersion Conferences" to discuss and share ideas on practical implementation of Afrocentric content throughout the curriculum in public and private schools (Hilliard, 1990). Some of the fastest-growing churches in large urban centers are those which are part of the so-called neo-pentecostal movement (Lincoln and Mumiya, 1990) that focuses on both an Afrocentric cultural and political perspective and a charismatic worship style. Practical research and theoretical construction are being implemented in the fields of psychology (Akbar, 1985; Nobles, 1985), history (Carruthers, 1984; Keto, 1989), ethics (Karenga, 1984), political theory (T'shaka, 1990; Karenga, 1980), and other disciplines. Afrocentricity is a significant and growing movement within the New Afrikan communities and among both African and Euro-American intellectuals and academics. As the Afrocentricity movement has grown, there has been a corresponding growth of theoretical and philosophical literature which defines, describes, and shapes the direction of the movement.

This chapter will examine the social and political implications of Afrocentric theoretical models put forth by several leading Afrocentric thinkers as these models are applied to existing cultural situations. Particular focus will be applied to the Afrocentric intellectual ideas of Molefi K. Asante, Maulana Karenga, and others. I will also begin the task of offering a critique of the dominant Afrocentric intellectual trend. Finally, I will suggest a rethinking of the Afrocentric paradigm that will lay the foundation for a theory of Critical Africentricity.

DEFINING AFROCENTRICITY

Afrocentricity refers to an intellectual discourse which is concerned with integrating an interdisciplinary field of study from a common world view. Afrocentricity is the philosophical basis for black studies (Karenga, 1982) or, as some call it, Afrology—the study of Africa, Africans, and related issues (Asante, 1987). Asante (1983) states that Afrocentricity is "the logical heir to Negritude." In The Afrocentric Idea in Education, (1991), he writes:

Afrocentricity is a frame of reference wherein phenomena are viewed from the perspective of the African person. The Afrocentric approach seeks in every situation the appropriate centrality of the African person (p. 5).

Defining a *classical paradigm* is essential to Afrocentric thought and praxis. Bayo Oyebade (1990) writes:

Since Afrocentricity adopts Africa as a takeoff point in any discussion of African civilization, it is Diopian in methodology. Indeed the Diopian school of Afrocentric thought insists that the ancient Kemetic (Egyptian) civilization should be the classical reference point for the study of African civilization, as the Greek civilization is for analysis of European civilization (p. 234).

Karenga (1988), who is the creator of his own Afrocentric social political theory, which he calls Kawaida, also relying on Diop, writes:

[The Afrocentric] world view must evolve from the rescue and reconstruction of the classical African legacy of Egypt. Diop (1981, p. 12) writes that "for us, the return to Egypt in all fields is the necessary condition to build a body of modern human sciences, and renew African culture." In fact, "Egypt will play, in a rethought and renewed African culture, the same role that the ancient Greco-Latin civilizations play in Western culture" (p. 411).

Both Oyabade and Karenga see the use of ancient Egyptian civilization's classical paradigm as a fundamental step toward establishing the groundwork of modern black civilization. The question of an authentic African-centered way of knowing the world and an African epistemology, as well as an African-centered ontology, is essential to Oyabade, Asante, Karenga, and other Afrocentric writers. Norman Harris (1992) writes that:

The significance of Afrocentric ontology and epistemology is profound. The way one constructs reality, one's place in it, and the way one validates knowledge determines one's life chances. For example, the individualistic ontology into which we have all been socialized makes it all but impossible for many African Americans to conceptualize the idea of racial responsibility, particularly as it relates to racial empowerment (p. 156).

Harris asserts that the questions of individualism and communalism are key differentiations between Eurocentric and Afrocentric ontologies. This communal Afrocentric ontology stretches beyond human relationships into the African relationship with nature, which humans from an Afrocentric perspective should be in harmony with. Harris locates Afrocentric epistemology in a combination of historical knowledge and personal intuition. He continues,

History is key because when the individual appropriately submerges himself in the reservoir of African history, then that submersion allows the individual to discover him or herself in the context of that history and thereby judge the reality of any given phenomenon (p. 157).

The concept of a centrist world view and cultural perspective which makes the observers subjects in their own discourse is the starting point of Afrocentric theory. This counter-hegemonic strike against Euro-American domination of cultural discourse in a multicultural society is of great importance. However, there are some problematic areas within the discourse of Afrocentricity which must be examined in order to move it to a truly counter-hegemonic position.

THE PROBLEMS OF AFROCENTRICITY

The basic Afrocentric argument of a need to create a major shift in the hegemonic Eurocentric epistemology, which also sets the foundation of U.S. society, is a correct one. However, Afrocentrists generally tend to reduce the issue of Eurocentric epistemological hegemony to an issue of racial proclivity (biological determinism) and ethnic domination. A deeper economic and political analysis of hegemonic Eurocentric culture and structuring of society will provide a more functional understanding of the social political and cultural solutions to the New Afrikan situation in the United States.

It could be argued effectively that there is no monolithic European culture, though there is a European cultural ethos dominated by one class view. Eurocentric culture as we know it today is largely a product of the coming to power of the bourgeois merchant class in Europe, and later in the Americas, over the European aristocracy within the past five hundred years. The culture of the European bourgeoisie with all of its accompanying philosophical assumptions has guided the thinking of most Europeans and affected the lives of New Afrikans and other colonized and formerly colonized peoples in the world.

Asante's argument cited above and his focus on making African people subjects of their own lived experience, rather than objects of European and Euro-American study, is relevant and necessary. This also raises the question of the place and possibility of intellectual objectivity in the study of human societies and social political relationships. The myth of intellectual objectivity has historically been used as a tool of repression by the European and Euro-American bourgeoisie to maintain a position of power in matters of race, gender, culture, and social discourse. This has allowed the mainly white male bourgeoisie to set the parameters of academic legitimacy and limit the control of intellectual discourse to white men of that class or those people of color and white women culturally loyal to that class.

The ideology of the Eurocentric bourgeoisie was born out of the matrix of the Protestant Reformation, the development of capitalism, and the expansion of European imperialism in the fifteenth century. The ideological development of the European bourgeoisie occurred in the historical context of ongoing contention between the mercantile capitalist class and the last remnants of the Roman Empire represented by the European aristocracy and the Roman Catholic Church.

The new bourgeois class striving to break the restrictive, anti-intellectual bonds of the Roman Catholic Church sought a model for the new society which the class was striving to shape. The new bourgeois society which they envisioned, unlike the powerful Church of Rome, was open to new knowledge and learning. The leaders of the European enlightenment found a model for the new society in the precursor to Rome—ancient Greece.

By the eighteenth and nineteenth centuries the new class ideology was firmly entrenched as the ruling paradigm. The age of reason and "science" guided by the classic Greco-Roman ethos and aesthetic had propelled Europe and the European-dominated Americas into the position of political, economic, and intellectual rulers of the world. All of the leading influential thinkers of Europe would base their ideas on the Greek paradigm. Freud would use names from Greek mythology (id, ego, super-ego, Oedipal complex) to describe his theory of human psychoanalysis. Max Weber (1958) would write in *The Protestant Ethic and the Spirit of Capitalism*:

Only in the West does science exist at a stage of development which we recognize today as valid. Empirical knowledge, reflection on problems of the cosmos and of life, philosophical and theological wisdom of the most profound sort, are not confined to it, though in the case of the last the full development of a systematic theology must be credited to Christianity under the influence of Hellenism. . . . In short, knowledge and observation of great refinement have existed elsewhere, above all in India, China, Babylonia, and Egypt. But in Babylonia and elsewhere astronomy lacked—which makes its development all the more astounding—the mathematical foundation which it first received from the Greeks (p. 13).

The obvious Eurocentrism of Weber, writing in the nineteenth century, is placed in context by the work of Cornel West (1982), who is very helpful in explaining the relationship between the establishment of the Greek paradigm and the historical development of the European bourgeois class during the European Enlightenment.

The Enlightenment revolt against the authority of the church and the search for models of unrestrained criticism led to a highly charged recovery of classical antiquity, and especially to a new appreciation and appropriation of the artistic and cultural heritage of ancient Greece. For our purposes, the classical revival is important because it infuses Greek ocular metaphors and classical ideals of beauty, proportion, and moderation into the beginnings of modern discourse. Greek ocular metaphors—eye of the mind, mind as mirror of nature, mind as inner arena with its inner observer—dominate modern discourse in the West. . . . [M]odern philosophical inquiry is saddled with the epistemological model of intellect (formerly Plato's and Aristotle's Nous, now Descartes's Inner Eye) inspecting entities modeled on retinal images, with the Eye of the Mind viewing representations in order to find some characteristic that would testify to their fidelity. The creative fusion of scientific investigation, Cartesian philosophy, Greek ocular metaphors, and classical aesthetic and cultural ideals constitutes the essential elements of modern discourse in the West (p. 53).

Therefore, we can see how Eurocentric bourgeois ideology, focused on notions of class, racial, gender, and sexual hierarchy and domination, can in the name of reason, science, and the Greek paradigm come to be the basis for maintaining the "status quo." Moreover, this ideology of reason, science, and materialism relies upon a dichotomous world view which splits object from subject, mental from physical, and masculine from feminine, and attempts to reduce the world to essentials, ultimate truths, classical forms, and good or bad representations. In the end this represents a static, noncritical world view, even when it has been presented in the form of the historical materialism of Marxist philosophy.

THE LIMITATIONS OF AFROCENTRICITY

This bourgeois dichotomization of reality is precisely the place where the limitations within Afrocentricity emerge. If Afrocentricity is uncritical in its approach, it may only succeed in taking bourgeois Eurocentric thought, turning it on its philosophical head, painting it black, and calling it African. Asante (1991) specifically denies that this is the case. He writes:

It must be emphasized that Afrocentricity is not a Black version of Eurocentricity. Eurocentricity is based on white supremacist notions whose purposes are to protect white privilege and advantage in education, economics, politics, and so forth. Unlike Eurocentricity, Afrocentricity does not condone ethnocentric valorization at the expense of degrading other groups' perspectives (p. 171).

However, by focusing primarily on that aspect of bourgeois Eurocentric thought that emphasizes racial supremacy, while not fully assessing the dichotomous and essentialist nature of bourgeois thought as problematic in itself, Asante is able to avoid a critique of the dichotomous and essentialist nature of his own theories. This Afrocentricity implicitly accepts bourgeois theories of knowledge and cultural construction even while arguing for a new epistemological and ontological paradigm. This implicit acceptance of bourgeois philosophy often results in what appears to be empty worship and glorification of ancient "classical" knowledge and Kemetic esoterica while ignoring the ongoing construction of knowledge in the reflection of current African peoples on their lived experiences. The fact remains that failure to see the class basis and connection of Afrocentricity to bourgeois Eurocentric thought in fact often does lead to Asante's description of "ethnocentric valorization at the expense of degrading other groups' perspectives."

The question of the nature of knowledge is most significant to this discussion. Knowledge does not rest in an eternal pool somewhere waiting for an aware human being to come and appropriate it and "pass it along." This traditional notion is the "banking" concept of knowledge challenged by Paulo Freire (1990). Yet Afrocentrists often conceive of knowledge in this way when they speak of "going back to the Ancient Kemetic knowledge." The banking approach to knowledge, which emphasizes a teacher to student hierarchy, serves to keep ownership of knowledge and culture from those who are co-participants in constructing it. The effort to set up a classical baseline of knowledge as "source," and canon, becomes a political issue in that the implicit seat of power rests with those who define and are most familiar with the canon and its parameters. Bell hooks (1990) writes that this dualism ultimately lends legitimacy to existing Eurocentric ideas.

It is no mere accident of fate that the ground of current discourse on black subjectivity is cultural terrain. Art remains that site of imaginative possibility where "anything goes," particularly if one is not seeking to create a hot commodity for the marketplace. Black folks' inability to envision liberatory paradigms of black subjectivity in a purely political realm is in part a failure of critical imagination. Yet even on cultural ground discussions of black subjectivity are often limited to the topic of representation, good and bad images, or contained by projects concerned with reclaiming an/or inventing traditions (expressed in literary circles by the issue of canon formation). Interestingly, both these endeavors are not in any essential way oppositional. Focus on good and bad images may be more fundamentally connected to the western metaphysical dualism that is the philosophical underpinning of racist and sexist domination than with radical efforts to reconceptualize black cultural identities. Concurrently, focus on canon formation legitimates the creative work of black writers in academic circles while reinforcing white hegemonic authorial canonicity (p. 18).

The question must be asked whether Afrocentrists, by focusing on the so-called baseline knowledge of "classical" African civilizations, are in fact lending credence to the use of Greek civilization as the baseline of bourgeois Eurocentric cultural hegemony. This would imply that Afrocentrists do not see the accumulation of political power, control of knowledge, and cultural hegemony by one class in society over other classes as problematic in itself.
     Consequently, Afrocentrists do tend to assume an avoidance posture toward questions of conflict, power, and politics. This ties Afrocentricity strongly to the black cultural nationalism of the 1960s which emphasized a dualistic separation of "political" struggle and "cultural" struggle, assuming that the cultural struggle must be won prior to and distinct from the political struggle. This cultural nationalism was marked also by a denial of the political significance of class contradictions and power inequalities among New Afrikans. For example, Karenga, as chair of the cultural nationalist "Us" organization, could say in 1967,

We say with [Sekou] Toure that for Us there are no intellectuals, no students, no workers, no teachers; there are only supporters of the organization. . . . We do not accept the idea of class struggle; for today in Afro-America there is but one class, an oppressed class [of blacks] (p. 25).

Today, Afrocentricity as a theoretical model has failed to develop a class analysis which takes into account the significance of political and economic power differences and the problems which may arise within the African community as a result. Asante (1990) provides a descriptive assessment of class relationships which seems to be based on Weberian notions of class structure, but which again does not extend sufficiently to assess the political significance of this structure.

Class distinctions for the Afrocentrist consist in four aspects of property relations: (1) those who possess income producing properties, (2) those who possess some property that produces income and a job that supplements income, (3) those who maintain professions or positions because of skills, and (4) those who do not have skills and whose services may or may not be employed (p. 10).

Asante (1988) goes no further in his analysis of class structure because within his theoretical framework, analysis focused on class contradictions is based on a Eurocentric model of conflict. This idea of historical conflict being Eurocentric and antithetical to Afrocentrism is reflected in Asante's critique of Marxism:

Marxism . . . allows open warfare on the bourgeois class. Operating on the European values of confrontation developed from the adventures of Europeans during the terrible White Ages, both of these systems (capitalism and Marxism) believe in utter destruction of aliens. This, of course, is contradictory to the Afrocentric value which respects difference and applauds pluralism. Strangers exist in that they have not been known . . . [but] Marxism's Eurocentric foundation makes it antagonistic to our worldview; its confrontational nature does not provide the spiritual satisfaction we have found in our history of harmony (p. 79).

The Afrocentricity of Asante and other leading thinkers stresses an avoidance of conflict with the capitalist system and poses solutions which remain in the context of existing capitalism. Asante (1988) asserts:

We must struggle to gain a foothold in every sector of the American economy. . . . Our path to economic survival will not be based upon landholdings but owning secure industries, creative breakthroughs in art and music, exploitation of all fields of athletics and salaried positions based on education and talent (p. 94).

This failure to confront asymmetrical power relations outside of a cultural critique of Eurocentric racism within existing capitalist society is a serious weakness of Afrocentricity. By secluding the Afrocentric view to primarily a critique of white racist ideology, the Afrocentrists seem to be carving out a comfortable and acceptable Afrocentric niche for themselves in established Eurocentric academia. The primary emphasis of this academic Afrocentrism seems to be in promoting a pluralistic, multicultural society where no one culture has hegemony over any other, yet it resists the idea of conflict or antagonism which would seem to be necessary in overcoming the power inequities inherent in current political cultural relations. These political cultural relations are evident in disproportionate poverty, disease, crime, police oppression, and other realities of the lived experience of New Afrikans in U.S. cities.

The dichotomous, static, and ahistorical view of knowledge prevalent in Afrocentric discourse reflects the hegemonic influence of bourgeois Eurocentric thought on Afrocentric writers even as they strive to construct "pure" Afrocentric epistemologies. The reification of culture and the focus on ancient civilizations (and more specifically, the ruling classes of those civilizations as models for current Afrocentric social structure) betrays an apparent desire to replicate European hierarchical social structure even as Afrocentrists criticize Eurocentric society. Asante (1988) writes, "Walking the way of the new world means that we must establish schools which will teach our children how to behave like the kings and queens they are meant to be" (p. 47). Little or no mention is made in Afrocentric writing of the role of the ancient African peasantry and the laborers who actually constructed the ancient monuments of Kemet, Ethiopia, and Great Zimbabwe. The illusion is maintained that these human efforts were all accomplished in totally harmonious relations, with each person, whether king or laborer, male or female, mystically happy to stay in her/his place assigned by the universe.

This harmonious social order is the key to civilization for the Afrocentrists, who insist that there were no antagonisms or class contradictions in the "classical" civilizations. However, this view is not even upheld by the patriarch of many Afrocentrists, Cheikh Anta Diop. Diop (1974) describes a revolutionary situation which occurred in the Sixth Dynasty of the Old Kingdom of Kemet under the Pharaoh Zoser, who clashed with the priests of the city of Heliopolis and proclaimed himself "Great God" and outside of the control of any human authority. Diop writes:

Thereafter the regime again evolved toward feudalism. The courtiers constituted a special corps of dignitaries which would make itself hereditary by usage and soon by right. The feudal system that had just triumphed with the Fifth Dynasty reached its peak with the Sixth. It then engendered general stagnation in the economy and the administration of the State in urban as well as rural areas. And the Sixth Dynasty was to end with the first popular uprising in Egyptian history (p. 206).

The target of the uprising was the oppressive state bureaucracy, which most affected the Egyptian poor. The rebellion challenged the absolute political and religious power of the Pharaoh, which even reached to the grave. According to the theology of the time, only the Pharaoh had a right to the "Osirian death," or the hope of resurrection. "After that revolution," writes Diop, "all Egyptians had a right to the 'Osirian death.' . . . The discontent was strong enough completely to disrupt Egyptian society throughout the entire country" (p. 207).

It is evident in Diop's research that the "classical" Kemetic civilization was (1) repressive and divided by class contradiction and (2) historically changed and democratized by antagonism and conflict between the classes, in spite of the Afrocentrist assertion that conflict is antithetical to the African ideal of social harmony.

When considered in this light, Afrocentricity (like bourgeois Eurocentricity) seems more concerned with codifying knowledge, history, and social structure into a status quo that can only be comprehended and defined by a chosen few. Repeated references to harmony as a principle, while ignoring the existence of unequal social relations of power, functions to maintain power in the hands of those who define the arena of discourse.

Asante is correct when he says that Afrocentricity is the legitimate heir of Negritude. But like the philosophical movement of the Franco-African petty bourgeoisie, Afrocentricity is vulnerable to the same critique which was so eloquently leveled by Frantz Fanon (1963). Speaking of the colonized African intellectual struggling to find a place for himself in his own society, Fanon writes:

Thus we see that the cultural problem as it sometimes exists in colonized countries runs the risk of giving rise to serious ambiguities. . . . Culture is becoming more and more cut off from the events of today. . . . It is true that the attitude of the native intellectual sometimes takes on the aspect of a cult or of a religion. . . . He sets a high value on the customs, traditions, and the appearances of his people; but his inevitable, painful experience only seems to be a banal search for exoticism (p. 217).

Fanon points out that this effort to codify traditions and place virtual religious value on reconstructing the past out of forgotten cultural practices is in conflict with the nature of cultural knowledge. Asante with his Njia system (1988), and Karenga with Kawaida thought (1967), have focused on constructing whole new cultural, religious systems which are based on "classical" African ethos, customs, and traditions. These systems codify the past, and it is emphasized that their acceptance and practice are minimal requirements for "authentic" Afrocentric cultural praxis. There is an underlying suggestion in these systems that the lived historical culture of New Afrikans is somehow less than African because it lacks "purity" due to contamination by Euro-American culture. Culture is not a static set of customs, formulas, or traditions. To attempt to locate culture in specific customs, traditions, and ways of thinking which are not allowed to change actually leads to the death of culture. I agree with Fanon (1963) when he writes, "the desire to attach oneself to tradition or bring abandoned traditions to life again does not only mean going against the current of history but also opposing one's own people" (p. 224).

Fanon warns that this static search for a reconstruction of the "glorious past" and defining what is "African" according to the petty bourgeois intellectuals is problematic in that this class often ends up simply replacing white masters with Black ones. At the same time no fundamental changes in the structure of society are made. The legitimacy of the status quo is maintained in the name of reconstructing and preserving so-called pure African culture.

It is probably no coincidence that Afrocentrists and cultural nationalists in the United States have often been the most vocal supporters of dictators like Mobutu in Zaire, Amin in Uganda, Burnham in Guyana, the Duvaliers in Haiti, and many other despots who have exploited and oppressed Africans for their own ends. All of these men have done so while supposedly promoting "traditional" African customs and culture.

RETHINKING AFROCENTRICITY

Do these criticisms mean that Afrocentricity as an intellectual discipline and theoretical model should be abandoned? On the contrary, while some New Afrikan intellectuals have condemned Afrocentricity as irrelevant or re-actionary (Gates, 1991; Steele, 1990), Afrocentricism's strongest argument is in its call for a counter-hegemonic discourse to break the intellectual and moral legitimacy of the Eurocentric bourgeoisie on the minds and lives of the African, Asian, and Latin American world majority. I would add that it is strategically necessary to total human liberation to also break the hegemonic domination on the minds and lives of working men and women of European descent who are also in cultural and political control of the ruling classes.

The Afrocentric claim, that African people must construct a new African identity and must begin to perceive and interpret the world in its entirety from an African psychological, spiritual, and cultural frame of reference, is a correct one. Africans must engage with problems and issues from our own contexts as subjects in the world. This is not a neutral project. It requires an ongoing critical assessment of both subjective lived experience and objective conditions.

The major weakness of Afrocentricity exists in limiting its social critique to the role of white supremacist racism and abstracting and dehistorisizing culture in its relationship to politics and power. Afrocentricity for the most part implicitly accepts the legitimacy of static, positivist epistemology. In its refusal to deepen the critique of existing capitalist social structure and capitalism's relationship to oppression and exploitation, Afrocentricity implicitly accepts the legitimacy of the politics of domination outside of the racial paradigm and fails to examine the relationship to racism of other forms of oppression such as sexism, heterosexism, and ecological destruction at this point in history.

I would argue that some form of Afrocentric theory is necessary in this historical period in which, while there are no significant legal restrictions to black freedom, New Afrikans of all classes are expressing more cynicism and despair about the relationship between Africans and U.S. social and political life. It is also a time when the New Afrikan urban poor, employed, and un-employed are feeling isolated and powerless in a society where the majority of Euro-Americans and even some middle-class people of color are demanding more tax cuts, less spending, more jails, more police, and less government help for affirmative action programs.

This social, political, and cultural context seems to call for a radical world view with a vision of a restructured society. The restructured society developed out of the new world view would be one committed to cultural democracy and equality for the various ethnic, sexual, class, and other groups within the society. This new world view would be culturally centrist and committed to critical analysis of both the state and civil societies.

A THEORY OF CRITICAL AFRICENTRICITY

Critical Africentricity is a philosophy of praxis aimed at creating effective strategies of liberation from the multiple forms of domination experienced by African people born in the United States in particular, and African people throughout the diaspora in general. Because Critical Africentric theory is related to critical pedagogy and is concerned with developing a humanitarian world view, it is also aimed at developing and participating in a worldwide liberatory practice which will benefit all of humanity. For the Critical Africentrist, the discourse of social analysis about Africans in America is derived from both an understanding of the precolonial African experience and the collective lived experiences of New Afrikans in the struggle against racial colonialism.

In rethinking some of the issues of Afrocentricity, and applying a Critical Africentric analysis, I will look at four major questions. These include (1) the nature of culture; (2) the construction of knowledge; (3) hegemony, power, and political oppression; and (4) Critical Africentricity and Consciousness. In the following section I will further explain the key issues which define Critical Africentric theory.

Critical Africentricity and the Nature of Culture

Definitions of culture are usually either anthropological, focusing on what particular cultures look like, or they are sociological, focusing on lists of elements of culture. Most definitions of culture assume that culture is an expression of monolithic, ethnic/racial communities through phenomenon such as art, food, music, clothing, religion, or other outward forms. In the same vein, Karenga (1980) lists seven elements in his Afrocentric Kawaida theory which he says that every culture possesses.[3]

Critical Africentric understanding of culture would posit that cultural phenomena take their form in the dialectical tension which exists in the asymmetrical power relationships between groups and within groups. Culture is constructed as the more powerful and the less powerful segments of society contend for positions of power and privilege between themselves. This means that any given culture is actually a complex of cultures between unequal class, gender, religious, language, sexual, and other elements within groups. H. E. Newsum (1990) describes how this phenomenon functions between language groups:

Intergroup activities between members of opposed sociolinguistic and socioeconomic realities produce a language which reflects the class roles of persons acting in the situation and sometimes there is noticeable condescension on the part of the upper class participants and defiance or passiveness on the part of lower class participants. ... The consciousness of exploiting groups and the consciousness of exploited groups respectively are in constant opposition, each group advancing the collective cause of the two respective divisions (p. 23).

As Newsum explains from his perspective as a sociolinguist, these systems of culture are defined by often oppositional individual and collective subject positions within a society. This is the dialectic of culture. This notion suggests that there are really no homogeneous national cultures so much as systems of contending social groups within national groups or ethnicities, which are in constant struggle with one another over positions of power and influence.

A cultural dialectic occurs between economic classes, geographical locations, color/caste groups, religious sects and denominations, language dialect groups, sexual orientation groups, gender groups, and perhaps other currently unrecognizable groupings, all within the context of New Afrikan ethnicity. This same cultural dialectic which occurs within ethnocultural groups also exists between such groups. For instance, as the New Afrikan middle class strives to place its values at the center of the agenda to define black people's social and political direction, there is a response from the New Afrikan poor and working class, both in defense of their own values and in an effort to exert itself and survive as a group. Yet, even in the contention, there is mutual influence between groups.

This then is an argument against notions of cultural purity and permanence. It is the nature of culture to adopt from and adapt to outside influences, both as acts of resistance and as acts of domination striving for recognition from the other. Culture is constructed in the constant process of dynamic change motivated by shifts in asymmetrical power relationships within complexes of various subject positions. The resulting material manifestations of cultural phenomenon—for example the artistic, social, and political expressions of groups and individuals—are behaviors of resistance and survival which assist and motivate cultural actors to make sense of and give meaning to their collective existence. At best we can only identify cultural historical moments in any civilization's process, as opposed to identifying classical paradigms which define a culture for all time.

From this perspective, rather than accepting the notion that Black people in the United States have been passive objects of a process of de-Africanization and Americanization, they can be understood as being active subjects in the process of Africanizing the European culture which they encountered. Whatever religious, linguistic, familial, or social-political form was thrust upon them has been appropriated, internalized, and Africanized into the collective ethos. There is no need to seek "pure" classical African cultural forms to prove the Africanity of blacks in the United States. There have never been such forms, even on the continent.

Critical Africentricity and Knowledge

Critical Africentricity maintains a historical view of knowledge. Knowledge is socially constructed and culturally mediated within societies and is affected by historical context. Human beings construct knowledge in their critical reflection upon lived experiences, out of which they are able to define and name their own social, political reality.

Antonia Darder (1991) speaks to the importance of constructing knowledge from the lived histories of oppressed peoples.

With this in mind, a critical approach must appropriate [oppressed people's] own histories by delving into their own biographies and systems of meaning. . . . [A] critical perspective opposes the positivist emphasis on historical continuities and historical development. In its place is found a mode of analysis that stresses the breaks, discontinuities, and tensions in history, all which become valuable in that they highlight the centrality of human agency and struggle while simultaneously revealing the gap between society as it presently exists and society as it might be (p. 80).

These "stresses and breaks" are the contradictions, situations, and problems to be solved between individuals and social groups in order for society to prosper. These social group issues are the motive force of history and the locus of the construction of knowledge. This challenges both the notion of pure classical knowledge, which is handed down from one generation to the next, and the idea that societies can be perfected by reconstructing old systems and traditions of knowledge, as well as the notion of knowledge as an individual pursuit.

People act as subjects in the world on objects of knowledge. These objects of knowledge may be environmental material conditions, social historical situations, challenges of nature, or psycho-spiritual challenges. Using information gained from "old knowledge," subjects reflect, share, and strive to understand as a community. In the act of challenging new situations and problems, "new knowledge" is constructed, which will eventually itself become "old knowledge" to be challenged by new situations. This construction, challenge, and new construction of knowledge provides the context in which, as Fanon (1963) says, "each generation must out of relative obscurity, discover its mission, fulfill it or betray it" (p. 206).

Hegemony, Power, and Political Oppression

Gramsci's (1987) concepts of domination and hegemony are helpful in a discussion of the relationship between power and political oppression. Prior to the Civil Rights movement, the primary means of colonial control of New Afrikans was by domination. The use of direct force, violence, and intimidation through laws, police, the military, and civilian forces was sufficient to keep the people of the colonized ghetto in place. In more recent years, since the fall of Jim Crow segregation, global capitalism in the United States has tended to rely primarily on cultural hegemony and only secondarily on domination as a means of social control.

While Afrocentrists have raised the issue of hegemony in discussions of culture, they have used the term mainly in its instrumental form, referring mostly to cultural or ideological predominance. Critical Africentricity understands hegemony as the psychological and social manipulation of one or several groups by another group for the purpose of establishing moral and intellectual leadership. Hegemony is the gained consent of a group to the domination by another group even when the consent may not be in the interest of the consenting group. Hegemony is enforced primarily through the institutions of civil society, which are the cultural institutions, such as churches, social clubs, sororities/fraternities, educational institutions, artistic institutions, print and electronic media, and private enterprise. All of these institutions of "civil society" are to varying degrees independent from the state and its apparatus.

The core of U.S. cultural hegemony is based on maintaining the myth of a common and collective heritage for "all Americans" regardless of race, creed, or national origin. This myth is symbolized in various ways by Plymouth Rock, Thanksgiving, the American Revolution, the Liberty Bell, the Constitution, and various other representations. Cultural hegemony is codified in the manufacturing of a common desire, the ubiquitous "American Dream." Hegemony and desire are manufactured in songs, hair spray, deodorant and automobile commercials, movies, novels, and comic books. The theme of this hegemonic desire is always the same: "You ought to want this fantasy life. And if you work hard enough it can be yours."

Hegemony is exerted by what is allowed in the cultural discourse and what is discouraged or muted from the discourse. When ideas are discounted, denied, or ignored, possibilities and alternatives are cut off. The targets of hegemony are forced to "settle" for what they are presented with and can only figure that "this is the best (country, car, economic system, solution to racism) there is." This is the manner in which false or uninformed consent is garnered, through legitimation and delegitimation. Hence the main objective of cultural hegemony is to create an assimilated society under the leadership of the ruling class to ensure the smooth running of the dominant system. When assimilation fails, domination and intimidation result.

Critical Africentricity and Consciousness

Consciousness is closely related to the question of hegemony. Consciousness is the personal awareness possessed by individuals of shared collective experience and connected interests with a group in the context of common social, political, and cultural conditions. Consciousness may be identified within and by the group according to specific discoveries related to racial, class, ethnic, national, or other collective experience.

Consciousness is primarily a subjective act of collective will. It is constructed in the social engagement of humans with each other and the environment. Material conditions play a part in shaping consciousness; however, the subjective wills of collectives acting on their environment are primary.

Critical Africentricity posits the need to develop a collective liberatory consciousness as a necessary act against Eurocentric control of New Afrikans. Both Malcolm X (Perry, 1989) and Frantz Fanon (1963) focused on counter-hegemonic action as the source of liberatory consciousness. This is also the locus identified by Critical Africentric theory. Again there is agreement with Afrocentric and cultural nationalist thought in identifying the need to gain moral cultural authority in the hearts and minds of the oppressed through cultural revolution. Where Critical Africentricity differs with cultural nationalism and Afrocentricity is at the crucial points of misidentifying the reconstruction of classical civilization and cultural traditions as the primary ground of resistance and of identifying the so-called cultural revolution as a separate and prior act to political revolution. Critical Africentricity posits that these are mutually interrelated processes. Cultural action is political and politics is cultural action. As discussed earlier, because these Afrocentric/cultural nationalist pursuits are based on the implicit acceptance of Eurocentric cultural assumptions, they in fact serve to reinforce the legitimacy of Eurocentric hegemony. Afrocentricity therefore ends up serving as part of oppressive, hegemonic civil society. In contrast, counter-hegemonic, cultural action seeks to discredit or refute the pillars of the dominant value system, not legitimate them by posing similar, albeit "Afrocentric," values and assumptions about social structure, history, and epistemology.

CONCLUSION

Critical Africentricity can be summed up by outlining nine major characteristics of its theory and praxis. These are the components which form the basis for the theory and which define Critical Africentricity as a distinct theory from Afrocentricity.

1. Critical Africentricity is a cultural/social theory based on a dynamic epistemology drawn from the historical and current experiences of New Afrikans born in the United States.

2. Critical Africentricity is dedicated to self-determination action as essential to the liberation of New Afrikans born in the United States.

3. Critical Africentricity refuses to accept cultural compartmentalizing of knowledge based on false notions of biological determinism and racialism. For the Critical Africentrist, all knowledge is potentially useful for freedom.

4. Critical Africentricity values African cultural knowledge and traditions and emphasizes its historicity and ongoing change against notions of "classic," unchanging forms of cultural knowledge.

5. Critical Africentricity emphasizes cultural historical identification with Africa by New Afrikans as essential both to ethnic/cultural survival and as a means of resistance to racial colonialism and cultural hegemony.

6. Critical Africentricity utilizes a dialectical social analysis which opposes the stratification of society along unequal ethnic, class, gender, and sexual lines.

7. Critical Africentricity posits that there are contradictions such as racialism, sexism, heterosexism, and ecological domination which are *transhistorical* (not dependent on and prior to) capitalism. To challenge the legitimacy of these interrelated social contradictions is a necessary revolutionary act for social change.

8. Critical Africentricity is committed to radical democracy and a redistribution of economic, political, social, and cultural assets and power.

9. Critical Africentricity posits that the development of a national cultural consciousness by New Afrikans as a people for themselves is a necessary counter-hegemonic strategic action toward liberation from racial colonialism, capitalism, and cultural domination.

These criteria can serve as a guide in developing further work and praxis around Critical Africentricity, emphasizing the radical struggle against bourgeois philosophy whether it is African or European. Critical Africentricity seeks to break down the dualistic divisions between cultural discourse and political discourse. It is a challenge for us to value the everyday experience of common people as the place to begin defining what is real. This everyday experience is the place from which New Afrikans will shape their own liberation. At its best, Critical Africentricity should be cultural action for the freedom of a colonized people.

NOTES

1. The form *Africentricity* is used rather than Afrocentricity to distinguish the two theories and to highlight that the term is a contraction of African Centric. Or in the words of Queen Mother Audley Moore, "Ain't no such land as Afro-land!"

2. Hereafter I will refer to "New Afrikans" as a cultural/national identification for Africans born in the United States as distinguished from Continental and other diaspora African national groups.

3. Mythology; History; Social Organization; Economic Organization; Political Organization; Creative Motif; Ethos.

REFERENCES

Akbar, N. (1985). *The community of self.* Jersey City, NJ: Mind Productions, Inc.

Asante, M. K. (1991). "The Afrocentric idea in education." *Journal of Negro Education, 60*(2).

————. (1990). *Kemet, Afrocentricity and knowledge.* Trenton, NJ: Africa World Press, Inc.

————. (1988). *Afrocentricity.* Trenton, NJ: Africa World Press, Inc.

————. (1987). *The Afrocentric idea.* Philadelphia, PA: Temple University Press.

————. (1983). "The ideological significance of Afrocentricity in intercultural communication." *Journal of Black Studies, 14*(1) (September).

Carruthers, J. H. (1984). *Essays in ancient Egyptian studies.* Los Angeles, CA: University of Sankore Press.

Darder, A. (1991). *Culture and power in the classroom: A critical foundation for bicultural education.* New York, NY: Bergin and Garvey.

Diop, C. A. (1974). *The African origin of civilization: Myth or reality?* Westport, CT: Lawrence Hill & Co.

Du Bois, W. E. B. (1989). *The souls of black folk.* New York, NY: Bantam Books.

Fanon, F. (1963). *The wretched of the earth.* New York, NY: Grove Press.

Freire, P. (1990). *Pedagogy of the oppressed.* New York, NY: Continuum.

Gates, H. L. (1991). "Afrocentricity: Beware of the new pharaohs." *Newsweek* (September 23).

Gramsci, A. (1987). *Note sul Machiavelli, sulla politics, e sullo stato moderno.* Cited by Joseph V. Femia, *Gramsci's political thought: Hegemony, consciousness, and the revolutionary process.* Oxford, England: Clarendon Press.

Harris, N. (1992). "A philosophical basis for an Afrocentric orientation." *The Western Journal of Black Studies, 16*(3).

Hilliard, A. G. III, L. Payton-Stewert, & L. Obadele Williams (eds). (1990). *Infusion of African and African American content in the school curriculum: Proceedings of the first National Conference* (October 1989). Morristown, NJ: JN Aaron Press.

hooks, b. (1990). *Yearning: Race, gender and cultural politics.* Boston, MA: South End Press.

Karenga, M. (1988). "Black studies and the problematic of paradigm: The philosophical dimension." *Journal of Black Studies, 18*(4) (June).

————. (1984). *Selections from the Husia: Sacred wisdom of ancient Egypt.* Los Angeles, CA: University of Sankore Press.

————. (1980). *Kawaida theory: An introductory outline.* Inglewood, CA: Kawaida Publications.

————. (1967). *The quotable Karenga.* Los Angeles, CA: Kawaida Publications.

Keto, T. (1989). *The Africa-centered perspective of history.* Pleasanton, CA: K. A. Publications.

Lincoln, C. E. & L. H. Mumiya. (1990). *The black church in the African American experience.* Durham, NC and London, England: Duke University Press.

Newsum, H. E. (1990). *Class, language education: Class struggle and sociolinguistics in an African situation.* Trenton, NJ: Africa World Press, Inc.

Nobles, W. W. (1985). *Africanity and the black family*. Oakland, CA: Black Family Institute Publications.

Oyebade, B. (1990). "African studies and the Afrocentric paradigm." *Journal of Black Studies, 21*(2) (December).

Perry, B. (ed.). (1989). *Malcolm X: The last speeches*. New York, NY: Pathfinder Press.

T'Shaka, O. (1990). *The art of leadership*. Richmond, CA: Pan Afrikan Publications.

Steele, S. (1990). *The content of our character*. New York, NY: St. Martin's Press.

Weber, M. (1958). *The Protestant ethic and the spirit of capitalism*. New York, NY: Charles Scribner's Sons.

West, Cornel. (1982). *Prophesy deliverance*. Louisville, KY: Westminster Press.

Chicana Identity Matters

Deena J. González

What is involved in the taking of a name, suggests the Chicana lesbian feminist theoretician Gloria Anzaldúa (1987), unites our search for a Chicano/a identity in this century. Other searches defy categorization. Disunited in our self-labelling—"Hi"-spanic, Latino, Mexican-American, even Chicano-American—our ruminations constantly project a homecoming that eludes us. This also unifies our condition in this century, and is instructive. "They caught us before we had a chance to figure it all out," Chicana/o activists protest. Our laments are ongoing proclamations, as enduring as José Vasconcelos' concept of "La Raza Cosmica," which he espoused in the 1920s. His concept of an enduring race was one thing; our self-identification is another. The word Chicana has always been difficult to use, especially if applied to women living in the previous centuries. Illusory even today, many Spanish-surnamed, Mexican-origin women refuse the term.

Still, we Chicana historians make an effort to apply the concept. Why? Our contemporary conditions are as illustrative as our histories, particularly the histories of the unnamed, of women. For women who have no name, Anzaldúa (1987) suggests this: "She has this fear that she has no names that she has many names that she doesn't know her names. She has this fear that she's an image that comes and goes clearing and darkening" (p. 43). For women who remain faceless despite their consistent presence in documents, this business of acquiring identity is the basis for living and for life, is the basis of the struggle for selfhood—in our (Chicana) present but also in "their" (Aztec/Native or mestizo) pasts (Hernández, 1993).

We find tremendous consolation in tracing the sources of our empowerment—the struggle for identity and for recognition is one, but only one, struggle in a long history of finding or locating identity. Lending identity, as historians do, is another important task, but it is often undiscussed although it lies on the flip side of the identity coin. Identity is both assumed and given; some people have "more" identity, some less. Every day, historians lift out of the records, or find in the records, or situate persons in records—our fundamental task is to organize this information in selective categories, and this is not easy. Who is denigrated one century is reified in the next. For mainstream historians, ignoring a group—say women of Mexican descent, as many have done—is part of a selection process; not naming women constitutes including them by omission. For the most part, in mainstream history texts and in the works of Chicano historians, Chicanas are absent. It is in these omitting spaces that Chicanas have found a place in the debates raging through the historical profession, and there we occupy a pivotal if uncomfortable role because we resurrect images and real persons from the past. Our task as Chicana historians is twofold—to resurrect and to delineate/revise. How do we do justice to both, and then translate our findings into languages that majority or dominant societies understand? Do we even want to do that? Our choices are neither simple nor clear. Here are examples from our very ordinary existences as historians and as self-identified Chicanas.

To the new generation of Western American historians—the revisionist brigade, as they have been called—the "West" is a place, a region, a state of mind, a culture, wide-ranging, long, far, distant, pockmarked by the dynamics of contest and conflict, consensus and contradiction. Not an easy place to reside, in other words. But to Chicana/o historians, the West is really the Mexican North.[1] The concepts we use and the configurations we bring to our work, whether of class—upper and working—or of the sexualized, gendered, racialized systems—in matrices traced like virgin, martyr, witch, or whore; or Native, mestiza, or Chicana—are different.[2] Never has the sunbonneted helpmate, sturdy homesteader, or ruddy miner or rancher been less useful to our projects. For us, teaching a class in Western American history, then, makes no sense. We ask, why not call it a history of the Mexican North? Why not call it a history of many names, of places termed by Native historians as far back as they can remember the Dancing Ground of the Sun, or by Chicano/a historians, Aztlán? You see our dilemmas and the new directions we are plotting. Add to this that few, except the most recent professionally-trained historians, were schooled in Chicano/a history. We are self-trained. Where do we begin, what do we name our undertaking, what organizes our chronology? Such matters of differences among historians often come down to nothing more—and nothing less—than the willingness of one group and not the other to suggest that we are in disagreement, or in what is quickly becoming a cliche, that our deliberations are contests taking place on suspect terrain.

These issues reflect my themes for this chapter: Chicana is a contemporary term, but can be applied to Spanish-speaking and Mexican-origin women in any area presently considered territory of the United States. Historians may well be bothered by the renaming, although established courtesies indicate that people should be known by their preferred terms. In 1980, the United States government ignored the protocol and lumped us together under the generic "Hispanic," rewriting history, so to speak, by suggesting that the tie to Spain was greater than the tie to our indigenous heritage. This may have suited other Latino groups living in the United States, but it caused a new wave of dissension among Chicano/as. As Luis Valdez (1994) postulated, "Why be an adjective, and not a noun? Why Hispanic? It doesn't compute. Why not Germanic, an Germanic?"

For Chicanas, one dilemma in self-identification set in not because we do not know who we are or are misguided in applying labels, but because like many other terms, Chicana has always been problematized as an identity in waiting, as an incomplete act. Philosophically, spiritually, or politically, Chicanas do not all look at the world in the same way, or even in ways Euro-Americans might understand. It is not true that we do not know who we are. If anything, we should suffer the accusation that we know too much who we are, have too much identity.

Add to this the internal, embattling ideological wars dominating our newly created spaces in the academy. Chicanas most agree on the name we have selected for ourselves; problematized, discussed, and assessed, it provided the point of departure, but everything since then has spun away from an assumed "core" of understanding. The fractures are rampant, and also hidden from the mainstream. (Unless you have followed the recent Chicano Studies debates at UC Santa Barbara, where at least one conclusion can be drawn—Chicanas and Chicanos do not agree on all issues.) Mainly, we least discuss our differences in favor of presenting a united front in the academic theater that would most often like to get rid of us all. To say fracture is to speak of secrets or to name lies. In our conferences of the past years, we have begun to witness that a resurgent Chicano/a nationalist student movement contradicts Chicano/a faculty agendas. Among Chicanas, lesbian/feminist pedagogies and scholarship parted ways with other types of Chicana [feminist] practices long ago. The majority of Chicana lesbian-feminist scholars do not feel comfortable operating within the confines and structures of the overwhelmingly male-identified, even "minority," organizations that exist within the academy. The majority of Chicana lesbian academics are not out, and many fear being outed. At last year's Ford Foundation Fellows gathering, gay/lesbian Chicano, African-American, and Native American academics discussed the policies of revelation, with one group decidedly arguing for secrecy, while those of us with tenure urged our colleagues to consider the fact that in most departments, very little is truly secret—least of all who pairs up with whom.

Continuing with the practices and politics of identifying, of self-identification, and the constructions of identity, mixed-race Chicana and Native/Chicana women decry the implicit racism that parades a Native/Othered guest lecturer before a Chicana conference not much interested in exploring this old division, but that would rather project a falsely unified consciousness listing the speakers as "foremothers." These are also examples from our daily lives as Chicana academics.[3]

Probing such politics and policies of identity and location, contemporarily as I have just done, or historically as I intend next, is difficult because self-designation is a twentieth-century exercise full of self-consciousness. Locating the identity of subjects long since dead, in the case of my work on nineteenth-century Nuevo Mexicanas, is equally problematic because the people I write about exist in the cultural and collective memories of the Chicano/Hispano families of Santa Fe. Ancestry remains exceedingly important in the lives of Northern Nuevo Mexicanas. The twin processes of naming and revealing engender further responsibilities and prerogatives and have been contextualized for that reason in these opening passages.[4]

Some might want to search the past for clues about how we came to our contemporary ideological impasses over the significance of our identities. Identity today, our autobiographical anecdotes reveal and the documents detailing the lives of nineteenth-century Spanish-Mexican women suggest, is not the same as identity once was. Nineteenth-century Spanish-speakers named themselves as village residents first, as members of particular families second, then as (Catholic) parishioners, and, continuously, as non-Indians. Without Native people—*against* whom they would identify—the Spanish-speaking, mestizo and non-mestizo might not have chosen specific identities at all, adopting instead a more colonialist attitude that rendered indigenous residents nonexistent.

As we know today, identity formulations have as much to do with what one carries inside as with what one encounters outside. Indigenous people thus existed as opposites to the Spanish, and then, in the case of the majority mestizo population (that is, after the first twenty-five years of conquest and colonization by the Spanish) their ongoing presence delineated a clearing space within which a small but tenacious conquistador class could continue to roam, relocate, and define itself, if uneasily. Physical appearance—or phenotype as geneticists might say—by itself helped identity concerns hardly at all, as we see in the present when we must piece together color, speech, dress, and many other "markers" to situate or locate one (an-other's) identity.

Mexico and the Southwest today see all manner of color representations and, as one friend reported, there is nothing funnier than to see North American visitors in Mexican towns run over to a blond or lighter-skinned local to pose questions in English. One of my points or theories, then, from my reading of colonial Mexican and New Mexican documents, is that after the first phases of initial conquest, Indian actually began signifying non-Spanish-speaking, not non-Spanish, as very few Spanish-speaking residents of the Northern frontiers could actually label themselves pure-blooded Spanish, even if they were of the criollo class (that is, were descendents of people self-designated as Spanish but born in the New World), even if color supported their sense of superiority. In the early part of the nineteenth century, in the midst of creating and adopting a *criolloized* existence, many used their labels not simply to delineate an ethnic identity, but to designate their classes primarily. This fragile existence as frontierspeople transcended other ponderings over and beyond their quests for specific regional identities—as Santa Feans, as Tucsonenses, as Tejanos. The migrations northward of mixed-race peoples, some studies suggest, signalled among the migrants an improved class status. Resettlement, they imply, hastened social and economic mobility, but were best considered locale by locale. The resulting identity formations were lodged in a hodgepodge system that was best understood by residents of a region, by insiders, and only loosely by those living throughout the distant territories of the former Spanish Empire (Morner, 1967).

Categorization primarily on the basis of any single identifying characteristic—that is, skin color, language skill, religious devotion, or birthplace—would be a mistake. Finally, on the question of the origins of the identity models I am asserting here, or on the origins of Chicana identity, it is important to bear in mind that insider/outsider concerns operated on a multitiered and in a multidirectional social system; a conquistador class may have sought to assert its power through identity manipulations. Wannabes—those seeking upper class status or non–lowest class status—in Tucson, Santa Fe, and San Antonio determined that harkening back to a conquistador heritage was better than to claim mestizo or indigenous ethnicity. The state, or Empire in this case, supported the denials readily enough: identity cards were common, and rules and regulations from both Church and State dictated marriage choices, to name only two examples of how race or ethnicity were also determined or ordained. From the beginning of Spanish contact, then, the search for identity hinged around questions of status and social location, as well as on relationship to the State or Empire, which is to say, pro-Crown, or later, pro-Spain or pro-Mexico, or later still, pro-Revolution.

In New Mexico, whose Spanish-Mexican women I speak about next, the hyphenations and terms were equally complex. "Spanish-Mexican" appeared as early as the colonial period (Castañeda, 1990). It was used interchangeably with "gente de habla español," at times to connote a criollo heritage, and otherwise to signify Spanish-Catholic background and Spanish linguistic dominance.[5] By 1820, a new sense of Mexicanness pervaded, with even criollos picking up the label "Mexican." Thus, Mexican still was recognized for the indigenous, Aztec word that it was (Me-shi-can), but it was Hispanicized sufficiently (Me-ji-cano/a) that it also came to be recognized as the basis for an evolving national identity. Mexico (the country) would not name itself until later, but already politicians, officials, criollos, mestizos, and Natives used the word and applied Mexican, if infrequently, to themselves. In the independence movements, adaptation of an indigenous word, of course, served to mark the severed bonds to Spain, and Mexico and Mexicanos continue to this day to glorify and uphold the concept of an indigenous, mixed-race inheritance. Unfortunately for we Mexican/Chicano residents of the Southwestern United

States, the federal government is abysmally ignorant of this rich heritage about naming and identity formations.

An added ingredient in the rumblings about Spanish versus Mexican, Indian versus non-Indian, criollo versus mestizo in the nineteeenth century was the steady reality of continuous race and cultural mixture. We might even say that non-Indian did not deny Indianness, but was also a realistic statement about Spanish-language dominance. In places like Northern Mexico and in the upper Rio Grande valleys that later constituted New Mexico and Colorado, few original settlers maintained "pure" Spanish blood. For one, immigration from the interior of Mexico was a constant phenomenon throughout the nineteenth century. Mestizos from central Mexico and mixed-race migrants with Spanish linguistic skills from such northern states as Sonora and Chihuahua moved north into New Mexico and Texas. This continued even after the United States invasions of the 1820s, 1830s, and 1840s.

Additionally, religion ordered other considerations: few Catholics married non-Catholics. In New Mexico, *genízaros*, or de-tribalized, Catholic converts of Indian descent, married Spanish-Mexicans. The hyphenated term, Spanish-Mexican, captures readily the forged race/ethnic, religious, and political minglings on the northern Mexican frontier and seems extremely appropriate in its application to the nineteenth century, but again, only if listeners recognize that Spanish-Mexican reflects mestizaje.

For Chicanas living after 1820, the changing political and economic configurations as Mexico declared its independence and the United States its interest in Mexico's northern territories mirrored other problems—not more choices, but different ones. Nuevo Mexicanos had sent Don Pedro Pino on a long journey to Mexico City and to Spain, as royal edict had decreed during the discussions about independence for Mexico. The familiar ditty, "Don Pedro Pino fue, Don Pedro Pino vino" (conveying roughly, he went, he saw, he returned), suggested that popular culture was not yet ready to concede any true change, in governance or anything else.

But change did in fact catch up to the frontierspeople. Soon, Missouri traders and merchants began pushing into the economic centers of the frontier, especially toward Santa Fe, with wagons loaded with manufactured items. The wagons creaked and groaned into this most populated Mexican community west of the Mississippi River, a town of over 4,000 persons that by frontier standards qualified it as a full-fledged city. The hardy perseverance of the wagons, the survival of goods on the pathways from the distant states along the Mississippi/Missouri corridor, and their knowledgeable drivers became images to be carefully considered by the locals. The long and short of it was that the Mexican frontier of the north had been neglected by the interior governing departments as they fought for or against independence instead, and this predisposed to a certain extent Santa Fe's residents toward embracing the North American articles, if not their purveyors.

Economic desires could not mask for long, however, lingering racial, cultural, and sexual tensions. Their appearance was aided by the underlying values and ideologies of impudent merchants from the United States. The trader/ trapper generation arriving in Santa Fe, men like James Ohio Pattie or William Messervy, despised the town's adobe structures and exhibited an unabashed disdain for local customs. Their comments conveyed far more than the typical anti-Mexican sentiment we know guided the travel literature of this period. Josiah Gregg in a famous volume published some time later preached a stereotypic notion of social status, "The arrival of the caravan at Santa Fe changes the aspect of the place at once. Instead of idleness and stagnation which its streets exhibited before, one now sees everywhere the bustle, noise, and activity of a lively market town." A physician by training, Gregg reported that nothing was wrong with Santa Fe and New Mexicans that a bit of merchandising could not cure.

No single character better symbolizes the way in which identity questions and issues were on the one hand central and important, or on the other, nearly ignored by historians, than Doña Gertrudis Barceló. Owner of Santa Fe's largest gambling saloon and bar, expert monte card dealer, and a fascinating businesswoman, she received the highest praise and worst criticism of every Euro-American in town. Matt Field depicted the saloon as a place "where her calm seriousness was alone discernable. . . . Again and again the long fingers of Señora Toulous swept off the pile of gold, and again were they replaced by the unsteady fingers of her opponent." In her, these restless wanderers recognized their own hungry search for profit, but they disparaged her for it. Josiah Gregg called Mexicans "lazy and indolent." James Josiah Webb determined that all Mexicans did was "literally dance from the cradle to the grave." In the Congressional Record of the period, speeches and statements equated brown skin color with promiscuity, immorality, and decay. Albert Pike in New Mexico in 1831 called the area around Santa Fe "bleak, black, and barren." New Mexicans, he said, were "peculiarly blessed with ugliness." Frank Edwards, on a military expedition—illegal at that—called Mexicans "debased in all moral sense," and they amounted to little more than "swarthy thieves and liars." Francis Parkman, historian of the West, would argue a decade later that people in this part of the country could be "separated into three divisions, arranged in order of their merits: white men, Indians, and Mexicans; to the latter of whom the honorable title of 'whites' is by no means conceded." When the United States conquered Mexico, the boundary commmisioner declared that the "darker colored" races were inevitably "inferior and syphilitic."

Literally thousands of other references mirrored the racist values and conquering ideologies of the United States, heightening the fervor over destiny and superiority, gloating over, as a *Harper's* reporter stated, "an ignorant, priest-ridden peasantry."

The racial idiom of these nineteenth-century illegal immigrants from the United States up until 1848, and subsequently when the territories were snatched from Mexico, suggest that sometime in this period, identity matters came to be shaped by anti-Mexican fervor as much as by proud ownership of the term Mexican. For women of the former Mexican north, the sexual idiom of the time, of the sort that denigrated the famous La Tules, but also others who labored for the newcomer class, is equally important to understand. Women were made active agents in a town that Gregg said bustled with activity, including sexual activity, or so they said. Prostitution in the period before conquest was illegal and its punishment was banishment from the town. Illicit sexual liasions, partner exchange, and all the rest were recorded in the court records, so sexual expression outside the confines of marriage was clearly evident; to read the newcomers' accounts, however, would suggest that all Spanish-Mexican women did, when not dancing, was have sex with the Euro-American men. For that reason, I have sought in my earlier work on widowhood to portray some of the harsher realities, to expose the ways in which women most often worked at several jobs, such as household manager, laundress, seamstress, and domestic; many operated carts on the plaza, and once a new wage, tax, and economic system was in place, these aspects of frontier life became even more necessary in explaining women's survival. Many students of history would like to make the case that La Tules operated a brothel and was doing her own share of exploitation, but there is no evidence to support the fantasy, and left unframed by the racial and sexual degradations colonization imposes, the conclusion encapsulates historically a form of misogyny.

Now where my discussion might go next, the effects of changes "measured" at another juncture (toward the end of the nineteenth century), remains primarily speculation. I am currently researching aspects of women's lives there, looking, for example, at women in Santa Fe's jails after 1880, when prostitution charges dominate the court records; what becomes clearer about the last decades of the nineteenth century is that until then, Spanish-speaking or sur-named women enjoyed some degree of mobility between towns and within extended family networks. That becomes much less the case in the twentieth century, and possibly until World War II, especially in the defense industries, with different wage-work based in the factories, where Chicanas were more locked into the lowest-paying and most depreciated jobs of all. Thus, our contemporary moves into urban centers followed in two stages. The first occurred between the Great Depression and roughly 1940, as rural to urban migration soared and when urban wage economies as well as migration from Mexico increasingly drew Mexicana and Chicana workers into the larger cities of Texas, New Mexico, Arizona, and California, and to a lesser extent toward selected states of the Midwest and the East. A second followed after World War II when the war machine actually drew them in, but only to lock them into war industry work or service occupations.

Identity formulations in those urban spaces, where bilingual skill was necessary for negotiating daily living, was still oppositional, but this time it resembled "a pulling away from" rural identity, small town identity, or extended or localized family. City migrants were often the first generation to leave their villages or small towns, often the first generation to travel such long distances (in that way, they resembled some colonial ancestors), and often the first generation to speak English fluently or to combine English and Spanish. Truly, what we see in this grouping, then, is a Chicana generation, if we understand Chicana as a twentieth-century phenomenon characterized by bilingualism, biculturalism, and shifting economic status—an economic status that was not necessarily better, but different—steady wage work as opposed to erratic wages, weekly paychecks as opposed to haphazard payments or by-the-piece or job payment. Also, a degree of independence, that is, a movement away from traditional racial, sexual, and religious governance, seems to prevail in the depictions by the few scholars who have begun to examine Chicanas in this era. I hesitate to argue too strongly that this is definitively the first generation of self-identifying Chicanas—that comes later in the 1960s, and I hesitate to mark it in the history books, to hail these women as "true" Chicanas, because if we have learned anything about authenticity and the power of authenticating, such differentiations proceed along contrary lines historically and contemporarily. Who is a real Chicana feminist is unanswerable in general terms and, so, who can be designated as the first discernible Chicana generation is equally ungeneralizable.

The search for home or homeland, another marker along the identity road, interestingly would be left to the next generation of urban Chicanas, and it is here that lesbian feminist theoreticians like Gloria Anzaldúa (1987), Cherríe Moraga (1983, 1993), Emma Pérez (1991), Alicia Gaspar de Alba (1989; 1993) and others take up the search for identities in the multiples; it is among this most recent generation of self-identified Chicanas that more fluid identities can be located. What may be important about each may be the linkage between identity and homeland. Here I am assuming that most have read Anzaldúa's *Borderlands*, Moraga's (1983) *Loving in the War Years*, Pérez's (1991) excerpt from *Gulf Dreams* and her article in *Chicana Lesbians*, called "Sexuality and Discourse," as well as the poetry and essays of Gaspar de Alba (1989; 1993) on border culture, in *Three Times a Woman* and *The Mystery of Survival and Other Stories*. Each author reflects a working-class heritage (or, for Gaspar de Alba, a strict Mexican, "untainted" ancestry/class, that is, non-pocho), a bilingual understanding of the world, and a centering of mother, grandmothers, or sisters in their memoirs and in their creative writing. Each longs for a space or site of reunification, and one can envision some generation of psychoanalysts, deconstructionists, and social historians engaging with these longings as a search for womb, mother, or homeland. The linkages could be dehistoricized, just for fun, but I would like to resurrect the historical for just a moment longer and then suspend it.

The political self-consciousness pervading the works of the Chicana lesbian feminist writers just named is one more marker along the path of their identities; another, I have suggested, is their nod to history and location, to family pasts and memory. In a version of her forthcoming novel, *Gulf Dreams,* Pérez recalls "the sound of the hammer reflected his love for us, pound for pound," as she gathers up memories of her father's upholstery shop located in front of their small-town, Texas home; or in Moraga's autobiographical essay, "There was something I knew at that eight-year-old moment that I vowed never to forget—the smell of a woman who is life and home to me at once"; in Gaspar de Alba's autobiographical statement when she names herself "the first Chicana fruit of the family."

Moraga (1993) claimed her mother's race, her brother claimed their (white) father's. Chicana, to this way of thinking, is racialized as blood (genetic) and not ethnicity or identity, something less true in Anzaldúa (1987) and Pérez (1991), who both have Mexican parents and see Chicana embracing mestiza pasts, more blurring rather than less; in Gaspar de Alba's (1989, 1993) poetry and reflections, Chicana becomes an identity assumed around linguistic borders because "English was forbidden at home and Spanish was forbidden" in her Catholic girls' school. Moraga privileges the color/blood connection, casting her choice in the direction of Chicana, whereas Anzaldúa, Pérez, and Gaspar de Alba search for and construct an ethnicity of the borderlands, the Rio Grande, and ultimately, México; for Anzaldúa and Pérez regional identity and ethnic identity or nationality derives from a rural Tejana experience, for Gaspar de Alba from a Mexican border zone. Their Chicana identities are lodged in *lo Mexicano* whereas Moraga's (1983), at least in the earlier volume, stems from a differently-assumed identity based on something chosen—either/or white or Chicana (the latter being the metaphorical land of her mother).

The bifurcations evident in Moraga's work reveal a personal journey that mirrors more than motherland/homeland searches. It is a search to be duplicated by many, evidenced alone that her posturings do not cause her any ostracism among Chicanas; indeed many young Chicana lesbians coming to their twin identities, first as Chicanas and then as lesbians, reify her as guru, understandably given the different stages of consciousness woven into her autobiographical ruminations. As Gaspar de Alba (1993) notices, in "Tortillerismo," a review of many of these texts,[6] Anzaldúa's mestiza consciousness is far more difficult to grasp for those whose racial and ethnic consciousness is absent, or de-historicized, or regarded as something that can be everchangingly shed or adopted at will. I would also say that Anzaldúa's and Pérez's Chicana lesbian identities are more fixed precisely because both are from villages in Texas, and Gaspar de Alba's because she is a fronteriza who traversed with agility the U.S.-Mexican border as she did the public/private, English/Spanish one. Moraga grew up in Los Angeles in a household with different borders, but decidely not with sustained geographic proximity to Mexico. It could also be argued that in her case, familiarity with Los Angeles is familiarity with the world. Her coming into a Chica*na* consciousness after 1980, a moment of consciousness explained by Anzaldúa who met Moraga at a conference and posed the inevitable, "Who/what are you?" is more than anecdote because the moment marks consciousness of the most intimate and powerful kind, the seconds of declaration, "I am" or "I think I am." Each of the writers listed here explains a similar process of identity-situating and each politicizes that moment radically by disavowal, rejection, or embrace. The moment configures itself distinctively and becomes not only a space for empowerment, but a space for departure—a signal of difference, if you will.

The question that emerges from the revelatory texts or writings of Chicana lesbian feminists is not who or what is to be made more of or less of, or who is more Chicana (those closest to Mexico?) or who less (those not?), but rather, as I am suggesting, how *much* to be Chicana and in what circles or locations to situate that identity, or, have it situated for one (as reflected in the question "who/what are you?"). Self-constructed, the lesbian memoirs of Anzaldúa and Pérez—more than Moraga's—locate their identity formulations across several centuries, Gaspar de Alba across two countries; theirs, I would argue, is in keeping with historical memory, even in their rejection of the masculinist aspects of that history. Their work exhibits the tendency to assert a "we," of family, community, or ethnicity, to speak of an historical "us"; far less evident is the focused "I," a tone detectable in many of Moraga's pieces.[7] Moraga's, then, might well be of the future because it patterns outward, from a dominant urban, First World existence (as she says in *Loving in the War Years*, a "passing," male-centric yet fatherless household/family, and importantly, an English-dominant domain). Anzaldúa, Pérez, and Gaspar de Alba did not share in the life of post–World War II Los Angeles such childhoods, emerged not from the gringo/Chicana parental racial dyad, or even cultural one. Thus, they stand apart from many contemporary movements that seek the move toward that next level of mestiza consciousness stretching beyond Spanish/Indigenous and embracing many other multiple ethnicities and identities; in a set of words, the transnational, transmigratory, First World cultural polyglot of the next century, in a name, Los Angeles. On that plane, then, Moraga meets up with Anzaldúa, Pérez, and Gaspar de Alba to complete a cycle or circle, a pattern not lost on historians or cultural anthropologists of the Southwest who recall Aztlán as the spiritual homeland of the scrappy Aztecs (scrappy here meaning in their beginnings as a group living in a rattlesnake-infested swamp and eventually dominating Tenochtitlán as they did). I am intrigued about future projections for this type of work and scholarship; perhaps Gronk's forecast is on the mark and we historians can state, "L.A. is [indeed] everywhere." In its most self-stylized or highly conscious form, one can imagine, for example, a Chicana/Native/Euro-American, or Third World Other/Transgendered person reinvoking Anzaldúa's mestiza consciousness and reinscribing it with new meanings. Similarly, a new generation of middle class, university-educated Chicanas may lay claim to a different mestizaje-ized identity altogether that revolves primarily around, or is lodged across the spaces of sexuality/class/

ethnicity/physical abilities. The step in that direction constitutes one Chicana (postmodern) condition.

Such problematizing also needs to take into account another departure, that is, the movement of these writers and other women of color like them into the academic theatre. Setting aside for a moment the trivialized pursuit of multiculturalism in education (what some scholars would call ethnomania unleashed in the academy or in the public schools), let me say that these writers must also be understood as a first generation of self-identified lesbians *and* first generation creative writers or scholar/activists. These linkages do denote some radical historical disjuncturing because, on the one hand, we have in them, in ourselves, a movement into Western European-patterned, formal educational systems, of the research type, and that move has come at a moment when the environments new to us are reorienting themselves in the very directions we argued for outside *their* walls. So although this means that, for the most part, we are ignored (the statistics on faculty hiring and on graduate student recruitment are appalling on the question of diversity), and our work is still most often ignored or disdained, we occupy, as a first generation, yet another *sitio*, a new site of, or for, identity; Anzaldúa's "she has this fear," with which I opened, can be understood, if contextualized against our invisibility or absence in the academy, but is less understandable if layered over the extremely rich pronouncements, creative and artistic expressions, of our poets, storytellers, and scholars.

This generational study of Chicana presence and perseverance on the question of identity, what may shape it, what may impose limitations on it, seeks to understand our concerns about identity, about names and naming, about consciousness of the self, against historical and contemporary backdrops. One is not divorced from the other, but as I have also tried to illustrate, when I as researcher am in one, I do not or cannot forget the other. Reinscribing both, evoking both, matters.

I want to conclude in overview that modern and postmodern self-constructions are differently linked by generations of Chicanas and that even designating a so-called generation of Chicanas is difficult because the Southwest and Midwest is demarcated by regions: Northern versus Southern, or in Southwestern states, border versus non-border, center versus margin in some, rural versus urban in others, by shifting demographies, and by differential relations to Washington. This makes the search for the appropriate application of the designation Chicana historically and contemporarily confusing. We continue to try, however, because our labels matter, race matters, and identity matters.

NOTES

1. See the forthcoming volume by Clyde Milner III (ed.), *The Re-signification of the American West* (New York, NY: Oxford University Press) for newer, "revisionary" work.

2. For a review of this literature, see Antonia Castañeda, "Women of color and the rewriting of western history," *Pacific Historical Review*.

3. The example is drawn about a MALCS Conference, 1993.

4. See D. González, *Refusing the Favor* (New York, NY: Oxford University Press, forthcoming).

5. On another labelling, "gente de razón," see G. Miranda, "Racial and Cultural Dimensions of Gente de Razón status in Spanish and Mexican California," *Southern California Quarterly 70*, (1988).

6. See *Signs*, Summer 1993.

7. See from *The Last Generation* the opening of the chapter reflecting on the changes in the Nicaraguan Revolution after Chamorro's election.

REFERENCES

Anzaldúa, G. (1987). *Borderlands/La frontera: The new Mestiza*. San Franciso, CA: Spinsters/Aunt Lute Press.

Castañeda, A. (1992). "Women of color and the rewriting of western history." *Pacific Historical Review*, pp. 501–533.

———. (1990). "Gender, race, and culture: Spanish-Mexican women in the historiography of frontier California." *Frontiers, 11*, pp. 8–20.

Gaspar de Alba, A. (1993). *The mystery of survival and other stories*. Tempe, AZ: Bilingual Review Press.

———. (1989). *Three times a woman*. Tempe, AZ: Bilingual Review Press.

Gonzalez, D. (Forthcoming). *Refusing the Favor*. New York, NY: Oxford University Press.

Hernández, I. (1993). "In praise of insubordination, or What makes a good woman go bad?" in E. Buchwald, P. R. Fletcher, & M. Roth (eds.), *Transforming a rape culture*. Minneapolis, MN: Milkweed Editions, pp. 376–392.

———. (1992). "Open letter to Chicanas: On the power and politics of origin," in R. González (ed.), *Without discovery: A native response to Columbus*. Seattle, WA: Broken Moon.

Milner, C., III. (forthcoming). *The Re-significance of the American West*. New York, NY: Oxford University Press.

Miranda, G. (1988). "Racial and cultural dimensions of Gente de Razón status in Spanish and Mexican California." *Southern California Quarterly, 70*, pp. 265–278.

Moraga, C. (1993). *The last generation*. Boston, MA: Southend Press.

———. (1983). *Loving in the war years: Lo que nunca pasó por sus labios*. Boston, MA: Southend Press.

Morner, M. (1967). *Race mixture in the history of Latin America*. Boston, MA: Little Brown.

Perez, E. (1991). "Sexuality and discourse," in C. Trujillo (ed.), *Chicana lesbians: The girls our mothers warned us about*. Berkeley, CA: Third Woman Press.

Valdez, L. (1994). "The Hemispheric American." Paper presented at the Claremont McKenna Athaneum, The Claremont Colleges.

Racialized Boundaries, Class Relations, and Cultural Politics: The Asian-American and Latino Experience

Rodolfo D. Torres and ChorSwang Ngin

"Race" and "ethnicity," though key concepts in sociological discourse and public debate, have remained problematic. Policy pundits, journalists, and conservative and liberal academics alike all work within categories of race and ethnicity and use these concepts in public discourse as though there is unanimity regarding their analytical value. Racialized group conflicts are similarly advanced and framed as a "race relations" problem, and presented largely in black/white terms.[1] A prime example of this confusion is the analysis of the causes of the April 1992 Los Angeles riots. In the aftermath of the riots, academics and journalists analyzed the riots as a matter of race relations—first it was a problem between blacks and whites, then between blacks and Koreans, and then between blacks and Latinos, and back to blacks and whites. The interpretation of the riots as a race relations problem failed to take into account the economic changes, the economic restructuring, and the drastic shifts in demographic patterns which have created new dynamics of class and racialized ethnic relations in Los Angeles (see, for example, Davis, 1990).

The analytical status of the ideas of race and race relations have been questioned for more than a decade within British academic discussion, and it is only more recently that some U.S. scholars have begun to consider the rationale and implications of this critique. A few U.S. writers have begun to shift from treating race as an explanatory construct to focusing on racism as a structure and ideology of domination and exclusion, and moving beyond race relations as black/white relations. David Theo Goldberg's (1993) innovative approach to mapping new expressions of multiple racisms and racialized discourse; Cornel West's (1993) call for a new language to talk about race; Michael Omi's (1993) recognition of the limits of race relations theories; Tomas Almaguer's (1989, p. 24) challenge "to remain open to lines of historical interpretation that do not resonate with the nationalist sentiments"; Barbara Fields' (1990) focus on race as an ideological construction; and E. San Juan's (1992) treatment of how race articulates with power, ethnicity, nation, gender and class all represent recent important contributions to the ongoing attempts at theorizing about racialized groups in the context of changing class relations in the United States. The parallel critique by British scholars has centered on the production and the reproduction of the concept of race within British society. Seminal writers of these works include Robert Miles (1982, 1989, 1993); Stuart Hall (1978, 1980, 1986); Paul Gilroy (1991); John Solomos (1988, 1989); A. Sivanandan (1982, 1990); and the recent works of Floya Anthias & Nira Yuval-Davis (1993).

In our analysis of the Latino and Asian American populations in California, we will move beyond the contemporary American debate by arguing for a complete rejection of the use of the terms "race" and "race relations" in academic and public discourses. We will introduce an alternative model that applies the concept of racialization to the California Asian and Latino populations and expands the concept of ethnicity to include both "ethnicity-for-itself" and "ethnicity-in-itself."

THE MUDDLES IN THE DEBATE

In everyday and academic discourse, the terms "race" and "ethnicity" are used interchangeably, creating much confusion over what is racial and what is ethnic in the designation of populations. In the U.S. tradition, the terms "race" and "ethnic" have been employed throughout as analytical categories to describe and "explain" various groups.

This muddle in the academic debate is also reflected in official governmental practices. The 1980 Census, for example, listed fifteen groups in the "race" item in the questionnaire: white, black, American Indian, Eskimo, Aleut, Chinese, Filipino, Japanese, Asian Indian, Korean, Vietnamese, Hawaiian, Samoan, Guamanian, and Other. Though the Census Bureau claimed that the concept "race" as used does not denote any clear-cut scientific definition of biological stock (Loh & Medford, 1984, p. 4), by categorizing groups as "races," the Census Bureau nonetheless is suggesting that each of the listed groups including "whites" are "races" (our emphasis). Even more complicated is the classification of peoples of Mexican, Central American, and Latin American origin. Because the Census uses a "white" and "black" category, Latinos were moved back and forth from a "white" or "ethnic" ("persons of Spanish mother tongue") category in the 1930 Census to a "black" or "racial" ("other non-white") category in the 1940 Census. In the 1950 and 1960 Census, the ambiguous category of "white persons of Spanish surname" was used. In 1970, the classification was changed to "white persons of Spanish surname and Spanish mother tongue." Then in 1980, Mexican Americans and Puerto Ricans, along with other Central and Latin Americans of diverse national origin, were classified as "non-white Hispanic" (Moore & Pachon, 1985, p. 3).

California, its dramatic changes in ethnic composition brought about by the liberalization of the 1965 Immigration and Naturalization Act and, more recently, the Amnesty Bill of 1988 which legalized the residency status of Mexicans and Central Americans, has brought to the forefront the ever-increasing confusion over these categories. Are Latinos an ethnic group or a racial group? Are Asians an ethnic group or a racial group? In this debate centered on a black/white dichotomy, Asian Americans and Latinos fall through these bipolar designations. The conceptual inadequacy of this dichotomy is most evident in California as the realities and the positions of the two populations bring into question the continued use of this model. The complexity of the class character and the differential integration of Asian Americans and Latinos into the U.S. political economy therefore calls for new paradigms to understand these changing populations in the post–civil rights era. To provide a critique and alternative framework of contemporary race relations, we will draw upon selected works of the innovative political economist Robert Miles.[2] As Miles' theoretical position on race and especially his advancement on the concept of "racialization" are central to our analysis, we will first outline his conceptual framework in substantial detail. This will provide a meaningful framework for analyzing the phenomena of racialized boundaries in "postmodern" capitalism.

ROBERT MILES' RECONSTRUCTION OF RACE

Central to Robert Miles' work is the notion of the generation and the reproduction of the idea of race as a social and ideological construct. According to Miles (1982, 1989), the idea of race has changed over time. It first entered the English language in the sixteenth century to mean lineage or common descent or history (see also Banton, 1987).[3] With European colonial expansion and colonization, contacts with Others increased. This contact was structured by competition for land, introduction of private property, demand for labor, and the perceived obligation of conversion to Christianity. Miles posited that European ideas of foreigners were based on the representation of the Others generated in the context of a stronger European economic and military force. During the eighteenth century, with the scientific assertion of the existence of different biologically constituted races, the term "race" came to mean discrete categories of human beings, based on phenotypical differences, and ranked with psychological and social capacities. Later, the emergence of the science of genetics refuted this idea of race as discrete and fixed subdivisions of the human species because no such link was ever found. This scientific discourse on race, however, did not replace the earlier conception of the Other: the idea of races as biological types persisted even though proven false by the weight of scientific evidence. Miles questioned why the scientific reconception of race has little influence in everyday discourse. He maintained, moreover, that an understanding of the continuing reference to the phenotyp-ical features suggested that "factors other than the development of biological sciences were fundamental to the formulation of the notion of 'race' and its continuing reproduction" (1982, p. 21). This use of "race" to denote pheno-typical variation, which is given social recognition and which in turn struc-tured social interaction, is what Miles referred to as the "social construction of race." Based on this historical understanding of the concept of race, Miles argues that race cannot be used descriptively to classify people in society, nor can the concept be used for either analytical or explanatory purposes.

Race itself is an ideological category that requires explanation. Thus Miles has carefully avoided the ambivalent employment of the term "race" except when he refers to its use by other writers. In challenging the analytical status of the idea of race, Miles (1982) also argues against the use of "race relations." Race relations, the central research focus of most British and American soci-ologists, is defined by its chief proponent John Rex as "the kinds of social relations that exist between people of the same race and ethnicity and between individuals or groups of different race and ethnicity" (1986, p. 2). Miles in-terpreted this conceptual transition from the social category of "race" to "race relations" as the product of the legitimation given to the belief that the "hu-man species consists of several distinct 'races.'" This "race relation" was then objectified as an area of study. Thus, Miles (1982) stated:

"Race relations" can only mean that 'races' have social relations, one with another. So, for relations to occur, "race" must exist. Indeed, they 'exist' in the sense that human agents believe them to exist, but uncritically to reproduce and accord analytical status to these beliefs is nevertheless to legitimate that process by giving it "scientific" status (p. 33).

Following Miles, several British sociologists have also carefully placed the term "race" within inverted commas (see Williams, 1989). Susan Smith, for example, notes that the meaning of "race" is ideologically biased, and therefore is fundamentally a social construct (Smith, 1989, p. 1). Other British writers, cognizant of Miles' work, have self-consciously defended their position to use the term "race" in their analysis. Gilroy (1987), for example, retains the use of the term "race" as an analytical category. For Gilroy, race is retained as "an analytical category not because it corresponds to any biological or epis-temological absolutes, but because it refers to investigation of the power that collective identities acquire by means of their roots in tradition" (1991). How-ever, Miles (1984) rejects such an approach by arguing against the confusion of ideological and political goals with scientific rigor in methodology.

Robert Miles' rejection of the category "race" is relevant to our attempt to provide insight to the current California "race" and "ethnicity" theoretical debate. In California, Asian Americans and Latinos comprise two extremely diverse populations. The population termed "Asian American" includes at least fourteen distinct groups: Chinese, Filipino, Japanese, Asian Indian, Korean, Vietnamese, Laotian, Thai, Cambodian, Hmong, Pakistani, Indonesian, Hawaiian, and people from the Pacific Islands of Micronesia and Polynesia. Each of these Asian American ethnic categories is further divided along linguistic, religious, and especially class lines. These changing demographic realities have reshaped the ethnic and socioeconomic relations of the populations of California. The majority of the recent Asian immigrants to California from Hong Kong, Korea, Taiwan, and the Philippines are of middle-class background. The Vietnamese, Cambodians, Laotians, and Hmong, on the other hand, are mostly refugees who entered the country without much capital. But, with time, class differentiation is emerging among these newcomers. While some Asian Americans within a sub-ethnic group are entrepreneurs, professionals, or managerial workers, others are dependent on the state for welfare. In terms of generational difference, some Chinese and Japanese Americans are direct descendants of the early pioneers who immigrated to the United States in the late nineteenth century. Still others are recent immigrants who have arrived within the last few years. Segments of the Asian American population are concentrated in ethnic enclaves such as Chinatowns, Little Saigons, and Manilatowns, while others are dispersed, living in middle- and upper-middle-class suburbs. Notwithstanding, these divergent groups are categorized in the U.S. Census as one single group—Asian Americans.

The use of a single category to represent the Asian-American population is also mirrored in the practice of classifying the Latino population as a single "non-white Hispanic" category. This group includes Mexican Americans of the Southwest, the colonized subjects from Puerto Rico, refugees from Cuba, and recent immigrants and refugees from Mexico, Central, and South America. These diverse Latino sub-groups are also differentiated by community, generation, and class origins. In describing the Latino community, scholars speak of the "barrio" to mean actual settlements but also in terms of the symbolic community that serves as a source of identity. The same generational difference that applies to Asian Americans and European Americans cannot be applied to Latinos, as there are Latinos who are the direct descendants of pre-conquest Southwest populations.[4]

The question of class and class structure is even more problematic among the Latino population. The existence of a Chicano class structure predates the Mexican American War of 1846–1848 (Barrera, 1979). This population includes the Chicano/Latino working class, petty bourgeois, recent immigrants from Mexico and Latin America, and the Chicano professional managerial class (Barrera, 1984). However, there is a paucity of studies on class divisions within the Latino community. As noted by Valle and Torres (1994), much needs to be learned about the nature and meaning of Latino class relations in a postindustrial society, and the manner in which these divisions manifest themselves in the changing organization of work, urban politics, and relation with the state.

Despite these varied and complex characteristics among both Asian Americans and Latinos, a distinction can be made between the recent groups of immigrants and the earlier groups: the recent groups have not been subjected to the same harsh legal exclusionary practices and therefore do not share the lived historical memory of virulent racism. This distinction is important—it determines how ethnicity is perceived by others and how it is used by the ethnic groups involved. All immigrants, however, are connected to their native countries by transnational economic and social processes. The material forces that determine their migration, their present production relations, and their class positions are similarly determined by the larger social structure and the global economy.

This class diversity within the immigrant population makes representing them as either "race" or "ethnic" problematic. Segments of the immigrant population might conceivably be regarded as a "racial" group in the tradition of the "race-centered" theorists, as this group is subjected to hate crimes and other discriminatory practices. Others might be regarded as an "ethnic" group in the tradition of the "ethnic-centered" theorists: their middle-class status proclaimed by the neoconservatives as evidence of equal opportunities for all groups in the United States. We must be cognizant of the fact that the material success among the middle-class immigrant population should be attributed, in part, to their professional education received abroad and to the capital immigrants brought with them, and not to some inherent cultural entrepreneurial essentialism found among certain Asian Americans and "Hispanics" as argued by the new entrepreneurial cultural determinists (Kotkin, 1992).

Given the existence of class divisions within the Asian American and Latino populations, we find the key to Miles' insight—the unequivocal rejection of the notion "race"—useful in solving part of the Asian American/Latino "race/ethnic" muddle. The category "race" as applied to Asian Americans and Latinos (along with African Americans, Native Americans, and European Americans) has no heuristic value. That is, racialized social groups in the United States do not constitute "races." What about the classification of Asian Americans and Latinos as "ethnic" groups? For this, we will first briefly define the term "ethnicity" as used in the sociological literature and Robert Miles' critique of its uncritical use.

ETHNICITY

The actual term "ethnicity" (from the Greek word "ethnos," meaning "people" or "nation") has been defined by Milton Yinger (1994) as

a segment of a larger society whose members are thought, by themselves and/or others, to have a common origin and to share important segments of a common culture and who, in addition, participate in shared activities in which the common origin and culture are significant ingredients (p. 3).

Milton Gordon (1964) similarly defines ethnicity as "a shared feeling of peoplehood" (p. 24). The research on "ethnicity" and "ethnic group" as a dominant paradigm in contemporary British and American sociological writings has defined the "culture" of the social group as their major focus.

Miles (1982), a major critic of the use of the term "ethnicity," argues that assessing a group's beliefs and behavior in terms of its

culturally determined distinctiveness can lead to a simple cataloguing of cultural difference (a dictionary of the "exotic") at one level, while at another it presents an analysis of the interaction between culturally distinct groups either without reference to or even in direct opposition to class relations (p. 67).

Furthermore, "by abstracting cultural differentiation, and the notion of group identity which derives from this difference, from production relations," Miles continues, "the consequence is either a failure to identify class divisions within the culturally distinct populations . . . (or) the class position that migrants come to occupy . . . (and) the material forces which determine the migration" (1982, pp. 67–69). Thus, Miles (1982) argues that "ethnic relations" cannot be used as an analytical framework as it contains a number of "analytical, logical and empirical contradictions and/or errors." Furthermore, he argues that research of "ethnic" culture would constitute an analytical trap if it is divorced from its historical and material context (p. 70). However, Miles also recognizes there is a certain ambiguity in his work on the concept of "ethnic" and "ethnicity" (Miles, 1991, personal correspondence).

While we share Miles' rejection in assigning analytical status to "ethnic" groups, we argue for the modified use of the term. We propose the concepts "racialization of ethnic groups," "ethnicity-in-itself," and "ethnicity-for-itself" to examine the dynamics of Latino and Asian American group relations. But first, we will draw on Miles' explication of the concept of racialization.

RACIALIZATION

Miles argues that the employment of the idea of race in structuring social relations should be more appropriately termed "racialization" rather than "race relations." Writing in *Racism* (1989), racialization is referred to as

those instances where social relations between people have been structured by the signification of human biological characteristics in such a way as to define and construct differentiated social collectivities. . . . The concept therefore refers to a process of categorization, a representational process of defining an Other (usually, but not exclusively) somatically (p. 75).

Three characteristics are attached to the notion of racialization. First, "racialization entails a dialectical process of signification. Ascribing a real or alleged biological characteristic with meaning to define the Other necessarily entails defining Self by the same criterion" (Miles, 1989, p. 75). Thus, "the African's 'blackness' reflected the European's 'whiteness'; these opposites were therefore bound together, each giving meaning to the other in a totality of signification" (Miles, 1989, p. 75). Second, the concept of racialization should take into account "the emergence of the idea of 'race' and its subsequent reproduction and application." Third, "the racialization of human beings entails the racialization of the processes in which they participate and the structures and institutions that result" (Miles, 1989, p. 76). That is, in racialized societies, institutions and political processes, both formal and informal, are necessarily also racialized. An example of racialization would include a political process where demands are made that certain "racial" groups be represented in positions of power or be given special privileged status. In the United States, this process is commonly known as the "politics of entitlement."

The concept of racialization has been employed by U.S. scholars Michael Omi and Howard Winant (1986) in their landmark work, *Racial Formation in the United States: From the 1960s to the 1980s*. Omi and Winant use the concept "racialization" to "signify the extension of racial meaning to a previously racially unclassified relationship, social practice or group" (p. 64). Regrettably, Omi and Winant do not fully develop this concept, nor do they use it in a sustained analytical manner. The authors' concept of racialization is grounded in race relations sociology—a sociology that reifies the notion of race.[5] This reification of race implies that racial groups constitute a monolithic social category. In suggesting that race is an active subject—"an unstable and 'decentered' complex of social meanings—the authors advance the notion that the idea of race is socially constructed. Yet they implicitly embrace and anchor their analysis of social movements and racial formation on the illusionary concept of race.[6] Omi and Winant (1986) furthermore assign analytical status to the idea of race by claiming that "the concept of racial formation should treat race in the United States as a fundamental organizing principle of social relationship" (p. 66). Whereas we maintain that racialization is grounded in class and production relations, and the idea of race need not be explicitly employed for a process of racialization to occur.

The Racialization of Ethnic Groups

The notion of racialization set forth in Miles' writing—the representation and definition of the Others based on the signification of human biological characteristics—is particularly useful in understanding the U.S. discourse of the non-European immigrants and natives. Until recently, discourse on Native Americans, African Americans, Latinos, and Asian Americans has largely depended on a phenotypical representation and evaluation. Both color and physical appearance were given social significance. By reason of their color and physical features, these populations were perceived as bearers of diseases and as endangering European American morals and "racial" purity. This discourse based on "race" provided the ideological context, in part, for the enactment of past restrictive immigration laws and discriminatory policies. Even though fewer phenotypical characteristics are employed in contemporary discourse of the immigrant groups in formal legislative policies, the racialization process continues to inform many group practices and individual actions. We would include as instances of racialization in California the "hate crimes" directed at Asian Americans and other racialized groups, the violent attacks, vandalism, racial slurs, and hateful mail directed at immigrant institutions, churches, and individuals, and racialized code words such as "welfare queen," "Willie Horton," "illegal alien," "model minority," among others.

To understand this antipathy toward Asians and Latinos, we suggest that this is the result of categorization of immigrants and foreigners based on their physical features (skin color, mostly). Past signification of immigrants, by ascribing them with real or alleged biological or cultural characteristics, are available as part of the American culture for reinterpretation, given the existence of certain stimulus. In contemporary U.S. society, the stimuli that lead to the renewed attack on Asian immigrants can be attributed, firstly, to the decline of U.S. capitalism as an economic power, particularly its economic position in relation to Japan. Much of the political debate on what's wrong with the U.S. economy focuses on Japan's unfair trade practices and acquisition of American companies, landmarks, and cultural icons. Negative imagery of Japan in the form of "Japan bashing" is articulated by both the indigenous population and the politicians, and often reproduced through political legitimation by the state. Secondly, acts of violence against racialized populations can be understood as attempts to define what is the local imagined community (Miles & Phizacklea, 1981; Anderson, 1991). The local American imagined community, a community based on the ethos of biblical foundation, republicanism, and individualism, is unable to regard those who express different values as part of the same community. This view of anti-immigrant antipathy is also echoed by sociologist Susan Smith. In her examination of working-class youth, she suggests anti-immigrant behaviors are attempts "to preserve both national exclusivity and neighborhood segregation" (Smith, 1989, p. 159).

Given these insights drawn from the works of Miles, Phizacklea, Smith, and Anderson, the bigotry and violence against racialized groups in California should be seen in the larger economic and political context. The authors attribute political and economic forces as having created and sustained racialized violence. These acts cannot be explained solely as the product of spontaneous violence perpetrated by psychologically aberrant gangs of white youth. The understanding of these multiple causes has enormous implications for directing effective policies designed to address and prevent racist violence against immigrants. New research needs to address the increased use of the signification of racial and cultural characteristics in political campaigns and the concurrent increase of intolerance against racialized groups in the United States.

RACIALIZATION FROM WITHIN

As immigrant groups are racialized by members outside their ethnic group, they are simultaneously engaged in defining and redefining their group identity. However, we maintain that this process of self-definition, racialization-from-within, and "ethnicity-for-itself" is but one form of ethnic activity. This is distinct from a process of activity and organization we regard as "ethnicity-in-itself." In "ethnicity-in-itself" immigrant groups are connected by their language and culture. Although it may be claimed that ethnicity is a subjective, constructed concept, and cannot be defined objectively with social cultural indicators (as some with the same language/cultural characteristics may not consider themselves part of the community at all), subjective ethnic identification can often lead to creation of ethnic institutions such as newspapers and schools in order to express that sense of peoplehood. Thus, the Asians and Latinos have created separate ethnic, cultural, and economic organizations to meet their multifarious needs in functioning in an urban society. These institutions and structures provide autonomous networks separate from the institutions and structures in the dominant culture. Examples of some of these Asian groups might be the Chinese language schools, the Korean churches, and the Chinese Lions Club, in areas with a critical mass of Chinese or Korean population. These affiliations are based on the members' linguistic and cultural similarity. These associations are no different from early Italian and Polish-American ethnic organizations. These ethnic activities are consistent with the traditional definition of ethnicity where the emphasis is on a socially defined sense of peoplehood based generally on concepts of shared culture and common origin. In California, this "ethnicity-in-itself" is created in part by the ethnic enclaves which serve as buffers between their group and the dominant populations. Furthermore, the recent immigrants do not share the historical memory of older immigrants and do not see themselves as victims of discrimination.

These "ethnicity-in-itself" activities, in the context of U.S. society, are noted by the indigenous populations as the unwelcome changes in their community. This "ethnicity-in-itself" is contrasted with what we observe as "ethnicity-for-itself." We would regard "ethnicity-for-itself" as racialization from within. "Ethnicity-for-itself" includes associations with co-ethnic or other ethnic groups for the purpose of political empowerment and entitlement. The awareness of their common plight is what leads to the support of others who undergo similar experiences by emphasizing the community of memory, defining the boundary with which they can develop their own culture, and the sharing of common experience. This ethnic awareness is actively promoted to serve clearly defined ends. This racialization from within serves as a political defense strategy in the face of perceived adversity or disadvantage. It is this process of renegotiation and redefinition that defines the group's relationship with the dominant society. These groups see their existence within a larger ethnic formation. An example of "ethnicity-for-itself" is the increasing number of Asian-American and Latino organizations in Southern California. These organizations are themselves conglomerates of much smaller ethnic groups. A Los Angeles Asian-American organization, the Asian American Pacific Planning Council (APPACON), for example, represents thirty-three Asian-American organizations. Through this collective bargaining power, it is able to exert political pressure on the local government.

The politics of "ethnicity-for-itself" can be understood by employing Benedict Anderson's (1991) concept of "imagined community." "Ethnicity" used as a basis for organization is "imagined" because it suggests potential alliance across communities of diverse national origin, cultural background, and internal hierarchies within the ethnic groups. It also suggests a significant commitment to a sense of "horizontal comradeship" in the struggle for limited state resources. This "imagined community" leads us away from the essentialist notions of cultural and biological bases for alliance. So it is not race, or ethnicity, or culture which constructs the grounds for these politics; rather, it is the way ethnicity is internally racialized to constitute group alliance.

The ethnic consciousness and the politics that develops is an important line of cleavage and an important sociopolitical force shaping contemporary society. This often leads to pan-ethnic movements. An example is the multicultural movement that attempts to incorporate into the curriculum and the campus environment the wide range of cultures that coexist in the United States

Some of the "ethnicity-for-itself" members who engage in ethnic activities, speak in their native language, or celebrate ethnic cultural festivities, for example, might be considered "unassimilated" when judged from an assimilationist perspective. However, we are arguing that the question is not whether members of the group have assimilated, in the way Gordon (1964) uses the term where he refers to it as "a kind of ethnic change where people become similar to the dominant group." We argue, instead, that the way members continued to associate with one another is a conscious attempt to use ethnicity for the purpose of empowerment and entitlement. Most members of "ethnicity-for-itself" are in fact fully assimilated. Even if they are not, their distinctive cultural difference is not considered a handicap insofar as they are relating to other co-ethnic members. The "fully assimilated" may support "ethnicity-in-itself" activities because it is perceived as empowering the ethnic "cause." Others may support ethnic activities because they see these as opportunities to reinvent their own culture.

The attacks on expression of ethnicity are attacks on the activities of "ethnicity-in-itself." These activities are perceived by others as leading to the balkanization of American society. It represents a sort of social anxiety that Stuart Hall and his colleagues (1978) refer to as "moral panic." It is precisely these attacks or racialization from without that leads to the political consciousness of the members engaging in "ethnicity-in-itself." In response to the attacks, members see the need for associating and supporting other ethnic groups for political empowerment. In the process, the apolitical nature of "ethnicity-in-itself" gains a political consciousness, as minorities within a dominant society, and becomes "ethnicity-for-itself."

It is this political character of "ethnicity-for-itself" that we wish to retain. Therefore, we have departed from Robert Miles in that we recognize "ethnicity" as a powerful concept in understanding ethnic organization and group relations. We agree, though, with Miles that ethnicity cannot be used as an analytical category for research on ethnic groups for it often leads to "a catalogue of the exotic" and can constitute an "analytical trap" if "divorced from its historical and material context" (Miles, 1982, p. 70).

CONCLUSION

In applying Miles' argument, we have rejected the employment of "race" and "ethnic" groups as analytical categories, and the social relations between groups as "race relations." As discussed in our introduction, we found the traditional race relations approach grounded in the black/white paradigm incapable of providing insights into the complex nature of multiple racisms in an increasingly diverse society. We referred to the instances of racialization of Asian and Latino/Chicano populations as those social processes whereby social groups are singled out for unequal treatment on the social significance attached to physical or genetic differences. The significance of employing this theoretical approach is its application for examining any social group outside of the black/white categories. Furthermore, the process of racialization should be equally applicable in the examination of racialization within and between groups: the racialization of recent Southeast Asian immigrants by more established Asian Americans, the racialization of Central and Latin Americans by Mexican Americans, and the racialization of one ethnic group by another ethnic group, regardless of color. We have also made the distinction between "ethnicity-in-itself" and "ethnicity-for-itself" to account for the apolitical cultural practices of recent immigrants in the former, and the use of ethnicity for self-racialization and political alliance across ethnic lines in the latter. This distinction provides us with the analytical framework for understanding the dynamics of ethnic politics and multiple cultural identities within the context of a changing political economy.

Clearly, there are major areas where further research and theorizing is needed to move us forward in understanding the expression and consequences of racism(s). The first area is the need for comparative studies of racialized groups in the United States. As suggested in this chapter, this will require a radical break with the dominant race relations paradigm that assigns analytical status to the idea of race and frames racial matters in black and white terms. Second, more studies are required that treat with analytical specificity the nature and meaning of class divisions within racialized populations and communities, and the manner in which these changing class relations manifest themselves in community politics, and the relations with the state in a "post-industrial" political economy. Third, while different racisms have been hegemonic, they have always been the object of resistance and struggle. Studies of resistance must be undertaken, in particular, to demonstrate the complexities and contradictions that arise from the struggle against racism.

NOTES

1. A survey of recent book titles indicates the ubiquitous employment of the term "race" and the biracial theorizing. This uncritical theorizing and obsession with race only objectifies, obfuscates, and reproduces what is merely a social construct. Examples of some of these recent titles include *Two Nations: Black and White, Separate, Hostile, Unequal* (Hacker, 1992), *Chain Reaction: The Impact of Race, Rights, and Taxes on American Politics* (Edsall & Edsall, 1991), *Race in America: The Struggle for Equality* (Hill & Jones, 1993) and *Race Matters* (West, 1993).

2. In addition to the works of Robert Miles, there has been a growth of British literature that move forward the debate beyond race and its expression and significance in contemporary society. Other seminal writers of these works include the recent edited volume of articles drawing upon postmodernist, poststructuralist and feminist concerns by James Donald and Ali Rattansi (*"Race," Culture, and Difference*, 1992); John Solomos (*Black Youth, Racism and the State*, 1988; *Race and Racism in Contemporary Britain*, 1989); the liberal sociology of Michael Banton (*Racial Theories*, 1987; *Racial Consciousness*, 1988) and John Rex (*Theories of Race and Ethnic Relations*, 1986; *The Ghetto and the Underclass*, 1988; *Race and Ethnicity*, 1986); the Marxist-influenced work of the Center for Contemporary Cultural Studies (CCCS) of the University of Birmingham under the leadership of Stuart Hall (*The Empire Strikes Back*, 1982). Stuart Hall's seminal essay, "Race, Articulation and Societies Structured in Dominance" is a result of the UNESCO debate on race and racism (*Sociological Theories: Race and Colonialism*, 1980). Other important works included Stephen Castle's *Here for Good* (1984), Tuen Van Djik's *Racism and the Press* (1993), and the writings of A. Sivanandan, the director of the Institute of Race Relations (*A Different Hunger* [1982], and his recent *Communities of Resistance: Writings on Black Struggles for Socialism* [1990]).

3. Michael Banton (1987) has traced the entry of the word in the English intellectual thought to the beginning of the sixteenth century (p. 1), and the use of the term "race" through its several distinctive senses and the several changes. The most common use of the term speaks of the human "races" in the sense of subspecies, the common being the division of the humankind into Negroid, Mongoloid, and Caucasoid. Over the last few decades, it became clear that no meaningful taxonomy of human races was possible. A second common use of the term refers to a group of people who are *socially* defined in a given society as belonging together because of physical markers such as skin color, stature, and so on. The same social label may cover people with very different genetic relatedness and ancestry, for example, "blacks" in South Africa and "black" in Australia. In the United States, a person of black and European ancestry is labelled black, whereas the same person would be classified as white in Brazil.

4. This Latino "race" problematic and the social and political context of racial labels in the U.S. Census are explicated in the work of Lee (1993).

5. Miles (1982) refers to the term "reification" as the elevation of an idea, or concept, to the status of an object.

6. In their second edition (1994), the authors continue to assign analytical status to the concept of race despite its "uncertainties and contradictions" (p. 55).

REFERENCES

Almaguer, T. (1989). "Ideological distortions in recent Chicano historiography: The internal colonial model and Chicano historical interpretation." *Aztlan, 18*(1) (Spring).

Anderson, B. (1991). *Imagined communities,* rev. ed. London, England: Verso.

Anthias, F., & N. Yuval-Davis. (1993). *Racialized boundaries: Race, nation, gender, colour and class and the anti-racist struggle.* London, England: Routledge.

Banton, M. (1988). *Racial consciousness.* New York, NY: Longman.

———. (1987). *Racial theories.* Cambridge, MA: Cambridge University Press.

Barrera, M. (1984). "Chicano class structure," in Eugene E. Garcia, Francisco A. Lomeli, & Isdro D. Ortiz (eds.), *Chicano studies: A multidisciplinary approach.* New York, NY: Teachers College Press.

———. (1979). *Race and class in the Southwest.* Notre Dame, IN: University of Notre Dame Press.

Castle, S. (1984). *Here for good—Western Europe's new ethnic minorities.* London, England: Pluto Press.

Center for Contemporary Cultural Studies. (1982). *The empire strikes back: Race and racism in 70s Britain.* London, England: Hutchinson Library.

Davis, M. (1990). *City of Quartz.* London, England: Verso.

Donald, J. & A. Rattansi. (1992). *"Race," culture, and difference.* London, England: Sage.

Edsall, T. & M. Edsall. (1991). *Chain reaction: The impact of race, rights, and taxes on American politics.* New York, NY: W. W. Norton & Co.

Fields, B. (1990). "Slavery, race and ideology in the United States of America." *New Left Review,* 181 (May/June).

Gilroy, P. (1991). *There ain't no black in the union jack.* Chicago, IL: University of Chicago Press.

Goldberg, D. T. (1993). *Racist culture.* Cambridge, MA: Blackwell.

Gordon, M. (1964). *Assimilation in American life: The role of religion, race, and national origin.* New York, NY: Oxford University Press.

Hacker, A. (1992). *Two nations: Black and white, separate, hostile, unequal.* New York, NY: Scribner's.

Hall, S. (1986). "Gramsci's relevance for the study of race and ethnicity." *The Journal of Communication Inquiry, 10.*

———. (1980). "Race articulation and societies structured in dominance," in *Sociological theories: Race and colonialism.* Paris, France: UNESCO.

Hall, S., C. Critcher, T. Jefferson, & B. Roberts. (1978). *Policing the crisis: Mugging, the state, and law and order.* London, England: Macmillian.

Hill, H. & J. E. Jones, Jr. (1993). *Race in America: The struggle for equality.* Madison, WI: University of Wisconsin Press.

Kotkin, J. (1992). *Tribes: How race, religion and identity determine success in the new global economy.* New York, NY: Random House.

Lee, S. (1993). "Racial classification in the U.S. census: 1890–1990." *Ethnic and Racial Studies, 16*(1) (January).

Loh, E. & R. Medford. (1984). *Statistical sources on California Hispanic population 1984: A preliminary survey.* Chicano Studies Research Center, University of California, Los Angeles, CA.

Miles, R. (1993). *Racism after "race relations."* New York: Routledge.

———. (1991). Personal correspondence.

———. (1989). *Racism, key ideas series.* London, England: Routledge.

———. (1984). "Marxism versus the sociology of 'race relations?' " *Ethnic and Social Studies, 7*(2) (April).

———. (1982). *Racism and migrant labor.* New York, NY: Routledge and Kegan Paul.

Miles, R., and A. Phizacklea. (1981). "Racism and capitalist decline," in Michael Harloe (ed.), *New perspectives in urban change and conflict.* London, England: Heinemann Educational Books, pp. 80–100.

Omi, M. (1993). "Out of the melting pot and into the fire: Race relations policy." *The State of Asian Pacific America.* Los Angeles, CA: UCLA Asian American Studies Center.

Omi, M. & H. Winant. (1994). *Racial formation in the United States: From the 1960s to the 1990s,* 2d ed. New York, NY: Routledge.

———. (1986). *Racial formation in the United States from the 1960s to the 1980s.* New York, NY: Routledge and Kegan Paul.

Moore, J. & H. Pachon. (1985). *Hispanics in the United States.* Englewood Cliffs, NJ: Prentice-Hall.

Rex, J. (1988). *The ghetto and the underclass: Essays on race and social policy.* Brookfield, VT: Gower.

———. (1986). *Race and ethnicity.* Milton Keynes, England: Open University Press.

San Juan, Jr., E. (1992). *Racial formations/critical transformations: Articulations of power in ethnic and racial studies in the United States.* Atlantic Highlands, NJ: Humanities Press.

Sivanandan, A. (1990). *Communities of resistance: Writings on Black struggles for socialism.* London, England: Verso.

———. (1982). *A different hunger: Writings on Black resistance.* London, England: Pluto Press.

Smith, S. (1989). *The politics of "race" and residence.* Cambridge, England: Polity Press.

Solomos, J. (1989). *Race and racism in contemporary Britain.* London, England: Macmillan.

———. (1988). *Black youth, racism and the state: The politics of ideology and policy.* Cambridge, MA: Cambridge University Press.

Valle, V. & R. Torres. (1994). "Latinos in a 'postindustrial' disorder: Politics in a changing city." *Socialist Review, 23*(4).

Van Djik, T. (1993). *Racism and the press.* London, England: Routledge.

West, C. (1993). *Race matters.* Boston, MA: Beacon.

Williams, F. (1989). *Social policy: A critical introduction.* Cambridge, MA: Polity Press.

Yinger, M. (1994). *Ethnicity: Source of strength? Source of conflict?* Albany, NY: State University of New York Press.

Cultural Democracy and the Revitalization of the U.S. Labor Movement

Kent Wong

In November 1993, the AFL-CIO National Convention was held in San Francisco, California, one of the most culturally and ethnically diverse cities in the world. Yet when the convention began, and the members of the Executive Council appeared on stage in front of the convention, the predominantly older, white male leadership at the helm of the AFL-CIO was an obvious reflection of the lack of diversity within the leadership of the U.S. labor movement.

Of the thirty-five members of the Executive Council, thirty-one are white men. There is one white woman, one African-American man, one African-American woman, and one Latina. The first and only two women of color were appointed to the Executive Council a few months before the convention.

For many labor activists, the issues of cultural democracy and diversity have been an ongoing struggle within the ranks of the U.S. labor movement. It is a struggle for representation, for transformation, and to build a new identity and vision for the labor movement.

Unions are an important arena in the struggle for diversity in the United States. They are, by definition, democratic workers' organizations. Unions exist as one of the few institutions in this country that are multiracial in character, and have the capacity to advance a collective agenda that unites workers of all colors.

Forty years after the U.S. Supreme Court decision in *Brown v. Board of Education* challenging school segregation, and thirty years after the landmark Civil Rights Act of 1964, racism and segregation are alive and well in the United States today. Many communities, churches, and schools throughout this nation are segregated.

In contrast, unions are a critical institution where workers of all colors must interact with one another by necessity. History has shown that the success or failure of labor struggles has frequently rested on a union's ability to unite workers and to overcome attempts by those in power (management and its interests) to divide them based on race, gender, or immigration status. Yet the historic development of labor unions has frequently revealed a less-than-exemplary record in addressing diversity.

HISTORIC OVERVIEW OF LABOR UNIONS AND DIVERSITY

In the earlier part of this century, European immigrants played an essential role in establishing unions. European immigrants were integral players in the movement to build unions in the mines, mills, and factories throughout the country. To be successful, unions had to bridge cultural and language barriers between various European immigrant communities. As an example, early publications from unions in the garment industry were translated into numerous European languages to ensure the inclusion of immigrant workers. But although European immigrant labor was the backbone of the early days of the labor movement, African Americans and immigrant workers of color have historically been excluded by many labor unions.

The American Federation of Labor (AFL) was founded in 1881. At its 1890 convention, the Federation publicly opposed union provisions which excluded membership on account of race or color. Yet within a few years, the heads of the Federation came to realize that this idea was standing in the way of its expansion. Numerous unions within the Federation consistently practiced policies of racial exclusion. The Federation structure allowed considerable autonomy with regard to the affiliate unions; this included allowing unions to explicitly forbid African Americans and other workers of colors from admission (Northrup, 1944; Marshall, 1967; Jacobsen, 1968).

In addition, Samuel Gompers, the founding president of the American Federation of Labor who led the organization for several decades, was a lifelong opponent of Asian workers. Gompers steadfastly refused to allow Asian membership within unions, and denied charter to a multiracial farmworkers union from Oxnard, California in 1903 because of the participation of Japanese Americans (Ichioka, 1988).

In the early part of the twentieth century, the Federation explicitly adopted the policy of organizing African Americans into separate unions. When African Americans were denied admission to a union because of color barriers, separate unions were organized at either a local or national level.

During the 1930s, with the tremendous surge in union organizing throughout the country, including workers of color, African-American unionists called for an end to policies of exclusion. At the 1934 AFL convention, A. Philip Randolph, president of the Brotherhood of Sleeping Car Porters, demanded that "any union maintaining the color bar" be expelled from the federation. This resolution was defeated on the stated grounds that the AFL could not interfere with the autonomy of national and international unions (Marshall, 1967).

Unions in the building trades industry in particular were notorious for their opposition to workers of color. Many building trades unions acted as a close-knit fraternal club, where jobs and apprenticeships were handed down from father to son, and among relatives and close friends. African-American workers were excluded for generations before successfully breaking down color barriers enacted by unions in the building trades (Gould, 1977).

The Congress of Industrial Organizations (CIO), established in the 1930s, outlined in its constitution that one of its main objectives was "to bring about the effective organization of the working men and women of America regardless of race, color, creed, or nationality." Unlike AFL craft unions, generally organized on an exclusive and narrow basis, the CIO advocated industrial unionism to open union ranks to all workers in an industry. The CIO embraced a militant approach to organizing and advanced an agenda opposing racism and segregation within unions (Marshall, 1967).

The merger of the AFL and CIO in 1955 still did not bring about an end to policies of racial discrimination and segregation within the labor movement. At the AFL-CIO Convention in 1959, A. Philip Randolph and other African-American unionists again raised their voices to denounce racism and segregation within the labor movement. AFL-CIO President George Meany claimed that segregated unions existed in part because of support from black workers. When the debate escalated, Meany challenged A. Philip Randolph in anger, shouting "Who in the hell appointed you as guardian of the Negro members in America?" (Marshall, 1967). Many of the explicit racial barriers enacted by unions were not struck down until the height of the Civil Rights Movement and the enactment of the Civil Rights Act of 1964.

LABOR AND THE CIVIL RIGHTS MOVEMENT

As the civil rights movement gained momentum throughout the country, support from labor unions also grew. There was a growing collective interest among civil rights and labor leaders for social and economic justice. The historic march on Washington in 1963 brought together civil rights and union activists in unprecedented numbers to demand racial and economic justice.

The civil rights movement facilitated greater changes in the labor movement. A major target of the movement for equality was the workplace, and the passage of the 1964 Civil Rights Act included a significant provision to address the problems of employment discrimination.

In 1968, Dr. Martin Luther King, Jr. was assassinated while supporting African-American sanitation workers in Memphis, Tennessee. The Memphis sanitation workers used "I Am A Man" as their slogan to promote the struggle for unions as an integral part in the fight for civil and human rights (Beifuss, 1989).

In the late 1960s, black workers began organizing caucuses within unions to challenge established union leaders. Caucuses of black teachers were active in unions in New York City and Chicago, and black postal workers and other government workers also set up caucuses to oppose racism. Black workers in the basic industries, particularly auto, transportation, and steel, were among the most militant in advancing an agenda for action.

The most revolutionary black caucus movement developed among black auto workers in Detroit. In May 1968, black workers at Dodge Main launched a wildcat strike to protest speed-ups. When five black workers were fired, the workers organized the Dodge Revolutionary Union Movement (DRUM) to bring pressure against the auto maker as well as certain leaders within the United Auto Workers Union (Geschwender, 1977).

The United Farm Workers Union, built and led by Cesar Chavez in the 1960s, represented a significant coalescing between labor and community-based organizing. Chavez first began organizing through the Community Service Organization. The United Farmworkers galvanized broad-based support from the Chicano and Latino community. For many within the Chicano and Latino community, this was their first exposure to unions.

The farm workers' movement combined direct organizing in the fields with support from urban and rural community-based organizations, churches, and students. Thousands of college students and community activists were enlisted to support the grape boycott and other campaigns to pressure growers to sign contracts with farm workers. In the process, a new generation of labor activists was recruited and trained.

The civil rights, anti-war, and progressive social movements of the 1960s and 1970s also encouraged a new generation of labor activists. Some college-educated radicals chose to direct their energies and resources towards union organizing in factories. Other civil rights and community activists were also drawn into workplace organizing.

UNIONS IN DECLINE—CRISES AND OPPORTUNITIES

The percentage of organized workers within the U.S. workforce has steadily declined from a high of about 35 percent in the 1950s to a unionization rate of 15 percent in 1994. This decline has also been accompanied by a lowering in the standard of living of U.S. workers and a growing disparity between rich and poor.

The 1980s were especially difficult for unions, as the Reagan and Bush administrations never concealed their animosity toward unions. The Republican administrations appointed anti-union ideologues to the National Labor Relations Board and federal courts, which resulted in a steady erosion of the rights of unions and workers.

Yet in the midst of these attacks, there were also new opportunities for labor activists to advance an agenda for social change and for reaching out and organizing workers of color and immigrants. In part, this was due to a generational change in leadership from the old guard to younger, more progressive labor leaders. This was also facilitated by significant demographic changes in the workplace, where women and people of color were changing the face of labor.

At a national level, labor activists committed to organizing established the AFL-CIO Organizing Institute. The Organizing Institute's express purpose has been to train a new generation of labor organizers. Particular focus has been on women and people of color. This reflects a marked departure from the common practice of most unions to hire only from within, a practice that tended to promote gender and racial inequity.

At the national level, new organizations have been established to strengthen the participation of people of color within the labor movement. In 1992, the Asian Pacific American Labor Alliance (APALA) was founded. This was the first time in AFL-CIO history that a special organization promoting Asian-Pacific labor activism was established. While similar organizations had been established to address the concerns of women, African-American, and Latino workers, this was a long-overdue development for Asian-American workers, and resulted in the first new AFL-CIO support committee in nearly twenty years.

APALA has worked hard to advance a national agenda of civil rights and organizing. In addition, APALA worked in conjunction with the Coalition of Labor Union Women, the Labor Council for Latin American Advancement (an organization of Latino unionists), and the Coalition of Black Trade Unionists and the A. Philip Randolph Institute (organizations of African-American unionists) to organize the first national labor conference for women and people of color in October 1995.

TRANSFORMATION FROM WITHIN—EXAMPLES IN LOS ANGELES

The labor movement has been witnessing a generational shift in leadership. As older labor leaders are retiring or leaving office, newer labor activists are now emerging nationally and locally. In Los Angeles, as an example, two unions have undergone a fundamental transformation from within, and are now projecting a new identity for labor.

The Hotel Employees and Restaurant Employees (HERE) Local #11 is an example of a union that has been transformed from within. Local #11 has emerged as one of the most militant unions in Los Angeles, and is led by President Maria Elena Durazo, the daughter of Mexican immigrants.

Durazo first began work at Local #11 as a staff member. She became a leader within the union, and began to challenge the policies of union officers. Although over the years the membership had become predominantly Latino, the previous white male leadership of the union undermined Latino participation. They refused to translate the union contract into Spanish, and used union funds for legal action to prevent the meetings from being conducted bilingually.

Durazo challenged the old leadership in an election, but the incumbents flagrantly violated election rules and refused to turn over membership lists. Ultimately, the International Union placed the local under trusteeship because of the incumbents' mismanagement. In the elections held in 1989, Durazo was elected president (Siegel, 1993).

Since emerging as the leader of HERE #11, Durazo has energized the membership and concentrated union resources on organizing new members. Latino members who never before felt part of the union now embrace it as their own. The union has led high-profile actions, including civil disobedience and massive street demonstrations. HERE #11 recently won a major battle at the Radisson Wilshire Hotel in Los Angeles, and signed a four-year contract. The determining factor in the victory was the ability of the union to unite the Latino and Asian workers, who had previously been pitted against one another by management. HERE #11 is currently launching a series of ambitious organizing campaigns in downtown Los Angeles.

Another union that has undergone significant transformation is the Service Employees International Union (SEIU) Local #660, representing 40,000 Los Angeles County government workers. The County of Los Angeles is one of the largest employers in the state of California, and most of its workers are represented by SEIU #660. People of color comprise the majority of the work force. Within this ethnically diverse population, there have also been serious racial tensions.

In 1991, Gilbert Cedillo emerged as general manager of the union, the first person of color to lead the organization. He has developed an aggressive reputation for the union, built interethnic unity, and initiated labor and community alliances. In the fall of 1991, health care benefits for county workers were being threatened. SEIU #660 launched a series of militant job actions throughout the County, entitled "Rolling Thunder." Workers across the county staged a series of work stoppages, walk-outs, and sick-outs to demonstrate labor solidarity. The campaign resulted in victory, with the County agreeing to fully-paid health care coverage for 660 members and their families.

In 1993, in the midst of serious budgetary problems facing Los Angeles County, the County had proposed salary reductions of 8.25 percent for all County workers. Los Angeles teachers had just been forced to accept a 10 percent salary reduction, and it seemed inevitable that the County workers would also be forced to accept salary reductions.

The campaign to oppose the salary cut culminated in a massive demonstration in front of the Los Angeles County Hall of Administration on August 31, 1993. Thousands of workers, along with significant community and church support, marched for justice and against cutbacks in salaries and county services. This was one of the largest worker rallies in Los Angeles in the last decade. Within a week after this action, a contract was signed, and the County agreed to no salary reductions.

NEW ORGANIZING VICTORIES—REBUILDING THE LABOR MOVEMENT

In the past ten years, Los Angeles has emerged as a focal point for new organizing, especially among Latino immigrant workers. Los Angeles is a major point of entry for immigrants from throughout the world, especially from countries of Latin America and Asia. Over 40 percent of the population of Los Angeles is Latino. Southern California also has the largest concentration of Asian Americans in the country.

The new immigrant work force in Los Angeles and in California represent the best hope for a revitalized labor movement. Just as European workers were instrumental in building the U.S. labor movement over one hundred years ago, the hope and future of the labor movement's rebirth lies with new immigrant workers today.

One campaign involving the janitors of Los Angeles has attracted national attention. Fifteen to twenty years ago, janitors in Los Angeles were predominantly African American, and were predominantly unionized. They were employed directly by the building owners, were paid an average of $10–$12 per hour, and received full benefits. Yet due to the restructuring of the industry and transformation of the work force, the janitors changed from being predominantly African American to Latino, and from being predominantly a union work force to a non-union work force.

The janitors launched a highly visible public campaign, denouncing the gross inequities that allowed for corporations housed in high-rise office buildings to make billions while the workers who cleaned these buildings were paid close to minimum wage. Most of the janitors worked at night and after office hours, and served as an invisible army that would disappear before the work day began. The tactic utilized was to develop high visiblility and broad public support for the campaign. The walls of downtown Los Angeles and Century City, the two sites with the largest concentration of high-rise buildings in Los Angeles, were plastered with red posters declaring, "Justice for Janitors!" The janitors returned to their work sites during working hours wearing bright red T-shirts and marching through their high-rise office buildings in a series of spirited and noisy marches and demonstrations.

In summer 1990, janitors were brutally attacked by police during a peaceful march in Century City. Thirty-eight janitors and supporters were arrested, dozens were injured, and one woman suffered a miscarriage as a result of the police beating. However, as a result of the national attention generated and the intervention of public officials, this violent assault represented a turning point in the campaign. Within weeks after the beating, the five-year campaign to organize janitors in Los Angeles culminated in victory. Five thousand janitors were brought into the union, and soon more than 90 percent of the janitors in downtown Los Angeles and Century City were covered by a union contract. Workers won wage increases and health benefits (Olney, 1993).

As an expression of solidarity with the janitors in Century City, hundreds of Latino immigrant factory workers across town at the American Racing Equipment Company walked off their jobs. While the workers themselves had been involved in an organizing drive for many months, they were emboldened by the courage and determination displayed by the janitors in Century City. The American Racing Equipment Company workers launched a wildcat strike and demanded a raise, better working conditions, and a union.

The predominantly Latino immigrant workers at American Racing Equipment Company had been subjected to subhuman conditions. They worked on machines releasing hazardous fumes, and were not provided adequate face or headgear for protection. They walked out to protest low wages and poor working conditions.

The courage and dedication of the workers was remarkable. Hundreds of workers would congregate in the parking lot past midnight, after the end of their shift. At the makeshift union office nearby the plant, workers would sleep overnight on the concrete floors in order to wake up in time to leaflet the morning shift.

In December 1990, twelve hundred workers at American Racing Equipment Company voted in favor of the union, the International Association of Machinists. American Racing Equipment Company was the largest factory organized by a union in Los Angeles in the last twenty years.

In November 1992, more than four thousand drywall workers in Southern California signed a hard-won collective bargaining agreement. The workers, nearly all Mexican immigrants, had been subjected to intense exploitation. Wages had been reduced from $8–$10 per hour to $4–$5 per hour during the last ten years. Many worked up to twelve hours with no overtime pay, and virtually none had health care benefits.

When these workers walked off their jobs in June, the campaign spread like wildfire throughout Southern California. For seventeen weeks, the workers virtually shut down the drywall industry in Los Angeles, Orange, San Bernardino, Riverside, and San Diego Counties. During the course of the intense campaign, four hundred workers were arrested in a series of confrontations with police. At one point, the police chased a group of striking workers onto Highway 101, one of the busiest freeways in Los Angeles, causing a massive traffic jam.

The contract negotiated by the Carpenters Union covered four thousand drywall workers and thirty-two sheetrock subcontractors in seven counties. The workers won substantial pay increases, health care benefits, and, above all, the right to join the union (de Paz, 1993).

CHALLENGES AHEAD FOR THE LABOR MOVEMENT

Unfortunately, these organizing victories in Los Angeles do not represent a dominant trend within the labor movement today. Much of the labor movement, particularly at the leadership level, stubbornly refuse to embrace diversity, and refuse to make the necessary changes within their organization to meet the challenges for the future.

The victories won by some unions in Los Angeles and in other parts of the country represent a hope for the future. They also pose serious questions that must be addressed by the entire labor movement for its very survival. These fundamental challenges include the need to embrace diversity, the need to build labor and community alliances, and the need to build a culture of organizing.

Cultural democracy is essential to the growth of the labor movement. Women, people of color, and immigrants comprise the vast majority of new workers. Studies on union elections reflect that women and people of color are also more likely to join unions than other workers. The leadership and staff of unions must change to reflect the new work force. Unions must aggressively recruit and train women and people of color.

In a period when unions represent only 16 percent of the work force, it is essential for unions to build alliances within the community. Churches, students, community-based organizations, immigrants' rights groups, disability rights groups, lesbian and gay organizations, organizations within communities of color, and advocates for housing, health care, and the homeless are all potential allies of labor. Time and attention must be spent to develop and expand these relationships, and to forge a common agenda.

Finally, unions must organize the unorganized. Unions must transform a culture of business unionism to a culture of organizing. "Business unionism" occurs when unions are run like a business. Such unions collect dues from their members and in turn provide services. Workers are not encouraged to become active, workers do not embrace the union as their own organization.

In contrast, an "organizing" union advances a culture where everything the union does and everything the union represents is directed toward organizing its members and reaching out to organize the unorganized. Workers are challenged to embrace the union as their own organization, are encouraged to become active, and are motivated to work for social change. "Every worker is an organizer!" is a slogan currently being advanced by the United Farm Workers Union to embrace this organizing culture.

Unions must take the offensive in advancing an organizing agenda that represents the interests of the vast majority within this country. In this era of corporate greed and take-backs, unions must take the lead to defend the standard of living of all workers and demand universal health care. In this era of racism and anti-immigrant hysteria, unions must take the lead to build multiracial unity and defend immigrant rights. In this era when right-wing fanatics are attacking family planning clinics and attacking the rights of gay men and lesbians, unions must take the lead in defending the right of choice and in opposing all discrimination against lesbians and gay men.

For unions to meet the challenge ahead, they must emerge as a voice for all workers—for women and men, for young and old, for persons of diverse sexual orientations, for African Americans, Latinos, Asian Americans, European Americans, Native Americans, and other people of color. The struggle for cultural democracy within the U.S. labor movement is a struggle for its very survival.

REFERENCES

"Asian Pacific American workers: contemporary issues in the labor movement." (1992). *Amerasia Journal, 18*(1).

Beifuss, J. T. (1989). *At the river I stand: Memphis, the 1968 strike, and Martin Luther King*. Brooklyn, NY: Carlson Publishing Inc.

de Paz, J. (1993). "Organizing ourselves." *Labor Research Review, 20.*

Geschwender, J. A. (1977). *Class, race, and worker insurgency*. Cambridge, MA: Cambridge University Press.

Gould, W. B. (1977). *Black workers in white unions: Job discrimination in the United States*. Ithaca, NY: Cornell University Press.

Ichioka, Y. (1988). *The Issei*. New York, NY: The Free Press.

Jacobsen, J. (1968). *The Negro and the American labor movement*. New York, NY: Doubleday.

Marshall, R. (1967). *The Negro worker*. Westminister, MD: Random House.

Northrup, H. R. (1944). *Organized labor and the Negro*. New York, NY: Harper and Brothers.

Olney, P. (1993). "Rising of the million." *Crossroads* (July/August):

Siegel, L. (1993). "Local 11 takes on L.A." *Labor Research Review.*

Sumner M. R. (1968). "The CIO ERA, 1935–55," *The Negro and the American labor movement*. New York, NY: Doubleday.

Taylor, R. B. (1975). *Chavez and the farm workers*. Boston, MA: Beacon Press.

The Zone of Black Bodies: Language, Black Consciousness, and Adolescent Identities

Garrett Duncan

Scholars operating within the dominant academic framework rarely define language in terms of the ideology it embodies and the manner in which it reproduces power relations. Similar to the way in which they treat the idea of culture, scholars often mystify language, thus rendering it invisible or reducing it to an inert medium for the expression of individual ideas. Thus when the issue of language is raised for discussion, it is invariably defined as an instrument of communication, with infrequent brief mentions of its role in perpetuating dominant interests. For example, Patrick Courts (1991) writes, "Language is not simply a system of phonemes; it is not simply a set of surface structures (sounds or written marks of some kind. . . . *Language is the possibility of making meaning of and in the world*" (emphasis mine) (p. 7).

Although this viewpoint is necessary to understand the phenomenon of language, its hermeneutic undercurrents preclude factors that contribute to the richer, complex role of language in our everyday lives; it moreover fails to consider the role of language in perpetuating ideas of superiority and inferiority in the larger society.

In reference to Africans in the United States, dominant scholars initially framed the issue of language in a discourse that downplayed its political implications. Here the issue was one of "cultural deficiency," a theme that has permeated all aspects of Western science in characterizing people of color. This theme is a logical extension of white supremacist thinking in which positivist rationale posits a world that is reducible to objective and measurable parts; hence, a common dictum among researchers, even in the social sciences, is that *if a thing exists, it exists in some amount and can be measured*. Such a fragmented, particulate conception of the world fosters reification of abstract phenomena and the ranking of ostensibly related but fundamentally disparate

phenomena; these models, depending on the particular brand, invariably locate dark-skin peoples last, on the bottom, or in the margins as the most
deviant representation of humankind.

The reasoning that inspired the current Ebonics[1] research emerged out of
the political milieu of the 1960s and the early 1970s. This work effectively
breaks away from the dominant conceptual configuration by relocating the
center of black language in America to Africa, the place of its origin. Clearly
scholars have traced certain traits in the language patterns of Ebonics to African roots. According to Lorenzo Turner (1973), for example, Wolof, Malinke,
Mandinka, Bambara, Fula, Mende, Vai, Twi, Fante, Gá, Ewe, Fon, Yoruba,
Bini, Hausa, Ibo, Ibibio, Efik, Kongo, Umbundu, and Kimbundu are West
African languages bearing features that are evident in linguistic patterns of
Diasporan Africans in America. The various language traits have persisted
primarily due to a noted lack of language mixing between Africans and Europeans, and among Africans during the earlier voyages of the slave trade. Slave
buyers who preferred Africans from specific groups in the same manner that
people favor certain breeds of dogs and horses further reinforced the integrity
of specific language characteristics. Thus, "African languages survived in the
New World for a time" (Dilliard, 1973, p. 74). What this means is that both
selective slave-trading practices and perhaps the reticence of the Africans during their voyages from Africa to the Americas reinforced the infrastructure of
present-day Ebonics. However, that certain distinct features persist as we
approach the twenty-first century is a reflection of the more blatant contradictions of a society that upholds itself as the model of pluralism and democracy. As Asa G. Hilliard (1983) observes, distinctive linguistic features
associated with the Black community demonstrate a pattern that "differs from
common American-English in predictable ways to one who knows African
languages and who knows about the history of oppression for African-
Americans" (p. 27). In a truly unified and pluralistic social system, society
would appreciate instead of disparage the contributions of Ebonics and the
Black speakers of Ebonics to America. But clearly this is not the case.

More recently, scholars have framed the issue of Ebonic language in an
important but narrow discussion that has barely, if at all, moved beyond a
dated discourse of justification or validation. Consequently researchers for the
most part still confine themselves to those issues that the dominant society
values (or confers with legitimacy), namely semantics, grammar, syntax, vo-
cabulary, and morphology. Discourse of this kind also promotes a myopic
conception of what constitutes legitimate language issues, thus negating other
avenues of creative and meaningful investigations into the different ways
members in the Black community perceive the world, ways that are in many
cases in conflict with the perceptions of the dominant white population (Smith,
1992).

In this chapter, I will attempt to connect the construct of Black consciousness and adolescent identity formation to the issue of language. Drawing on

interviews conducted with high-school age, American-born Black adolescents in a small urban community in southern California, I shall advance the discussion to include the "zone of black bodies." The zone of Black bodies, as used in this work, is that ideological terrain upon which Black youths contest racist artifacts in the process of constructing their adolescent identities. As we will see, this terrain often intersects with the discursive grid that fosters white supremacist notions; also, it will be apparent that this terrain implicates, but is irreducible to, both the conceptual level and the enfleshed level of people activity.

BLACK CONSCIOUSNESS, LANGUAGE, AND DEVELOPMENT

George Lakoff and Mark Johnson (1980) write in their book *Metaphors We Live By* that:

understanding our experiences in terms of objects and substances allows us to pick out parts of our experience and treat them as discrete entities of a uniform kind. Once we can identify our experiences as entities or substances, we can refer to them, categorize them, group them, and quantify them—and, by this means, reason about them (p. 25).

The imagery that informs how we perceive our experiences is not mere happenstance, however. Rather, hegemonic forces structure social reality in ways that obscure the connections between phenomena that have surface differences, leaving the purveyors of dominant interests to organize the fragments of our everyday lives to meet their needs. In other words, not only do illusions distort everyday representations, but dominant institutions, such as the media, construct these necessary illusions in a systematic fashion that serves to reproduce oppressive arrangements in the larger society. This idea is persuasively argued, for example, in the work of Noam Chomsky (1987, 1989, 1991a, 1991b), Jerry Fresia (1988), Edward Herman (1982), Clarence Lusane (1991), and some of their co-authored works (e.g., Herman & Chomsky, 1988).

The relevance of the above to the present discussion is that it provides a basis from which to elucidate the impact of the historical vilification and brutalization of black, brown, red, and yellow bodies in the popular imagination. This process of demonization is not merely the culmination of discrete and isolated acts but is rather the consequence of a constellation of forces that reinforces racist imagery. These forces act with impunity upon the psyches of the oppressor and the oppressed alike. For example, in his book *Fantasies of the Master Race*, Ward Churchill (1992) describes the role of American popular culture in "manufacturing" the image of Native Americans through literature and cinematography. For instance, speaking of the way in which the cinema has romantically portrayed the "Old West" and "Cowboys and Indians," Churchill observes that:

[A] bitter irony associated with this is that Indian as well as non-Indian children heatedly demand to be identified as cowboys, a not unnatural outcome under the circumstances, but one that speaks volumes to the damage done to American Indian self-concept by movie propaganda. The meaning of this ... can best be appreciated if one were to imagine that the children were instead engaging in a game called "Nazis and Jews" (1992, p. 240).

In a similar fashion, dominant ideologies and institutions have worked to construct the image of the *colored body* on the physical level to symbolize filth, deformity, and violence. Dominant society has long associated the colors black and brown, for example, with dirt and feces and all sorts of uncleanness. Similarly, the real victimization of black, brown, and red bodies through rape, lynching, and castration interweaves with the persistent representations of colored bodies as indefatigable breeding machines to underpin the complex and contradictory patterns of sexualized, gendered, and cultured metaphors that are pervasive in the larger culture. Religious and academic scholarship also extends the image of colored bodies to represent moral and intellectual degeneration. The alleged diminutive stature of Asians and their "yellow" skin provides apparent evidence of moral inferiority. Metaphors such as "black lie," "darker side," and "blackened heart" conjure up images of dishonesty, cruelty, and hatred.

Given the sociohistorical context of America, it is not unusual that these images influence the attitudes of even those that the dominant culture disparages. For, contrary to unexamined assumptions of Black family pathology related to cultural deficit mythology, Black children for the most part come from homes that are warm and nurturing. Keep in mind that "pathology is only the sign that valuable human resources are being neglected" (Erikson, 1980, p. 85). In addition, Margaret Beale Spencer (1988) has pointed out that Black parents often provide cultural emphasis to intervene between their children and a larger society that devalues their blackness. Her findings are supported elsewhere in reports that indicate that Black parenting strategies effect buffered environments in the rearing of healthy Black children (Barnes, 1972). I am proposing here that the vast majority of Black children enter society from supportive homes, expecting to be fully adaptive and successful in the larger society. However, I maintain, because of what scholars call violent cultural "discontinuities" (Bulhan, 1985; Erikson, 1980; Ogbu, 1987), public spheres such as schools do not reflect the lived experiences nor do they support the self-concepts of Black children; rather, social institutions represent literal battlegrounds for these children.

Besides the stares, the racial slurs, the distance kept, there are also elaborated cultural myths about the black person's body and sedimented stereotypes about his race. The Negro is ugly. The Negro smells. The Negro is a sexual beast. If not avoided, he is to be paternalized. . . . Gradually, he is thrown back to reexamine his corporal schema and his very being. A self-concept that started developing in the first few years of life is shaken to its foundation (Bulhan, 1985, p. 192).

That members of the dominant society connect black skin to fecklessness, promiscuity, physical deformity, violence, and dishonesty are evident in attitudes that still persist today. For example, the *Los Angeles Times* has reported that a large number of white Americans believe that Black and brown persons are "more violence-prone, less hard-working, less intelligent, less likely to be self-supporting and less patriotic than whites" (Fulwood, 1991, p. A13).

Clearly the American social, political, and economic milieus overflow with disparaging artifacts to be both appropriated and objectified by Black adolescents as they struggle with their identities. As Frances Cress Welsing (1991) powerfully argues, even the term "motherfucker," an appellation used with great frequency in certain segments of the Black community, and particularly among young Black males, is connected to objective and conceptual imagery that has shaped experiences of everyday life. I am not implying, however, that Black children fully capitulate to their surroundings. Not only is this not the case, it would also suggest that Black children lack the agency and the ability to resist oppressive circumstances. Sadly, this latter belief is the one that the dominant society popularly embraces, as suggested by the publicity and circulation given to books such as Jonathan Kozol's (1991) *Savage Inequalities.* Thus in the following section I will illustrate the resilience with which a group of young Black women and men engage oppressive artifacts as part of their struggle for identity—a resilience that is expressed through their words and their deeds.

LANGUAGE, RESISTANCE, AND THE ZONE OF BLACK BODIES

"Because men [and women] are historical beings, incomplete and conscious of being incomplete," observes Paulo Freire (1985), "revolution is a natural and permanent human dimension as is education" (p. 89). Among the young men and women with whom I spoke, the revolutionary human dimension is both implied and explicit in their language. For example, prominent in the discourse of these individuals is an acknowledgment of their incompleteness. For instance, Clayton,[2] a sixteen-year-old black male, describes himself:

I'm black and I'm a youth of 1993. And I have problems like every other youth that I know. And I just want to strive to help myself mentally. And that'll, I guess, when I help myself mentally, the physical will follow, because wherever the head goes, the body follows. Well, I still need improvement, really I do. And the past . . . in the past it was different.

(How was it different?)

Because I came into proper knowledge of myself. . . . You know, I really didn't think nothing of myself. I was just a kid who was just—I was always searching, striving to find something about me but I just didn't know, you know? I still really don't know.

Expressing a similar sentiment, Louise, a seventeen-year-old first-year college student who describes herself as African, tells me that she sees herself as "going through a metamorphosis." Elaborating, she explains:

Well, for me, it's that I'm out-growing the world that I live in right now. It's like, you know how people say they have to get out of the ghetto? That they need to get out of the ghetto? Well, I think that it's not really that they need to get out of the ghetto, but that their environment stifles them. And Pomona is stifling me right now. College is my escape route; if I don't get there, I am going to go crazy. . . . I find myself yelling at people about things that are really not even that serious or like getting mad at kids that call me for advice who I usually take time with. . . . It's to the point where I'm like, forget it, don't call me anymore and I won't call you—just leave me alone. I need to get out of here.

In addition, Veronica, like her best friend Louise, is also seventeen and a first-year college student. She notes:

I feel here lately . . . I feel real claustrophobic. It's like any little thing just pisses me off, I get upset, I don't care about who shot John, I don't care about anybody else. I want to go to school and I want to get there today. I want everything to be okay. But I have this feeling that when I get there that it's not going to be all that great. I don't know, I get scared: Am I going to succeed? What's going to happen when it comes time to get a job in psychology? What do I want to do? Do I want to get a job in the executive world? Do I want to do this? Do I want to do that? I don't know because my world feels tight and I just want to explode. I just want to hit people! (laughter)

David, a seventeen-year-old high school senior, says that his "world is kind of confused and closed in." Daniel, Louise's sixteen-year-old brother, is even more vivid in his conception of the constraints placed on him by the world:

It's like every situation that we get into is like a microcosm of what actually happens in this society. That's just like the Pentagon, to use that example, the Pentagon telling NASA that they are not to make that new space thing. That's not the way it's supposed to go. We are not doing that. It's everybody and every little thing is trying to control you in some way. And you have to break past that and have on the blinders that the horse has on—just go.

Their thoughts project understanding of a world that is complex, dynamic, and constantly changing. This conception of their milieus—both psychological and social—is in direct contrast to the unproblematic and unified image of the world that the various institutions of this society convey. Their words, typical of the responses of their peers, also indicate an awareness of constraints, both imagined and real, imposed upon their personal development. Also, their desires for growth and change coincide with an awareness of their incompleteness. Growth, as Clayton notes, entails coming into a "proper knowledge of self." This knowledge takes on two trajectories. It involves, on the one hand, a new way of thinking or reasoning about the world and everyday life. Youths more often than not express this new way of looking at things in terms of what they disdain. Invariably, this includes things that are "weak" and "shallow." The following exchange powerfully illustrates the sentiments of many of those interviewed:

Daniel: The shallow and weak part of it is the biggest thing. I would say weak more than shallow. Because I hate a weak person—I hate them to death. I can't be around them. Weak means that you have no backbone, you have no point of view; you are like a chameleon . . .

Veronica: Weak people, weak minds. When it's about us and fun, we sit at this table and talk about nothing and enjoy ourselves. A weak person will come and feel bored. They don't know how to adapt to us; they want to change their attitudes— they want to get upset. Maybe they don't fit in . . . it's something—I don't know.

Louise: We have this joke about Taunia. We call her Stepford Wife. It's like she goes with the wind and she just changes. It's not to knock her because a lot of it stems from the way she was brought up. Well, her mother sheltered Taunia a lot in her life. And then she's Christian; her mother is like real Christian, heavy Christian. Taunia thinks she's supposed to be heavy Christian and if she has any nasty thought at all, it's like "oh my God! It's not happening!"

(By nasty, do you mean sexual?)

Louise: Yes. She wants to tap into the bad part of [the] world but then keep her good image.

(Do you mean like being on both sides of the fence; straddling the fence?)

Louise: She'll do something and then she won't tell anyone because she feels that she did something wrong. We used to share all kinds of things with her, but she felt that when she did wrong she couldn't tell anybody. Then later on, she would judge us. Shallow means that they have no substance. It means that they don't stand for nothing; they will fall for anything. They blow with the wind.

Veronica: When you tell them something, they're blind in one eye and can't see out the other. And they don't hear what you are saying.

Louise: And got everything to say in the world about what you are doing.

Veronica: But nothing's going on about what they are saying.

Louise: And they don't understand anything.

Veronica: And they are saying stuff that's not there. They want to talk about the world or what happened to the president, and it's like Reagan isn't the president any more—where were you?

Monica: I hate it when you are talking to someone and they want to change it to "yeah, I got a new pair of shoes today," or "I've got to go, my mom is here—bye."

Another way that adolescents recast their selves intimately connects them to the conception of their racialized somatic selves. In other words, Black youth wage resistance to the oppressive assumptions that converge to disparage the notions of race and gender at the site of "black bodies" on both a conceptual and a somatic level. This phenomenon is distinct to persons of color, including as it does both real and imagined aspects of their selves. For, unlike feeling the pressures of social constraints that many adolescents in general experience, to embrace one's "colored" body in the context of a racist society means to repudiate the ideals of beauty that are controlled by racialized metaphors and images. Hegemonic institutions such as schools and the electronic and print media mystify and elevate these representations to the status of common sense. Hence, loving black bodies as an act of reclaiming blackness is indeed a revolutionary act; "to love blackness is dangerous in a white supremacist culture—so threatening, so serious a breach in the fabric of the social order . . . death is the punishment" (hooks, 1992, p. 9). To love blackness entails reconfiguring the discursive grid of unexamined assumptions in order to augment the conception of what is beautiful and respectable; thus to embrace blackness means to also reclaim the derogated black body. Note, for instance, Veronica's remarks:

A woman is supposed to be quite feminine and very lady-like and dainty . . . and can't have any blemishes and must be perfect and prissy. That's not me. Like the song, "I may not be a lady but I am all woman." I don't have to be make-up down, have on some high-heels and some stockings, and a fancy dress to be a woman. I think that, though society says that I have to. But society says I also have to be blond and have blue eyes. So, since I am not that, then that tells me that I don't always have to have on heels and look a particular way. I can go and climb a tree and jump off a roof, if that's what I want to do. And then again, I can dress up and be feminine if that's what I want to do. But as far as society placing some images—they'll do that; they do that everyday and everywhere you look, that's all you see. God forbid, you turn on the TV and that's all you'll see. But I have to look at it my way. Matter of fact, the more you tell me no, the more I'm going to do. The more you tell me yes, the more I may do "no." The more you want me to be blond hair and blue eyed, the more I'm going to say that I'm the sun and cut all my hair off.

Veronica's words reverberate the knowledge that "race and sex have always been overlapping discourses in the United States" (hooks, 1990, p. 57). However, youth racially enflesh their selves in other, more abstract forms as well. For instance, according to the popular images and metaphors that represent virtue and evil, to embrace blackness means to strip white supremacy of its moral authority. As James H. Cone (1990) states in his book *A Black Theology of Liberation*, "Black consciousness is an attempt to recover a past deliberately destroyed by white slave masters, an attempt to revive old symbols and create new ones" (p. 12). Consider seventeen-year-old Kwesi's remarks:

First of all let me say that I am not a Christian. That I don't have a religion. And for a long period of time I didn't believe in God. If I were to describe myself to myself, I would say that I'm a God. Let me break it down to you. First of all, I don't think that . . . I have full belief in that the white man is the devil . . . but I do know that I am God, and that our people are Gods. If the King James Version is right, of the Bible, it says there in the Bible, in Genesis I believe, that first the earth was created and then on the seventh day, men were created. It said, "God created man in His own image." What's the image of man? Is it blood, is it bones? So, I would think that God is man. And we were the first men, we are God. And then even Allah . . . Allah, what does it mean? Hands? Arm, leg, arm, leg, hand, or something like that?

(Do you mean Arm, Leg, Leg, Arm, and Head?)

Yes! And what is that, it's not a man, but it's human. So, I consider myself to be a God for that reason. Also I have trouble believing the Bible, but that's just historical . . . if I were to consider myself to be strong and I consider myself black. Even though I don't consider myself to be black, because I'm brown, because that is my skin color.

The discourse that frames the racialized and somatic language explicitly stated in Kwesi's remarks and implied in Clayton's statement can trace its origins to the teachings of the Honorable Elijah Muhammad; I consider these implications elsewhere. However, the religious-spiritual nexus to the conception of the self is particularly important, permeating as it does many aspects of our conversations. In the United States, received notions of flesh, sexuality, and emotionality generally relate to *Christian* views of the body as a weak and sinful vessel (Shilling, 1993). Interwoven with the Victorian perspective on sexuality, normal bodily functions are vulgar and are subject to societal repression: "while farting, belching, and nose picking may be socially unacceptable in many public spheres of waged work, they are often carried out unselfconsciously in the privacy of the home" (Shilling, 1993, p. 172). This logic also extends to body *language*, the uninhibited expression of which is connected to moral weakness, intellectual poverty, and suggestive of sexual permissiveness. That Black youths make these connections and further attach them to "Christian" ethics is particularly salient in Louise's comments. She elaborates upon this as she describes an incident in which the issue of language and body behavior clearly relates to Christian standards of respectability:

> At a basketball game at Pomona High, for half-time entertainment, Coach T. invited Palomares' basketball teams and Emerson's basketball team to play against each other. Palomares' cheerleaders—they weren't even cheerleaders—they were just little kids who go to the school, who were showing pride. They were in the stands, whooping and hollering in the stands, cheering on their team. They were having fun; I didn't see anything wrong with it. Taunia and Bettina are sitting in the back of the bleachers saying, "Now see my mother wouldn't allow me to act like that in public." What were they doing? I didn't understand what they could possibly be doing wrong—I didn't understand that. You guys are entirely too judgmental—"my mother didn't raise me to be such and such and such, to be good wholesome Christians." They have to wear dresses down to their ankles and sit with their legs crossed and not say anything unless somebody speaks to them. And they're passing their own judgment onto other kids. They were kids and they were having fun! And it's a trip because those kids probably understand more about themselves than Taunia and Bettina will ever understand or at that time they could possibly know. And just seeing how those kids could just have fun—they didn't care what people thought about them.

Although common to our discussions, the sentiments presented up to this point in connection to black bodies are not uncontested. From a sociogenetic perspective, it is not at all unreasonable that Black youth internalize or, as Frantz Fanon (1967) would say, *epidermalize* certain attitudes that disparage Black life and culture. In fact, the young men and women in this chapter, to a person, describe periods in their lives during which they held "pseudo-humanistic attitudes." I call pseudo-humanist thinking those conceptions of humanity that negate the human capacity to act upon the world by reducing men and women to simply flesh and blood. For example, most individuals express a primary attachment to Black families and communities while they also acknowledge an awareness of social injustice. Yet, at some point in their lives, they consider themselves to be "Americans" who by mere chance happen to have brown and black skin. However, as they become aware of personal injustices, they also become cognizant of the social oppression that people of color in general and Black people in particular suffer at the hand of dominant institutions. Hence, many of the young men and women eventually form attitudes that prime them to challenge the symbols and mechanisms of white supremacy.

However, individuals do not always appreciate racialized illusions for the distorted images they convey, particularly with respect to black bodies. One salient issue in this regard has to do with the conception of the "ghetto." The term ghetto generally conjures up a place rife with violence, poverty, ignorance, and general despair. Moreover, despite its original designation as a place where European Jews were forced to live or the recent demographic shifts in the purported modern-day slums or, for example, South Central Los

Angeles and Compton, the racialized image of the ghetto is still endowed with the attributes of the so-called Black underclass. Even in William Julius Wilson's (1980) influential book, *The Declining Significance of Race*, he in spite of his explicit attempt to do otherwise racializes the concept of the underclass or ghetto by equating them with social backwardness and emphasizing this disproportionality in the Black community (Goldberg, 1993). Thus, Wilson effectively endows *black bodies* with the criminal pathologies that he argues define the *social dynamics* caused by educational disadvantagement.

If only implied in Wilson's work, this idea is explicit in an arguably more potent medium of television programming that emerged from the mid-1960s. A review of situation comedies in which Black characters are central to the shows reveals a distinct trend that is consistent with the so-called "Moynihan Report" that trumpeted the crisis of the "Negro" family in the mid-1960s (Office of Planning, 1965). Programs such as *Good Times, Sanford and Son, That's My Momma*, and *What's Happening* reinforce the perception and deduction that black families and black people are socially deviant. These specific themes still permeate media coverage of the Black family although they have mutated to enjoy the respectability of the "news" format. As Carl Ginsburg (1989) argues, the basic structure of the Moynihan report has endured to inform the journalistic media's portrayal of the Black community on both national and local levels. For instance, the featured story of the August 1993 *Newsweek* magazine is entitled "A World Without Fathers: The Struggle to Save the Black Family," and bears the angelic black portrait of seven-year-old George Martin on its cover. This representation is the most popular spin-off of the alleged pathological configurations: The Black family and the absent father. The dominant media frequently alert the public to the implications of this purported sickness.

On a nightly basis, news coverage sensationalizes "gang" violence, "reporting" on events with little or no verification of facts. Further, the uncritical use of non-specific terms such as "gang shootings" or "gang-related" effectively divorces certain events from *persons* and places them on *communities*, thus conflating criminal characteristics with demographic configurations. This kind of reporting was particularly blatant in the printed media during the rebellions of 1992, specifically concerning those events that took place in Los Angeles. Here, in an unprecedented way, newspaper editors replaced datelines to articles that would have previously read *Los Angeles* with the racialized *South Central* Los Angeles when stories were in reference to the more ostensibly brutal aspects of the uprising. Such editorial manipulations effectively evoke in the minds of its readers the images of violent black bodies engaged in the wanton "ghetto" acts of looting, arson, and mayhem. Thus, despite their reformulations, these measures still cohere to predictable and systematic racist mandates. Kwesi, in remarking that the "media is the fourth branch of government," demystifies these racial illusions to an extent. However, certain comments concerning appropriateness and respectability seem to indicate that

Black youths accord certain representations with legitimacy. For example, according to fifteen-year-old Paige and her friend Roni, fourteen, "ghetto" is an attribute of certain human beings:

Paige: Well, certain black people are ignorant—they're ghetto. Because they live . . . they're just ghetto. They put all these pony-tails in their hair. I'm different from that because I wasn't raised that way. When I go out of the house, I'm going to look respectful and appropriate. I'm not going to have all kinds of pony-tails in my hair. Some people are that way and some are not.

Roni: Like Shonayné on "Martin" is ghetto.

Likewise, brothers Louis, fifteen, and Albert, fourteen, both sensitive to ghetto politics, affirm that "hegemony, which is inscribed in the physiognomic symbols of the student's bodies and compressed into gesture, is an act of corporeity" (McLaren, 1989, p. 194):

Albert: I'll say I'm different around . . . I'm not a racist or nothing . . . I'm different around other races, you know. Around other non-blacks, you know. I'm not a racist or anything, but I'm myself when I'm around, like . . .

Louis: Blacks?

Albert: Blacks, yeah (laughter). Whites, you know, try to stereotype, you know, most of the time. I try to make it so they won't think that—we are not all bad. Some of us are pretty good.

(So, does this include when you're at school? When you're in the store?)

Albert: The store, mainly, yes. You try to be more intelligent so they don't think you're a stupid nigger.

Louis: Like you don't walk how you usually walk when you with somebody else.

Albert: And you talk more intelligent, don't just say half the word, say the whole word, you know.

Clearly aware of the vicious stereotypes that characterize Black people in America, both Albert and Louis echo the words of Fanon (1967) when he lamented almost thirty years ago, "Yes, I must take great pains with my speech, because I shall be more or less judged by it" (p. 20). Their words also seem to affirm that "every body carries a history of oppression, a residue of domination preserved in stratum upon stratum of breathing tissue" (McLaren, 1989, p. 194). However, domination is not absolute and the resiliency of the human spirit is ever ready to exploit the opportunities for emancipation that contradictions in society create. Therefore, what dynamics contribute to the explication of contradictions and thus foster the environments in which Black youths construct identities characterized by boldness and the assertion of their Black selves?

DIALOGUE AND CONSCIENTIZATION

The process whereby young individuals empower themselves to assert their wills does not occur in a vacuum. As indicated above, Black youths are well aware of social contradictions and, moreover, direct experiences and empathic associations reinforce their perceptions. Clearly, individuals sometimes perceive contradictions to be too complex and thus to some extent acquiesce to their circumstances. However, a recognition of contradictions may also entail a repudiation of those things that they perceive to be "shallow and weak," as is the case with many of the youths with whom I spoke.

It is no oversight, therefore, that Black youth rarely mention schools as factors in their personal transformation; for to repudiate shallowness and weakness means to repudiate the forms of knowledge and strategies that teachers and administrators employ in schools. These practices, which I describe as fragmented pedagogies of consensus, detach or remove students from the realities of their lived experiences. These practices are made possible by the positivistic underpinning of American education that separates knowledge and truth from the power and interests they serve. This form of reasoning supports and is supported by uncritical notions of democracy and consensus that emphasize life as being unified and unproblematic. Employing strategies and curriculum engendered by these ideas, teachers often obscure the debilitating influence of racist artifacts, both conceptual and material, on the development of students of color (Duncan, 1993).

This is especially evident in teacher decisions concerning what children can and cannot do with respect to curriculum. Students of color, teachers allege, are too physical: They do not have the discipline to do labs, to go on field trips, or to participate in creative activities that require that they leave their seats. Behavioral perceptions, informed by the image of colored bodies, replace cognitive aptitude as the main factors in deciding educational programs for children of color. In fact, I will never forget the overwhelming response to a question I posed to students in a high school physical science class after the completion of their first laboratory exercise. When asked the purpose of the lab, the class of mostly Black and Chicano male students answered, "To determine whether we behave well enough to have future labs!" Conversely, students in my chemistry course, from which the exercise originated, responded with the more typical "to determine the identities of the unknown substances."

Hence, as implied in the students' comments, schools function to separate the chaff of active, vibrant students of color from the wheat of those students who comply with the standards enforced at school. On the other hand, however, the dominant society particularly valorizes the former attributes among white students: "This is evident," as Antonia Darder (1991) argues in her book *Culture and Power in the Classroom*, "in the nature of the behaviors that are rewarded in upper-class students (i.e., aggressiveness, original thinking, etc.) and those passive or allegedly civilized behaviors rewarded in bicultural students" (p. 5). It is obvious, therefore, that in addition to not having their lived realities affirmed in schools, by exerting their will to grow, Black students disproportionately experience a range of punitive actions ranging from limited access to college preparatory courses to suspensions and expulsion from school without due process. So in the absence of formal support from school personnel, other agents have emerged to validate the existence of Black youth. In addition to parents and traditional significant others, these individuals support and foster the consciousness necessary for making critical linkages that enable Black youths to act upon their worlds.

VERTICAL RELATIONSHIPS, NAMING, AND THE DEVELOPMENT OF BLACK CONSCIOUSNESS

In addition to the compensatory cultural emphasis that parents provide their young for coping in the larger society (Spencer, 1988), there are other categories of vertical relations that Black youth point to as significant to their personal development. I use the term "vertical" to describe those asymmetrical relations where individuals look up to other persons as authorities. Lev Vygotsky (1978) describes a similar interaction in his cultural-historical approach to development. The *zone of proximal development*, according to Vygotsky, is:

the distance between the actual developmental level as determined by independent problem solving and the level of potential development as determined through problem solving under adult guidance or in collaboration with more capable peers. . . . The zone of proximal development defines those functions that have not yet matured but are in process of maturation, functions that will mature tomorrow but are currently in an embryonic state. These functions could be termed the "buds" or "flowers" of development rather than the "fruits" of development (p. 89).

The vertical relationships that I seek to describe, although sharing similar dynamics, differ fundamentally from those that Vygotsky espouses in several ways. For instance, these relationships emphasize the *desire, self-assessment,* and *intentionality* of the "learner," in addition to *the explicit political resistance* that these types of relationships entail. These relationships in effect *name*. Naming is the process that affirms an individual's reality by the explication of dynamics that both liberate and incarcerate the self. Black youths accord the authority figures in these relationships legitimacy due to what they perceive to be these individuals' abilities to answer complex questions and to make nonsense of the common sense events that are a part of our everyday lives. Further, dialogue in these relationships are characteristic of the powerful content for which it provides a vehicle. For instance, Daniel provides insight into the dialogical process:

That's the magic of our friendship because it's not that we all agree with each other or that we are exactly alike. We fight a lot. We probably fight more than anybody else. But we accept different views. Like we said, "no holds barred": I might not agree, but I will respect you for what you are doing. I can say okay, I understand why you are doing it or whatever. I don't judge you, I don't inflict my views on you and say I don't like you because this is how I live my life. That's the key word, that's the key phrase: my life. So why should I put that on you? So, I think we do that.

As Daniel suggests, the dialogical process is not based on coercion, nor does it mandate consensus. It is indeed a confrontational method that is in direct conflict with the way in which white teachers regularly conduct their classrooms. Clearly the contrast has to do with teachers' ideas of respectability and perceptions of black bodies. Veronica implies this connection as she alludes to the issue of language as a form of intimidation:

But I feel the most comfortable with myself like at settings like this or in a classroom where . . . I like to intimidate people. It's fun, because I like to see where your intellectual level is and I want to see if you really are going to let me intimidate you. Like I will if you'll allow me to. And that's when I feel most comfortable, at peace with myself—when I can just control you. I feel more at peace when I can sit down and have an intelligent conversation.

(Now do you think intelligence and intimidation are one and the same?)

No. They are not one and the same, but they seem to run hand in hand because if your intelligence level is real good, you cannot be easily intimidated. If you have a high intellect and your confidence level is at its best, then intimidation and smarts would run hand in hand. If you got it up here, you wouldn't be as easily intimidated as someone who really didn't, who really didn't know what was going on in the world. . . . But I search for that in a person. Because I want to compete with you and if you are nothing to compete with, then you are nothing to be around. But if I can bring out something in you, and feed on it then we can make it. If you go away from my intellect and say "I cannot deal with it, I don't even want to talk to her anymore, I can't even hold two minutes with you"—bye . . . bye! Because if you are not smart enough to deal with me, you are not smart. If you are not intelligent enough to deal with me in terms of our conversation, then you are not intelligent enough to be next to me.

Hence, intelligence, as Veronica suggests, is inseparable from courage and integrity. It is not given to weak conversations and shallow interpretations. It necessarily entails relations whose dynamics characterize them as vibrant and full of vitality. *Informed peers* are one such group of these relations. Informed peers are those individuals who are knowledgeable about politics and culture as a consequence of their active participation in groups and organizations; in fact, the *organizations*, such as Saturday academies, cultural organizations, and religious and political study groups constitute vertical relationships in themselves. For instance, among young Black males in particular, prominent is an "Islamic" discourse that one can either directly or indirectly connect to the Nation of Islam and the teachings of the Honorable Elijah Muhammad. The "teachings," as Muslims commonly refer to them, emphasize the enfleshment of God (Allah) and the divine potentiality of human beings in the "here and now" as opposed to the "hereafter." In mosque meetings, ministers attach explicit messages of Black empowerment and self-determination to these concepts. Hip-hop and rap artists further publicize and popularize these messages through the medium of popular culture. Some of these artists include Kool Moe Dee, Public Enemy, KRS-1, Queen Latifah, X-Clan, Bran Nubians, Poor Righteous Teachers and, to a lesser degree, some of the so-called hard-core gangster rappers, such as Ice-Cube. Many artists sample segments of lectures by Malcolm X, Minister Louis Farrakhan, Ava Muhammad, and Khallid Abdul Muhammad, the latter two being special assistants to Minister Farrakhan. In addition, socioreligious organizations also disseminate the teachings among Black youth. The most popular, the Five Percent Nation, is a group of young Black men and women that congregates in central-city parks to "drop knowledge" and "kick science." The late Clarence 13X, credited with making the teachings available to the general public for the first time, founded the Five Percent Nation after he departed the Nation of Islam in 1964 (Cuba, 1990).

Thus, the teachings are accessible to a public beyond Muslim mosques. Kwesi, for example, although "not a Muslim," mentioned names of peers that are affiliated with the Nation of Islam whom he consulted for alternative and affirming points of views from those espoused at school. Similarly, Clayton frequents Leimert Park, a meeting place of the Five Percent Nation and the "new Mecca of Afrocentric culture in Los Angeles" (Renwick & Aubry, 1993, p. E3).

I do not emphasize the Islamic doctrine so much to validate it but rather to explicate its influence on the identity formation of Black adolescents. Clearly the teachings, as truth goes, are also "things of this world" (Foucault, 1980, p. 131) and have been implicated in perpetuating certain constraints on the self-realization of Black people. As many Black feminist critics of the various forms of black nationalist and civil rights groups have pointed out, many potentially liberatory organizations have failed to critique and eliminate the oppression within their own ranks. In fact, in addition to the Nation of Islam, many organizations whose social identities took form during the civil rights and Black Power struggles of the 1960s and 1970s tend to equate the liberation of black *people* with the liberation of black men. Consequently, critics point to authoritarian assumptions that underpin the language of the teachings; these assumptions inform attitudes that objectify women and perpetuate classist and elitist ideas. However, although hardly unproblematic and in need of examination in itself, the Islamic presence nonetheless is an influential force in black youths' struggle for identity.

Academic adult authority figures who work outside public schools and who generally locate themselves in the epistemological margins of their chosen disciplines comprise another group of vertical relations. An example of one such person is Frances Cress Welsing, a Washington, D.C.–based psychiatrist. The following exchange, for instance, illustrates this connection as a group of Black youths name their circumstances:

Daniel: So I had a problem, you know, with, am I . . . ? I was, you know, I guess in my subconscious—I never really said it—but I was a black American. And I came out here and it was like, I started learning, I started getting knowledge, I started obtaining . . .

Louise: Going and listening to Frances Cress Welsing . . .

Daniel: Yes, Frances Cress Welsing, you know, talking about America the pimp, the ho society and all this, you know, started to sink in. And slowly but surely it started, that American started to come out. But I had never really understood why until like this year when, I think I was in Mr. Clinton's class and he said stand up for the flag salute; stand up for the pledge of allegiance or something, whatever. And I was like, no. And he said, you're not going to stand up for the pledge of allegiance? And we had a discussion for the whole science class why I wasn't going to stand up. And it all started to come out why I didn't and why I never have since I've been out here. And it was because, you know, if there was a war I wouldn't, you know, fight. If there was an altercation between a police officer and a brother, I'd get on the brother side no matter what the problem. So, it was like why should I pledge allegiance to this flag?

Veronica: You'd be lying.

Daniel: Lying and aligning yourself with a country with which you don't stand for its principles or how it got started. So, how can you . . . it's like you're lying to yourself, pimping yourself.

Of note is the appropriation of "ghetto" metaphors in making linkages that name the students' realities. In particular is the "pimp and ho" analogy. University representatives who deliver on-site lectures to students as well as teacher-initiated classroom discussions have also employed this analogy. I should also point out that in the latter case the teacher in question creates in the public sphere of school "private spaces" by allowing students who choose to excuse themselves from certain lectures to do so. The compromises that this teacher makes reveal not a breach in integrity but rather the repressive character of schools and other public spheres. However, the racist and gendered "ghetto" metaphors, although serving a clear and effective purpose, still reinforce masculinist thinking that is fundamentally exclusionary. Along these lines are explicit remarks attributed to Welsing. Welsing, whose work is well-received in the Black community, equates homosexuality and bisexuality with male passivity and acquiescence. She asserts that:

Black women must learn to rear sons who will learn from the cradle that their major function as men is not to get a good job and a fine car, but to defend, protect and support their people (in that order), even should death be the consequence.

Black male bisexuality and homosexuality have been used by the white collective in its effort to survive genetically in a world dominated by colored people, and Black acceptance of this imposition does not solve the major problem of our oppression but only further retards its ultimate solution (1991, p. 92).

Commenting on homophobia in the Black community, bell hooks (1989) invites us "to think about the shit [we have] been saying and ask [ourselves] where it's coming from" (p. 120). Clearly Welsing's position stems from the uncritical acceptance of oppressive assumptions intrinsic to the homophobic context of the United States. Indeed this is problematic as the notion of sex and identity is a serious issue among Black youth. Many of those with whom I spoke, for instance, told stories of how society in general and Black culture forces them to wrestle with their sexualities in silence, sexualities that include homosexual feelings and same-sex erotic experiences.

CONCLUSION

Implicit in reconstituting the boundaries of truth and knowledge is the contestation of power. "Power is needed to disobey the white cultural imperatives. . . . The only power is people" (Sizemore, 1972, p. 163). This assertion of Black power is a challenge to what Michel Foucault (1980) describes as the "regime of truth" that "exists in a circular relation with systems of power which produce and sustain it, and to effects of power which it induces and which extend it" (p. 133). Although people generally conceive power in terms of what it represses, power also has emancipatory capacities. In terms of the Black adolescent experience in America, this means asserting selves that defy the common caricatures that inform popular attitudes; hooks (1990) declares, "assimilation, imitation, or assuming the role of the rebellious exotic other are not the only available options" (p. 20). The youths with whom I spoke affirm this, revealing identities that reflect at once "conscious and unconscious, contradictory, oppressive and emancipatory responses" (Darder, 1991, p. 54) to the events that constitute everyday life.

Contradictions in the larger society provide openings that allow Black youth to challenge prevailing conceptions of beauty, truth, and authority. This occurs as Black youths gain multiple and contested knowledges of who they are through interaction with others whom they accord status as authority figures. In addition, as adolescence is also a period during which youths explore their sexual selves *and* due to the contradictory repression and glorification of sex in the larger society, Black adolescents often assert their identities in a manner that converges somatic features with racialized images. This means that in a very problematic way cultural reclamation is associated with an increasing refutation of black bodies as aesthetically and sexually denigrated entities. Hence, the link between consciousness, language, and Black adolescent identities materializes as a direct historical conflation of blackness, black bodies, sexuality, and violence. That these representations converge and diverge in the Black adolescent imagination is apparent in their creative language.

Pedagogically it means that teachers need to address issues directly and openly. Just as adolescents desire to penetrate the veneer-like or superficial representations of culture and politics, they also desire to explore more deeply and honestly other aspects of their lives. However, the weak curriculum and unfair arrangements that emerge from deeply embedded assumptions in the larger society cannot stand up to the truth and power that increasing numbers of Black youth bring to public spheres. Hence, in order to effect any substantial changes, educators must transform the fragmented and shallow way of thinking reproduced in schools. These transformations will only occur, however, when the dominant society finds the courage to come to terms with what it is and what it is not.

NOTES

1. The term Ebonics, derived from ebony and phonics to mean literally "black sound," was developed by Black linguists to challenge the pejorative conceptualization of the phenomenon as implied in the oxymoron "Black/African-American English/dialect" which denies the integrity of African language systems, glosses over the sociopolitical and historical realities of segregation in America, and perpetuates the stereotypical image of Black people as inchoate beings (Smith, 1992; Smitherman-Donaldson, 1988).

2. All references to participants will employ pseudonyms primarily to protect the identities of others who may be implicated by their words. For the record, the vast majority of those who participated in this project requested that their real names be used in publications that contain our discussions. The interviews were conducted during August 1993 as part of a larger project. The discussions varied from two to eight hours in length; the longer interviews were conducted over two sessions. Also, interviews were conducted one-on-one, with pairs and small groups. Interviews from the sessions that were comprised of the following individuals are included in this chapter: Louise, Veronica, Monica, Daniel, & David (small group); Kwesi & Regina (pair); Louis & Albert (pair); Clayton (individual); Paige & Roni (pair).

REFERENCES

Barnes, E. (1972). "The black community as the source of positive self-concept for black children: A theoretical perspective," in R. L. Jones (ed.), *Black Psychology.* New York, NY: Harper and Row, pp. 166–193.

Bulhan, H. A. (1985). *Frantz Fanon and the psychology of oppression.* New York, NY: Plenum Press.

Chomsky, N. (1991a). *Media control: The spectacular achievements of propaganda.* Westfield, NJ: Open Magazine.

———. (1991b). *The new world order.* Westfield, NJ: Open Magazine.

———. (1989). *Necessary illusions: Thought control in democratic societies.* Boston, MA: South End Press.

———. (1987). *The Chomsky reader,* ed. J. Peck. New York, NY: Pantheon Books.

Churchill, W. (1992). *Fantasies of the master race: Literature, cinema and the colonization of American Indians,* ed. M. A. Jaimes. Monroe, ME: Common Courage Press.

Cone, J. (1990). *A Black theology of liberation* (20th anniversary ed.). Maryknoll, NY: Orbis Books.

Courts, P. (1991). *Literacy and empowerment: The meaning makers.* New York, NY: Bergin & Garvey.

Cuba, P. (1990). *Master Fard Muhammad: "Detroit history."* Newport News, VA: United Brothers & Sisters Communications Systems.

Darder, A. (1991). *Culture and power in the classroom: A critical foundation for bicultural education.* New York, NY: Bergin and Garvey.

Dilliard, J. (1973). *Black English: Its history and usage in the United States.* New York, NY: Vintage Books.

Duncan, G. (1993). "Racism as a developmental mediator." *Educational Forum,* 57(4), pp. 360–370.

Erikson, E. (1980). *Identity and the life cycle.* New York, NY: W. W. Norton.

Fanon, F. (1967). *Black skin, white masks.* New York, NY: Grove Press.

Foucault, M. (1980). *Power/knowledge: Selected interviews and other writings 1972–1977,* ed. C. Gordon; trans. L. Marshall, J. Mepham, & K. Soper. New York, NY: Pantheon Books.

Freire, P. (1985). *The politics of education: Culture, power, and liberation.* New York, NY: Bergin & Garvey.

Fresia, J. (1988). *Toward an American revolution: Exposing the constitution and other illusions.* Boston, MA: South End Press.

Fulwood, S. (1991). "Attitudes on minorities in conflict." *Los Angeles Times* (January 9), p. A13.

Ginsburg, C. (1989). "Race and media: The enduring life of the Moynihan report." Monographs of the Institute for Media Analysis, Inc., no. 3.

Goldberg, D. (1993). *Racist culture: Philosophy and the politics of meaning.* Oxford: Blackwell.

Herman, E. (1982). *The real terror network: Terrorisim in fact and propaganda.* Boston, MA: South End Press.

Herman, E. & Chomsky, N. (1988). *Manufacturing consent: The political economy of the mass media.* New York, NY: Pantheon Books.

Hilliard, A. (1983). "Psychological factors associated with language in the education of the African-American child." *Journal of Negro Education*, 52(1), pp. 24–34.

hooks, b. (1992). *Black looks: Race and representation*. Boston, MA: South End Press.

———. (1990). *Yearing: Race, gender, and cultural politics*. Boston, MA: South End Press.

———. (1989). *Talking back: Thinking feminist, thinking black*. Boston, MA: South End Press.

Kozol, J. (1991). *Savage inequalities: Children in America's schools*. New York, NY: Crown Publishers, Inc.

Lakoff, G. & Johnson, M. (1980). *Metaphors we live by*. Chicago, IL: University of Chicago Press.

Lusane, C. (1991). *Pipe dream blues: Racism and the war on drugs*. Boston, MA: South End Press.

McLaren, P. (1989). "On ideology and education: Critical pedagogy and the cultural politics of resistance," in H. Giroux and P. McLaren (eds.), *Critical pedagogy, the state, and cultural struggle*. Albany, NY: State University of New York Press.

Office of Planning and Research of the U. S. Department of Labor. (1965). *The Negro family: The case for national action*. Washington, D.C.: U.S. Government Printing Office.

Ogbu, J. (1987). "Variability in minority school performance: A problem in search of an explanation." *Anthropology and Education Quarterly*, 18(4), pp. 312–334.

Renwick, L. & E. Aubry. (1993). "Art and soul: Leimert Park is emerging as the New Mecca of Afrocentric culture in Los Angeles." *Los Angeles Times* (December 1), p. E3.

Shilling, C. (1993). *The body and social theory*. Newbury Park, CA: Sage Publications.

Sizemore, B. (1972). "Social science and an education for a Black identity," in J. Banks and J. Grambs (eds.), *Black self-concept*. New York, NY: McGraw Hill.

Smith, E. (1992). "African American language behavior: A world of difference," in P. Dreyer (ed.), *Reading the world: Multimedia and multicultural learning in today's classroom*. Claremont, CA: Fifty-Sixth Yearbook of the Claremont Reading Conference, The Claremont Graduate School, pp. 38–53.

Smitherman-Donaldson, G. (1988). "Discriminatory discourse on Afro-American speech," in G. Smitherman-Donaldson & T. van Dijk (eds.), *Discourse and discrimination*. Detroit, MI: Wayne State University Press, pp. 144–175.

Spencer, M. (1988). "Self-concept development," in D. T. Slaughter (ed.), *Black children and poverty: A developmental perspective—new directions for child development, vol. 42*. San Francisco, CA: Jossey-Bass, pp. 59–72.

Turner, L. (1973). *Africanisms in the Gullah dialect*. Ann Arbor, MI: University of Michigan Press.

Vygotsky, L. (1978). *Mind in society: The development of higher psychological processes*, ed. M. Cole, V. John-Steiner, S. Scribner, & E. Souberman. Cambridge, MA: Harvard University Press.

Welsing, F. (1991). *The Isis (Yssis) papers: The keys to the colors*. Chicago, IL: Third World Press.

Wilson, W. (1980). *The declining significance of race: Blacks and changing American institutions*. Chicago, IL: University of Chicago Press.

The Alter-Native Grain: Theorizing Chicano/a Popular Culture

Alicia Gaspar de Alba

How does one theorize Chicano/a popular culture? The word "theory" itself, both in its present academic application as well as in its archaic context, conscientiously excludes the popular and the marginalized. Etymologically, the word stems from the Greek *theoria*, which signifies an act of viewing; archaically, it meant an imaginative contemplation of reality.[1] Contemplation, in ancient Greek culture, did not refer to the fleeting moments of time during which the slave or the housewife, for example, mused about her life; it was, instead, the contemplation indulged in by "thinkers," philosophers, scholars—a foreign language, deeply abstract, meaningless to the masses, self-referential and privileged. The words "scholar" and "school" come from *scholes*, another Greek referent, signifying leisure. Theorizing, then, was an activity of the leisure class, whose members could afford the time needed to contemplate, formulate, and explicate their theories.

In contemporary usage, the word Theory with a capital "T" has remained the sovereign right of the academy; education affords Theory, as Theory is the privileged contemplation engaged in by those who have the leisure to pursue speculation beyond need. To "do" formal Theory, the kind that gets validated within the academy, is first to belong to the social class that gets "educated," and second, to cultivate a particular language that expresses the ruling vision of academic Theory. As historical objects of that vision (equivalent to the male gaze in cinema and the colonizing gaze in anthropology), women, people of color, the working classes, and oral traditions have all been *overlooked* by theory. Hence, Chicanos/as, like other colonized "Others" in the United States, have had to devise our own theories, following a strategy of appropriation and subversion rooted in resistance to academic and cultural hegemony. As Gloria Anzaldúa (1990) says in her introduction to *Haciendo Caras*:

[W]e need *teorías* that will enable us to interpret what happens in the world, that will explain how and why we relate to certain people in specific ways, that will reflect what goes on between inner, outer, and peripheral "I" 's within a person and between the personal "I" 's and the collective "we" of our ethnic communities. *Necesitamos teorías* that will rewrite history using race, class, gender and ethnicity as categories of analysis, theories that cross borders, that blur boundaries—new kinds of theories with new theorizing methods (p. xxv).

Theorizing Chicano/a popular culture, then, involves primarily analyzing resistance in Chicano/a cultural production and inventing theories, or views, of resistance that mirror our colonized realities.

Given the above cogitations on the classist history and meaning of Theory, the phrase "theories of resistance" is paradoxical. Yet it is in paradox, in contradiction and ambiguity, that postmodern theory especially finds its more dynamic expressions, as evidenced by the current debates on subject/object, margin/center, identity/difference, insider/outsider, high/low culture, quality/diversity, butch/femme. We can define resistance by what it is (the power to oppose) and what it is not (submission). Because the former definition includes the word "power," any theory that would illuminate resistance must consider power relations. The negative definition points to an analysis of ways by which people comply or are made to submit. Thus, it seems necessary to historicize Chicano/a resistance within the context of the U.S.–Mexican War, the Mexican Revolution, the Zoot Suit Riots, and the Chicano Civil Rights Movement; we must also situate Chicano/a resistance within theories of representation and identity politics, particularly at the crossroads of race, class, gender, and sexual orientation; and, finally, we must attempt to analyze the expression of Chicano/a resistance through a deconstructive critique of cultural texts.[2]

The purpose of this chapter, however, is to focus on three theoretical approaches to reading resistance: (1) poststructuralist semiotics, used specifically to analyze the ways in which a popular text can signify and elicit *concientización*, or cathartic moments of political awareness; (2) ethnographic criticism, which explores different forms of audience reception to popular texts, particularly those that resist dominant ideologies in radical ways; and (3) *rasquachismo*, the theory and praxis of popular pleasure as a subversive and uniquely working-class strategy, demonstrated by Chicano/a humor and by artistic appropriation of Chicano/a cultural "kitsch." The entire analysis, moreover, is informed by a Chicana feminist perspective.

A POSTSTRUCTURALIST READING OF SIGNS

One way of interpreting resistance in Chicano/a cultural production is through a semiotic reading of signs from a poststructuralist perspective; that is, a perspective that illuminates the many voices and meanings of a given sign—its multivocality—as well as the intertextual dialogue that exists in all cultural production. This primarily linguistic approach is especially prescient in the theoretical framing of an ethnic identity that has been, in large part, historically determined by language difference. How, for example, do the signs "Mexican" and "Chicano," which are inscribed with linguistic as well as racial and cultural codes, affect subjectivity? Structuralists believe that human understanding of the self and the self's relationship to the world is organized through language—language as "an abstract system, consisting of chains of signs. Each sign is made up of a *signifier* (sound or written image) and a *signified* (meaning)" (Weedon, 1987, p. 23). Ferdinand de Saussure's theory that the meaning of a sign could be derived from the sign's negative definition, from its difference from other signs, was extended by Jacques Derrida's concept of "*differánce* in which meaning is produced via the dual strategies of "difference and deferral" (Weedon, 1987, p. 25). Whereas Saussure's theory ended in fixed definitions which failed to account for historical circumstances and their impact on a person's sense of him/herself (i.e., his/her subjectivity), Derrida and his poststructuralist cohorts conceived of subjectivity, because of its continual process of deferral to historical specificity, not as "unified or fixed" but rather as "precarious, contradictory, and in process, constantly being reconstituted in discourse each time we think or speak" (Weedon, 1987, p. 33). Because the historical moment is always changing, the definition is always changing, as is the subject engaged in the process of defining, whose ever-changing subjectivity is shaped by the language or languages he/she is using for that definition. Thus, a sign has no singular meaning, and no singular subject preserves fixed meanings.

This decentering of the subject proves to be problematic for those who have just entered into the discourse of subjectivity, those cultural "others" whose lives have been deferred by the historical reality of colonization and oppression. But the poststructuralist idea of a decentered subject is an accurate description of Chicano/a subjectivity. If it is true that, as Gloria Anzaldúa (1987) believes, "ethnic identity is twin skin to linguistic identity" (p. 59), and if a Chicano/a's linguistic identity is, itself, "precarious, contradictory, and in process" because of the heterogeneity of languages that interface Chicano/a discourse, then an ethnic identity that has *language* as a basic component of difference is equally ambiguous and unstable. Anzaldúa (1987, p. 55) names eight different languages that converge on Chicano/a identity:

1. Standard English
2. Working class and slang English
3. Standard Spanish
4. Standard Mexican Spanish
5. North Mexican Spanish dialect
6. Chicano Spanish (Texas, New Mexico, Arizona and California have regional variations)

7. Tex-Mex

8. *Pachuco* (called *caló*)

The bridges that stretch across the U.S.–Mexico border simultaneously separate and join two nations. Conceptually, the different languages that bridge Chicano/a subjectivity perform the same functions: they separate and join two cultural realities across the landscape shared by both—a geographical, political, and personal space known as the border. The border epitomizes the contradictions and conflicts of a binational, tricultural, and multilingual identity; the border incorporates both difference and *differánce* because Chicano/a identity is always in the process of defining itself in contrast to "the other side," and that process is/has been always historically specific.

The overriding question of Chicano/a subjectivity is not, primarily, "Who am I?" (that one comes later) but "*What* am I?"[3] The "what" in the question refers to nationality. Given the relational and oppositional nature of Chicano/a citizenship in an Anglo-dominated country, "what am I?" is further complicated by the mirror-image projected from without: "what do they think/say I am?"

Cheech Marín's *Born in East L.A.* (Universal Studios, 1987) is a low-budget Hollywood production which criticizes the racist notions of "nativism" and American citizenship that the Border Patrol enforces. The film satirizes the racist assumption that Chicanos/as are not "real" Americans who need to carry documentation to prove our identity/citizenship. Marín is both the subject and the object of *Born in East L.A.* As the object, he is described in the jacket copy of the video as the "illegal alien" who gets "accidentally deported" and tries time upon unsuccessful time to "sneak back into the United States," only to realize that he was not "born to run . . . from the immigration service." As the subject, Marín is the Chicano filmmaker using the issue of citizenship and the cinematic device of mistaken identity as metaphors for a state of cognitive disorientation, a psychological effect of colonization that I call *cultural schizophrenia*. The perception of this state is fundamental to the evolution of Chicano/a consciousness. Culture, as defined by *Webster's* and as it applies to my use of the term cultural schizophrenia means "the customary beliefs, social forms, and material traits of a racial, religious, or social group." Apart from its clinical definition of mental disorder, schizophrenia signifies "the presence of mutually contradictory or antagonistic parts or qualities." Integrating these denotations, cultural schizophrenia is the presence of mutually contradictory or antagonistic beliefs, social forms, and material traits in any group whose racial, religious, or social components are a hybrid (or *mestizaje*) of two or more fundamentally opposite cultures.

Because this hybridity, in the case of all "New World" peoples, is a product of conquest, we can deduce that cultural schizophrenia is a psychological effect of colonization. The colonized mentality is first and foremost a split identity, part conquered, part conqueror, "both tyrant and slave," "the victor, and the vanquished," as Corky González (1972) says in his epic poem *I am Joaquín*.

Moreover, the history of colonization is directly linked to racism, which in colonial New Spain, as Tomás Rivera (1992) reminds us, was reinforced and normalized by a semiotic apparatus:

The colonial mind was preoccupied with color. When a child born to a couple was darker than the parents, he/she was called a *salto atrás*, a jump backwards, but if the child was lighter, he/she was considered a *salto adelante*, a jump forward; and if the child was the same color as the parents, a *tente en el aire*, suspended (p. 410).

I argue that the awareness of cultural schizophrenia is fundamental to the evolution of Chicano/a consciousness because that awareness leads to identity crisis, to rupture between the outwardly-defined persona (or the colonized mind) and the inwardly-identified self. In this moment of differentiation, Chicano/a consciousness becomes aware of itself as not only separate from, but more importantly resistant to, the hegemonic constructs of race and class. Marín's tragicomic film enacts these constructs as the politics of assimilation and immigration.

Although the protagonist of the film, Rudy Robles (self-represented by Cheech), is a third-generation native of Los Angeles, he is being "sent back where he came from." Ironically, where he came from is where he is being deported from. But who is *he*? "Let's start with your name," says the INS official. "Rudy Robles," he says, sure of himself at first, but then he admits that this is not his "real name." "My whole name is Guadalupe Rudolfo Robles." Two names, two identities. Which is the real one? To the INS official who finds Rudy's "real name" in his computer records, Rudy is a 57-year-old "illegal alien" who has been caught and deported nine times. Rudy negates the imposed identity by pointing out his differences: "I'm not 57," and "I'm no illegal." But despite his fluent English (i.e., his East L.A. slang), without the proper documentation to "prove" his citizenship, Rudy is identified as the "Other" Guadalupe Rudolfo Robles, and "returned" to Mexico, where he is told he belongs. Rudy's "I'm an American citizen, you idiots!" serves as the central paradox of the film. He may think of himself as a citizen of the United States, but it is what the idiots think he is that determines his fate. As Rudy's case demonstrates, Chicano/a identity is, ultimately, a border identity: neither side wants you and you can't go home.

If neither citizen nor alien, what is a Chicano/a? Ultimately, this question leads to *concientización,* an epiphany of political consciousness—not for the mainstream audience who may find Rudy's "desperate attempts to sneak back into the States" hilarious,[4] but for the Chicano/a audience for whom issues of citizenship, borders, and identity are historically problematic, having plagued Chicano/a subjectivity for a century and a half. As Coco Fusco (1990) says in "The Latino 'Boom' in Hollywood," *Born in East L.A.* epitomizes the way "geographical frontiers have been internalized, creating a sense of fragmented identity" (p. 54). Awareness of the apparatuses that produce this fragmentation is a form of resistance both to the forces of assimilation and to the self-denigration and inferiority complex that infect the "colonized mind."[5]

ETHNOGRAPHIC CRITICISM AND THE NATIVE I/EYE

Another approach to an analysis of resistance is to monitor the audience reception to the text, as in ethnographic criticism. Reception theory, Tania Modleski (1991) explains in *Feminism Without Women*, has at its base the premise that audiences generate a plurality of responses to any given text. Unlike the Frankfurt School of criticism, ethnographic critics argue that there is not merely one response, or one meaning, or one effect to be gleaned from a text. The radio, for example, was read by Frankfurt critic Theodor Adorno as a text that produces passivity and subservience in the audience. By creating a "false consciousness" in the consumer of mass culture, a demand for products and entertainment that are ultimately forms of oppression, mass culture manipulates the audience into complacent acceptance of the status quo.

Informed by their Marxist underpinnings, the Frankfurt critics see mass culture only as the modern opiate of the people. Ethnographic critics, on the other hand, taking their cue from the poststructuralists and the Birmingham School of cultural studies, believe that mass culture elicits multiple responses from its audiences that range from submission to resistance. One way to probe that multiplicity, then, is to monitor audience reception in the way that Janice Radway did for her study on romance novels and their impact on midwestern housewives—by traveling to the site to observe, survey, and interview the participants and letting them speak for themselves. A danger that Modleski (1991) sees to the ethnographic criticism approach is that "by focusing on the audience member's response to texts, the critic might wind up re-subscribing to an apolitical view of the individual as sole producer of meanings and unwittingly endorsing a pluralist, anything-goes kind of criticism" (p. 37).

Traditional ethnography is narcissistic, another problem. The ethnographer sets him/herself apart and above his/her subjects and passes judgment, as it were, on the data. Audience reception, though it reveals the multiplicity of meanings inherent in any text, still depends upon the ethnographer to filter those findings through the lenses of his/her own ideologies. Moreover, traditional ethnography is a form of domination, a way of condescending to the natives under study. Because both native and alter-Native cultures are "othered" and exoticized in order to be quantified and studied, they get categorized as "subcultures." Such categorization poses two problems: by definition, "subculture" implies the presence of a superior culture; and, rather than being analyzed in their own right, subcultures are used as filters for analyzing the effects of the messages that the ethnographer's own culture, the dominating culture, projects onto the so-called subculture. Though this may be a powerful source of knowledge, it reduces the subjects of study to cultural guinea pigs.

An analysis of audience reception to a Chicano/a text performed by a Chicano or Chicana would minimize the ethnographic filter and illuminate a discourse community based on shared cultural values, practices, and beliefs, albeit nuanced by the critic's own class, gender, and political and sexual orientations. Working within the contradictions of what Renato Rosaldo (1993) calls a "native ethnographer,"[6] the Chicano/a critic of Chicano/a popular culture seeks out multiple audience responses that resonate with his/her own diverse subject positions. This approach may not qualify as "ethnography," native or otherwise, if it fails to employ "the ethnographer's elevated, distanced, normalizing discourse" (p. 109). Nonetheless, it is a critical endeavor that draws on ethnographic methodologies (i.e., participant observation and oral interview) without subscribing to or perpetuating its colonizing gaze. As another critical strategy, the ethnographic method can be used to describe and interpret that colonizing gaze.

In an intriguing essay depicting Hollywood as "the ethnographer of American culture" (p. 404), Ana López (1991) argues that a power relationship exists between the ethnographer and the culture that he/she is interpreting. This power relationship is equivalent to a colonizer/colonized duality. Hence, because "Hollywood does not represent ethnics and minorities [but rather] creates them, and provides its audience with an experience of them" (p. 405). Hollywood, in effect, colonizes "Other" cultures. Hollywood directors interpret "Other" cultures, choosing specific images and narratives to create the ethnic experience on the screen, and thus, act as agents/representatives of the industry.

In this respect, the director of a mainstream film or the curator of an exhibition about ethnic "Others" can fill the role of the traditional ethnographer. Like the traditional ethnographer, the director/curator is in the position of interpretive authority without accounting for the sociopolitical differences that comprise the ethnographer's subjectivity—the very subjectivity that not only interprets the data, but chooses from it the images to be used for representation. In the case of the *Hispanic Art in the United States* exhibition (1987), for example, curators Jane Livingston and John Beardsley (1992) decided to organize a survey of thirty artists (painters and sculptors only) in the United States who were "of Hispanic descent," and therefore shared some "stylistic affinit[ies]." The very premise of the show reflected the melting pot mentality of the curators: in the interest of "coherence and a strong underlying assertion of aesthetic will" (p. 106), racial and cultural differences were erased. Furthermore, only two forms of artistic expression were chosen to promote the curatorial interpretation of the Hispanic "subculture" in the art world. Writing in defense of the "Hispanic" label, Livingston and Beardsley (1992) outline the difficulties they had in selecting an accurate signifier for their exhibition:

No other term seemed any better. To use *Latin American* seemed to suggest that the artists were not North American; in fact, nearly two-thirds of them were born in the United States. *Latino* seemed to exclude the Spanish Americans of the Southwest. *Chicano* excluded those not of Mexican origin. Compelled by necessity to include some descriptive term in the title of the exhibition, we decided *Hispanic* was the least incorrect . . . . Moreover, we think it reflects fairly the fact that there are legitimate shared characteristics, both in terms of subject matter and style, among artists in the North American environment who share New World Spanish-Native American roots. That is, there are ways in which "Hispanic" culture, no matter how diverse internally, is distinct from mainstream European American or African American culture (p. 116).

They were, of course, deeply criticized for their patent homogenization and for the vision they created of "Hispanic" art as primitive, folksy, and religious. The real issue, however, is not how accurately or realistically Livingston and Beardsley (or Robert Redford, as we will see below) represented the cultures under scrutiny, but how the exhibition revealed the social and historical discourses about those "Others" which the curators themselves represented (Stam, 1991).

In *The Milagro Beanfield War* (1987), the object of Redford's film (as we are told in the jacket description of the video) is the stereotypically unemployed "Chicano handyman" who becomes a "spirited rebel" and instigates a "humorous culture clash" between Big Business and the "everyday people" of a "magical New Mexican village." The subject of the narrative (i.e., the one telling the story) is the sensitive liberal outsider, or rather, John Nichols, the Anglo author of the novel, and Robert Redford, the Anglo director of the film. These Anglo *auteurs* are represented in *Milagro* by the hippie journalist/ex-lawyer, Charlie Bloom (John Heard) and the aspiring sociologist/graduate student, Herbie Platt (Daniel Stern). Both Bloom and Platt are the ethnographers of Milagro (actually, the Northern New Mexican village of Truchas). Bloom writes and publishes *La Voz del Norte*, a weekly periodical that purports to be *the* "voice," not only of Milagro, but also of northern New Mexico. Platt has received a grant from New York University to "study the indigenous cultures of the Southwest." Thus, Bloom and Platt serve as narrative devices for *Milagro* that, like the Anglo reporter in *The Ballad of Gregorio Cortéz*, "incarnate the dominant discourse of the film" (Fregoso, 1985, p. 128). That dominant discourse, verted on the metaphor of the land grant disputes of New Mexico, is bourgeois capitalism, and its principal method is appropriation.

The purpose of a Chicano/a ethnographic criticism of *The Milagro Beanfield War* would not be simply to criticize Redford for his romantic appropriation of Chicano culture and his gross oversimplification of the land grant problems in New Mexico, but also to emphasize that the romantic tourist interpretation and the colonizing directorial gaze represent Hollywood's hegemonic discourse about the Mexican "Other." Similarly, a native ethnographic criticism of the CARA exhibition[7] can deconstruct the "insider" and "outsider" polemics at the heart of both the show and the "Quality" debate in the mainstream art world. The native eye/I does not assume only one correct, authentic interpretation (if that even exists), but allows for an interpretive stance framed by the politics of self-representation. As Rosaldo (1993) points out, "[n]ot unlike other ethnographers, so-called natives can be insightful, sociologically-correct, axe-grinding, self-interested, or mistaken . . . [but] they do know their own cultures" (p. 108).

My own native ethnography resists the "subculture" model imposed by ethnographic methodology, which presupposes the monolithic influence of the dominant culture, and uses the "subculture" as a filter by which to analyze that influence. This model is also used in all levels of scholarship in the field of cultural studies, from introductory course readers in popular culture to recent feminist scholarship. In *Feminism Without Women: Culture and Criticism in a "Postfeminist" Age*, for example, Modleski (1991) writes: "By focusing on subcultures and studying the values and beliefs associated with them, the analyst is able to make sense of the ways in which 'messages' are 'decoded' according to the shared cultural orientation of particular groups" (p. 38). Though it is true that Modleski is invoking an ethnographic criticism that can monitor revolutionary responses to dominant ideologies, she fails to question the hierarchical assumptions that organize cultures into "sub" categories.

Similarly, Dick Hebdige (1993), a cultural critic of the Birmingham School and author of *Subculture: The Meaning of Style* (1979), finds that the cultures of subordinate classes and groups represent challenges to hegemony, primarily through a recoding of dominant styles. Again we have a critic who, although he can lucidly explain the power dynamics of hegemony and the insidious ways in which the "rhetoric of common sense" (p. 361) penetrates our everyday lives, himself normalizes the vertical stratification of cultures, thus reifying the ideology that creates those categories in the first place and that the field of cultural studies is supposed to question. When "minority" or "other" groups are relegated to the status of "subcultures," they are *sub*sumed by and *sub*jected to an ethnocentric methodology of cultural studies. This, in effect, produces academic segregation, which in turn reproduces the hegemonic view of popular culture.

This is not to say that subcultures do not exist in the genealogy of the dominant culture; but rather, that the term "subculture" is applicable only to those cultures which derive from the dominant one, as in white youth cultures like hippies, punks, and fraternities, or in the separatist communities of senior citizens. These are subcultures, though not necessarily subordinate ones, because they are enclaves of difference within the same ethnicity as well as by-products of the dominant culture's values. Although subcultures appear to resist the dominant value system, they are not, in fact, resisting the dominant culture as much as dominance itself. A subordinate culture, on the other hand, lives in a direct power relation with the dominant culture; it is not a recalcitrant offspring, but a disenfranchised colony of the dominant ethnicity. Although I agree with Hebdige (1979) that "[s]ubcultures . . . express, in the last instance, a fundamental tension between those in power and those condemned to subordinate positions and second-class lives" (p. 132), I disagree with his premise that white youth cultures are sentenced to second-class lives and that "minority" groups who have a history of colonization can be compared to groups who, though they may be at the bottom of the capitalist structure, historically represent the colonizer. Rather than the restrictive and reductive prefix "sub," I propose that we re-think cultures that are racially and ethnically different from the dominant one as "alter-cultures." Issuing from the Latin word for "other," alter means to change, to make or become different, as in the altering of consciousness or the alteration of an outfit. Moreover, the concept of "alter ego" represents another self, another identity. In postmodern, poststructuralist discourses, the word "alterity" is used to connote the condition of Otherness; a "subaltern," therefore, as in the British colonial notion of a "subaltern continent," is the underground, the Fourth World, the lowest rung of Otherness. But the term "subaltern" is a colonialist construct, reinforcing the connection between inferiority and people of color. I suggest that Chicano/a culture is not only an "alter-culture" that simultaneously differs from, is changed by, and changes the dominant culture, but is also an *alter-Native culture* (i.e., an Other culture native or indigenous to the United States).

RASQUACHISMO: THE SUBVERSIVE POWER OF PLEASURE

Like the Frankfurt School and the postmodernists, even critics of postmodernism such as Roland Barthes and Fredric Jameson see popular culture as a weapon of hegemony that manipulates the audience through pleasure. The masses, the argument seems to run, are controlled by the hegemonic messages couched in the pleasure of the text. Reading the horror film as oppositional cinema, however, Modleski (1987) shows how the perverse pleasure of horror films can be subversive to the status quo. "Many of these films," she argues, "[such as *The Brood* and *The Texas Chainsaw Massacre*] are engaged in an unprecedented assault on all that bourgeois culture is supposed to cherish—like the ideological apparatuses of the family and the school" (p. 158). Thus we have two views of pleasure: as resistance, as complacency—but we also have, according to John Fiske, two kinds of pleasure.

In *Understanding Popular Culture*, Fiske (1989) explains the difference between hegemonic pleasures which exert social control by producing meanings and practices in the interest of power, and popular pleasures which subvert the meanings and values of hegemony and thereby evade being controlled. "High" culture, for example, is said to uplift, edify, and inspire, while "low" culture merely entertains, amuses, or distracts. The former occupies the spiritual, mental domain, and is considered "good for the soul"; the latter focuses on the excesses of the body—eating, drinking, vocalizing, being physically stimulated rather than mentally challenged or spiritually renewed. Fiske finds popular pleasures inherently subversive because they "arise from the social allegiances formed by subordinated people[;] they are bottom-up and thus must exist in some relationship of opposition to power (social, moral, textual, aesthetic, and so on) that attempts to discipline and control them" (p. 49).

Perhaps the best example of a popular pleasure in Chicano/a culture is what Tomás Ybarra-Frausto (1991) calls *rasquachismo*, a uniquely working-class aesthetic of Mexican origin—resourceful, excessive, ironic, and, in its transformation of utilitarian articles into sacred or aesthetic objects, highly metaphoric.

Bright colors (*chillantes*) are preferred to somber, high intensity to low, the shimmering and sparkling over the muted and subdued. The *rasquache* inclination piles pattern on pattern, filling all available space with bold display. Ornamentation and elaboration prevail and are joined with a delight in texture and sensuous surfaces (pp. 133–134).

In the context of Minimalism and Modern art, *rasquachismo* is more than an oppositional form; it is a militant praxis of resistance to hegemonic standards in the art world. Therein resides its popular pleasure, for in subverting dominant ideologies, in "[turning] ruling paradigms upside down ... [this] witty, irreverent and impertinent posture that recodes and moves outside established boundaries" (Ybarra-Frausto, 1989, p. 5) both evades power and empowers itself, as we see in Guillermo Gómez-Peña's video performance, *Border Brujo*.

In his essay, "Surrealism Without the Unconscious," Frederic Jameson (1991) offers three ways of interpreting a postmodern video: (1) thematic interpretation, which seeks to understand the meaning of the text in general (not all video texts will have meaning, though); (2) referent interpretation, which identifies specific references or allusions in the text that shape, change, or even dissolve the general interpretation; and (3) an analysis of the production process itself, meant to foreground connections between the technical and the abstract or conceptual elements of the text. Though not exactly applicable to non-mainstream videos, these three methods tender good starting points for analyzing a text as oppositional, intertextual, and polyphonous as Guillermo Gómez-Peña's *Border Brujo* (1991a).

A thematic interpretation should examine resistance, since that is the theme of this essay. But *Border Brujo* is not a text in which to *analyze* resistance; resistance is the *modus operandi* of the text; it resists analysis, meaning, classification, order, closure. Any detailed description of the text, short of presenting the full transcript, is an exercise in futility. To describe it in broad strokes, then, *Border Brujo* is a low-tech video adaptation of a performance poem of the same name that Gómez-Peña wrote and rendered in 1989 as part of a series entitled "Documented/ Undocumented."[8] The performance is divided into three parts, subtitled respectively: Language Is the Border/El lenguaje es la frontera; Identity Is an Optical Illusion/La identidad es una ilusión óptica; Toward a Post-Colombian Future/Hacía un futuro post-Colombiano.

The organization is arbitrary at best, meant to underscore not a unifying theme in each section but a postmodern analogy: the fragmented, illusive, and existential nature of the border. Thus we have a fragmented and schizophrenic performance packaged as a B-grade video.

Jameson (1991) believes that "video—so closely related to the dominant computer and information technology of the late, or third, stage of capitalism—has a powerful claim for being the art form par excellence of late capitalism" (p. 76). Resisting this affinity between technology and capitalism, however, Gómez-Peña (1991b) finds it "obscene to put half a million dollars into a performance piece" (p. 159), explaining that Latin American artists, "[u]nlike Northern artists . . . cannot avoid the political and moral implications of technology" (p. 159). Nonetheless, video is more accessible and enjoys wider distribution than performance art, and so constitutes a logical medium for dissemination, if not commodification, of Gómez-Peña's border politics. Because it is an adaptation of a written and performed piece, the staging of which is largely static except for the speaker, and because of Gómez-Peña's stance on technology, camera work is minimal, and the production process is limited mainly to editing and altar construction. It would, of course, be interesting to investigate the Sushi Performance Gallery and CineWest Productions, but this would take us away from the actual experience of the performance, wherein the power of *Border Brujo* lies. This leaves me with an interpretation of the historical references and cultural allusions in the text. Indeed, this reading may not render any holistic meaning to the piece (nor am I intending to do that), but it will, at least, provide some frame of reference by which to approach *Border Brujo* on its own terms, and perhaps even traverse the border that it conceptualizes between a Mexican and a Chicano identity. Even though Gómez-Peña is not by birth a Chicano, he works in the installation and performance modes of Chicano/a art and has assumed border citizenship and the culturally-schizophrenic problematics of Chicano identity.

Born in Mexico City in 1955, Gómez-Peña crossed the line in 1978, not to work in the fields or the factories of el Norte, but to study at the California Institute of Arts, a four-year education from the UNAM (Universidad Nacional Autónoma de México) already under his Panama hat.[9] Here we see one of the primary contradictions of *Border Brujo*: the privileged auteur and the marginalized subject. Gómez-Peña in the guise of his character refers to himself as not only a performance artist, but also "a cultural prisoner, a refugee, a migrant poet, a homeless shaman, and the village fool" (p. 195). He is aligning himself to the folk traditions of *santería, brujería*, and *curanderismo*, and yet he is formally trained in Latin American literature, linguistics, and art. In this videotaped seánce, so to speak, fifteen personas, wildly divergent, speak through him: from the undocumented immigrant to the Border Patrol agent, from the Gregorian monk to the Cholo punk. Is he attempting to represent a cultural schizophrenia that may not be authentic to his experience as a "chilango,"[10] or is he establishing the multivocality of border culture? And finally, is *Border Brujo* meant to be *teatro, testimonio,* video, ritual, or simulation?

Produced by the independent CineWest Productions in collaboration with Sushi Performance Gallery of San Diego, *Border Brujo*, as described by the author in the manuscript version of the piece:

. . . is a ritual, linguistic and performative journey across the U.S.–México border . . .
. . . unfolds into 15 different personas, each speaking a different border language . . .
. . . fuses postmodern techniques with popular voices and dialectical forms borrowed from a dozen sources, such as media, tourism, pop culture, Pachuco and pinto slang and political jargon . . .
. . . speaks in Spanish to Mexicans, in Spanglish to Chicanos, in English to Anglo Americans and in tongues to other brujos and border crossers . . .
. . . articulates fear, desire, trauma, sublimation, anger and misplacement . . .
. . . creates a sacred space to reflect on the painful relationship between self and other. . .
. . . negotiates several artistic traditions, including performance art, Chicano theater, ritual theater, border poetry and Latin American literature (Gomez-Peña, 1991, pp. 194–95).

This preface, which is not available in the video version, forewarns the reader that s/he is about to enter a Twilight Zone; it is in a way a referent interpretation of its own. The video adaptation, however, simply thrusts the viewer into the experience. The bizarre "ceremony of memory," officiated by a man in a banana necklace and čalavera earrings who is speaking in unknown tongues, begins with the Brujo lighting the multifarious candles on his altar, thus illuminating the conceptual space of the "other." Let me do some illuminating of my own by examining the cultural allusions embodied by a few of the objects on Border Brujo's *rasquache* altar.

"Kitsch" is not an accurate translation or example of *rasquachismo*, but, in terms of the dominant culture, it signifies a kind of cultural production that also originates in and represents the popular, the vernacular, the working class. In her study on religious paraphernalia, Celeste Olalquiaga (1992) describes three kinds of kitsch: "first-degree kitsch" is the real thing, so to speak, a tradition that goes back at least a hundred years. As she explains, "[s]tatuettes, images, and scapularies embody the spirits they represent, making them palpable. Consequently, this imagery belongs in sacred places, such as home altars, and must be treated with utmost respect" (p. 42). Next, Olalquiaga names "second-degree kitsch" or "neo-kitsch" which is bereft of history and devotional qualities and "leaves us with an empty icon, or rather an icon whose value lies precisely in its iconicity, its quality as a sign rather than as an object" (p. 45). Whereas first-degree kitsch is bought by devotees, neo-kitsch is mass-marketed and sold as souvenirs and collector's items. Finally, "third-degree kitsch" includes icons and paraphernalia that have been recycled by the art world in the making of "happenings," assemblages, and mixed-media installations. In Chicano/a and Latino/a art, this takes the form of *altares*, such as Amalia Mesa-Bains' altar in the CARA exhibit,[11] constructed as an homage to Mexican movie star Dolores del Rio. This artistic installation differs from home altars of the first-degree kind, says Olalquiaga (1992).

As a recent exhibition title suggests, the recasting of *altares* is often meant as a "ceremony of memory" that invests them with a new political signification and awareness. This artistic legitimization implies formalizing home altars to fit into a system of meaning where they represent the culture that once was (p. 48).

Border Brujo's altar is clearly composed of third-degree kitsch. Apart from the votives that spread on the table before him, and the bottle of Herbal Essence shampoo from which Border Brujo is drinking, there are objects of arcane significance such as the papier-mâché sculpture of the Big Mac sitting in its own little shrine and a statuette of the *Star Wars* droid R2D2 flanked by two statuettes of Cantinflas, Mexico's Charlie Chaplin. Crowning the altar behind him is the head of Mexican wrestling champion Superbarrio, masked hero of the working class. Small kachina dolls, a cow's skull, a bust of Popeye next to a Mexican señorita, a collage with the Virgin of Guadalupe in relief, a statuette of a zoot-suited Pachuco, calaveras of different sizes—all of this is third-degree kitsch, meant to show the *mestizaje* of border culture, the collaborative possibilities of border existence, the postmodern "flattening of history in one eternal present that contains all pasts and futures" (p. xiii). There is also an oblique critique of the pan-American sacralization of popular culture.

Rooted in the vernacular traditions of Mexico, *rasquachismo* is a politically-charged aesthetic that flies in the face of elitism and affirms the dynamic environment of everyday life in the barrio. Like kitsch, *rasquachismo* comes in at least the three flavors noted by Olalquiaga: we have first-degree *rasquachismo*—icons, objects, and practices that are rooted in the oral and popular traditions of Chicano/a culture; second-degree *rasquachismo*, which is appropriated from its original context by mainstream commercial enterprises such as stores that sell "ethnic" paraphernalia;[12] and third-degree *rasquachismo* that informs the work of Chicano and Chicana artists, writers, musicians, filmmakers, and other producers of Chicano/a popular culture.

One recurring icon in Chicano/a popular culture is the *calavera*, or skeleton, that is used primarily for Day of the Dead observances on November 2, but that also appears in ironic resistance to cultural annihilation. The tradition of using humor and irony for political commentary goes back as far as colonial Mexico, but it became an especially popular pleasure in the nineteenth century with the *calavera* caricatures of José Guadalupe Posada, from whom Chicano/a artists appropriated the tradition. "Posada's *calaveras* and broadside illustrations depicted crimes of passion, political and social events, religious imagery, natural disasters, and scenes from Mexican daily life" (Green, 1992, p. 65). Because they represented the common denominator between the rich and the poor, the skeletons spoke to all, judged all, respected none, and impersonated Everyman and Everywoman.

Commenting on the subversive power of caricature art, José Zuno (1967, author of *Historia de las artes plásticas en la revolución mexicana*) describes the caricaturist as a revolutionary and a social critic:

Como juzgador, el caricaturista usa de la ironía. De todo se burla, a todo se sobrepone. Hace notar los contrastes entre la belleza y la fealdad, entre la verdad y la mentira. . . . Llega, cuando es necesario hasta la crueldad, hasta la tragedia. Pero la ironía sólo es destructora y negativa en apariencia, pues lo que destruye es lo falso, lo ridículo. Ella representa el esfuerzo que hacemos para triunfar de todo aquello que se opone a la ascensión del espíritu hacia el infinito (p. 151).[13]

Indeed, irony is what *Border Brujo* does best. Its humor, unless it is a sadomasochistic pleasure elicited through humiliation, confrontation, condescension, and sarcasm, is not exactly funny. It is a harsh, jagged sensibility that strings together one insensitivity after another, and in that way serves to alter the mainstream concepts of art and popular culture. Perhaps the best description of *Border Brujo* would be the word "eulogy," a Day of the Dead commemoration for the " 'wetback' with amnesia" whom every Chicano/a is in danger of becoming.

Comedy is another popular pleasure of *la Raza*. Cheech Marín (1988) says that when the message is slipped into the coffee of the audience, "You don't taste it, it goes down smooth, but later you feel the effect" (p. 37). In *Born in East L.A.*, the pleasure engendered by comedy is the vehicle for Marín's very serious treatise on Chicano/a identity and border politics. Because of its social and oral qualities, comedy is the performance art of the working classes, a direct descendant of the vaudeville tradition of acting and theater.

An analysis of the *rasquache* elements in the early forms of Chicano theater, *carpas* (circus-like pantomime shows), and *tandas de variedad* (similar to vaudeville reviews) unveils the humorous strategies by which Chicanos/as historically have critiqued and survived dominant ideologies.[14] Says Ybarra-Frausto (1991):

In ensemble, the *carpa* sketches are some of the earliest artistic projections of the *rasquache* sensibility. Through the characters of the *peladito* and *peladita* (penniless urban roustabouts), one enters a lively picaresque world of ruffians who scamper through life by the seat of their pants. Always scheming and carousing, the *pelados* personify the archetypal Chicano everyman and everywoman who live out a life-on-the-margin sustained by laughter and a cosmic will to be (p. 6).

Mario Moreno, more commonly known as Cantinflas, whom the *Los Angeles Times* ("The Mexican Everyman," 1994) called "the century's greatest symbol of popular culture in the Spanish-language world" (Sec. F, p. 1), was the prototype of the *peladito*. As a comedian who bridged the underdog world of tent show skits and vaudeville theater and the developing world of Mexican cinema, Cantinflas represented the poor and the laboring classes. He was a loquacious Mexican "Little Tramp" who expressed the subversive power of comedy in his dirty-clothes and torn-shoes defiance to social mobility, his wily ways of making ends meet, and his linguistic improvisations "in which he twisted the thickly formal language with which working class Mexicans are expected to use when addressing people of higher position to make fun of those at the top" ("Mexico's Loved Clown Exists to Copious Tears," 1993, Sec. A, p. 4).

Cheech Marín is the contemporary Chicano version of the *peladito*. In *Born in East L.A.* this legacy is established abstractly by the concept of the deported Chicano, and concretely by images like the home altar—a syncretic composition of Catholic saints and santería objects assembled on a book shelf above a row of Encyclopedia Brittanicas—and the velveteen icon of Jesus Christ. Even in the home of a third-generation Angeleno who does not speak Spanish and who insists on calling himself an American (i.e., assimilated) citizen, strong cultural ties to Mexico are visible. With its $5 million budget (as opposed to the $30 million spent on Redford's *Milagro Beanfield War* released the same year) and its one-man show (Marín was the writer, director, main actor, and protagonist of the film), *Born in East L.A.* is as *rasquache* as Hollywood can get. Its sexist and homophobic issues notwithstanding,[15] the pleasure elicited by this text, like that elicited by the *pelado* sketches that preceded it, is the pleasure of survival, the most resistant act of all. Indeed, it is through resistance to cultural domination, psychological abuse, and physical hardship that Chicano/a identity has survived and evolved.

Not only was the Frankfurt School blind to popular culture's potential for disrupting the power relations (and the institutions that promote them) of the status quo, but also it focused exclusively on the popular culture of the hegemonic mainstream. Such ethnocentrism ignores the existence of "Other" populations and their different popular traditions and popular texts, and abolishes the possibility of "other" responses to and interpretations of mainstream mass culture. Audiences that occupy marginal status within Anglo patriarchy, however, necessarily develop protective devices against cultural annihilation; one of these is a critical awareness, what Anzaldúa (1987) calls *"la facultad,"*[16] capable of reading and rejecting mass-mediated, stereotypical representations of themselves.

Another protective device, related to the pleasure of survival discussed above, is the preservation and cultivation of cultural memory. In Chicano/a popular culture, we see this act of cultural preservation enacted by the oral tradition of *corridos* and *cuentos*, popular ballads and legends, respectively, whose forms originated in Mexican folklore. In *Memory and Modernity: Popular Culture in Latin America,* William Rowe and Vivian Schelling (1991) analyze the different faces of popular culture in Latin America and find that audience reception to serial melodramas, or *telenovelas*, for example, demonstrates "a tendency to resignification, which by mobilizing popular experiences and memories produces a margin of control, not over the ownership of media . . . but over their social meanings" (p. 109). Furthermore, as evidenced by the growing body of theoretical and analytical work on Black, Asian-American, and Chicano/a popular cultures, distinct "American" communities (that for too long have been called "subcultures") employ popular methods of distribution and representation specifically to oppose mainstream stereotypes and other injustices and to affirm their distinct realities and identities. Thus, audiences of color experience the subversive pleasure of their own popular texts.

If we pull popular culture from under the shadow of elite culture, it must also be yanked from the totalizing whiteness of Euro-America. Chandra Mukerji and Michael Schudson (1991) warn us in their introduction to *Rethinking Popular Culture*:

The legitimation of popular culture should not be taken—though it sometimes is—as an uncritical welcome to all that popular culture contains. The study of popular culture is too often its celebration. Although the celebration helps legitimate the aesthetic and political expressions of common people, the democratic aspiration of popular culture studies is sometimes undiscriminating. We can happily celebrate discoveries in popular culture of sociability, fellowship, and creative resistance to exclusionary cultural forms; but that should scarcely blind us to popular traditions of racism, sexism, and nativism that are just as deeply rooted. This is popular culture too (p. 36).

Indeed, those "popular [mainstream] traditions of racism, sexism, and nativism" are brought into sharp relief against the alter-native grain of Chicano/a popular culture.

NOTES

1. *Webster's New World Dictionary*.
2. Here I subscribe to the structuralist idea that "the world is a set of signs to be deciphered" as a text. See the introduction to C. Mukerji and M. Schudson (eds.), *Rethinking popular culture: Contemporary perspectives in cultural studies*. (Berkeley, CA: University of California Press, 1991, p. 44).
3. Am I American, am I Mexican, am I legal or illegal, am I a citizen or an alien? Indeed, the quest for identity, as any survey of Chicano/a literature and Chicano/a film will reveal, is perhaps the most prevalent leitmotif of the population of Mexican descent in the United States.
4. From the jacket description of the video.
5. Tomás Rivera argues that Richard Rodriguez demonstrates this self-denigration and inferiority complex throughout *Hunger of Memory*, preoccupied as he is with scraping off his brownness and with his schizophrenic split between a "public" identity in English and a "private" identity in Spanish. In other words, he perpetrates his own colonization by internalizing the racist and ethnocentric ideologies of the mainstream educational system, which dictate that an "individual," in order to succeed as a "mid-

dle-class American," must erase his differences and forsake his cultural memory, his native language, and his community. See Tomás Rivera, "Richard Rodriguez's *Hunger of Memory* as Humanistic Antithesis," pp. 406–414.

6. R. Rosaldo (1993), "After Objectivism," in S. During (ed.), *The Cultural Studies Reader* (New York, NY: Routledge, 1993, pp. 104–117). Here Rosaldo is referring to Américo Paredes's "diagnosis . . . that most ethnographic writing on Mexicans and Chicanos has failed to grasp significant variations in the tone of cultural events" (p. 108). Paredes's implication is that an ethnographer native to Mexican or Chicano culture would at least be aware of those variations necessary for accurate interpretation.

7. CARA, which means "face" in Spanish, is the acronym for the first major national exhibition of Chicano art that toured the country between September 9, 1990 and August 1, 1993. The full title of the exhibition is *Chicano Art: Resistance and Affirmation, 1965–1985*. My monograph on the exhibition is forthcoming from the University of Texas Press.

8. The reader will recall that Guillermo Gómez-Peña was one of the original members of the Border Arts Workshop/Taller de Arte Fronterizo that was appropriated in 1988 by the media imperialists of the so-called "Latino Boom."

9. See "On nationality: 13 artists," *Art in America* (September 1991), pp. 124–126 ff.

10. This is a derogatory expression for natives of Mexico City.

11. See the color reproduction of the Dolores del Rio altar in the exhibition catalogue *Chicano Art: Resistance and Affirmation, 1965–1985*, ed. Richard Griswold del Castillo, Theresa McKenna, and Yvonne Yarbro-Bejarano (Los Angeles, CA: UCLA and The Wight Art Gallery, 1991).

12. I am thinking specifically of businesses like the Tesoros store in Austin, Texas that has appliqued iconography from Mexican and Chicano culture (such as the Popocateptl/Ixxtacihuatl imagery taken from *calendarios*, the Guadalupe Posada *calaveras*, and reproductions of Frida Kahlo's work) to tee shirts bearing the "Tesoro Design" label.

13. Translation: "The caricaturist uses irony like a critic. He/she makes fun of everything, overcomes everything. He/she makes note of the contrasts between beauty and ugliness, between truth and falsehood . . . . When necessary, he/she reaches the point of cruelty, tragedy. But irony is only destructive and negative on the surface, for what it destroys is that which is false and ridiculous. Irony represents the effort we make to triumph over all of that which opposes our spiritual ascension toward the infinite."

14. See N. Kanellos, *A history of Hispanic theatre in the United States: Origins to 1940* (Houston, TX: Arte Publico Press, 1990).

15. Marín's film reinforces the sexist practice of using women's bodies to sell products or political messages. The French woman in the film, for example, is essentialized by her sexual apparatus, her accent, and her racial attributes. She functions primarily as the object of desire which Marín conflates with a national symbol, a contested territory, an immigration law, an historical event, and a naturalized American identity.

16. In the third chapter of *Borderlands/La Frontera*, Anzaldúa defines "la Facultad" as "the capacity to see in surface phenomena the meaning of deeper realities. . . . Those who do not feel psychologically or physically safe in the world develop this sense. . . . It's a kind of survival tactic that people caught between worlds unknowingly cultivate" (pp. 38, 39).

REFERENCES

Anzaldúa, G. (1990). "Haciendo caras, una entrada: An introduction," in G. Anzaldúa (ed.), *Haciendo caras/making face, making soul: Creative and critical perspectives by feminists of color.* San Francisco, CA: Aunt Lute Foundation, p. xxv.

————. (1987). *Borderlands/La frontera: The new Mestiza.* San Francisco, CA: Spinsters/Aunt Lute, pp. 55–59.

Fiske, J. (1989). *Understanding popular culture.* Boston, MA: Unwin/Hyman, p. 49.

Fregoso, R. L. (1985). "Zoot Suit and The Ballard of Gregorio Cortéz." *Critica, 1*(2) (Spring), p. 128.

Fusco, C. (1990). "The Latino 'Boom' in Hollywood." *Centro Bulletin, 2*(8) (Spring), p. 54.

Gómez-Peña, G. (1991a). "Border brujo," in R. Weiss with A. West (eds.), *Being América: Essays on art, literature, and identity in Latin America.* New York, NY: White Pine Press, p. 195.

Gómez-Peña, G. (1991b). Interview with Lilly Wei in "On nationality: 13 artists." *Art in America* (September), pp. 124–25, 159.

González, R. "Corky." (1972). *I am Joaquín/Yo soy Joaquín: An epic poem.* New York, NY: Bantam, pp. 18, 40.

Green, J. R. (1992). "Mexico's *Taller de Gráfica Popular*, part I." *Latin American Art, 4*(2), p. 65.

Hebdige, D. (1993). "From culture to hegemony," in S. During (ed.), *The cultural studies reader.* New York, NY: Routledge, pp. 366–367.

————. (1979). *Subculture: The meaning of style.* London, England: Methuen, p. 132.

Jameson, F. (1991). *Postmodernism, or, The cultural logic of late capitalism.* Durham. NC: Duke University Press, p. 76.

Livingston, J. & J. Beardsley. (1992). "The poetics and politics of Hispanic art: A new perspective," in I. Karp & S. D. Lavine (eds.), *Exhibiting Cultures: The poetics and politics of museum display.* Washington, DC: Smithsonian Institution Press, pp. 104–120.

López, A. M. (1991). "Are all Latins from Manhattan? Hollywood, Ethnography, and cultural colonialism," in L. D. Friedman (ed.), *Unspeakable images: Ethnicity and the American cinema.* Chicago, IL: University of Illinois Press, p. 404.

Marín, C. (1988). Interview. "Cheech cleans up his act." *Cineaste, 16*(3), p. 37.

"The Mexican Everyman." (1994). *Los Angeles Times* (April 23), Sec. F, p. 1.

"Mexico's loved clown exits to copious tears." (1993). *New York Times* (April 23), Sec. A, p. 4.

Modleski, T. (1991). *Feminism without women: Culture and criticism in a "postfeminist" age.* New York, NY: Routledge, p. 38.

————. (1987). "The terror of pleasure: The contemporary horror film and postmodern theory," in T. Modleski (ed.), *Studies in Entertainment: Critical Approaches to Mass Culture.* Bloomington, IN: University of Indiana Press, 1987, p. 158.

Mukerji, C. & M. Schudson (eds.). (1991). *Rethinking popular culture: Contemporary perspectives in cultural studies.* Berkeley and Los Angeles, CA: University of California Press, p. 36.

Olalquiaga, C. (1992). *Megalopolis: Contemporary cultural sensibilities.* Minneapolis, MN: University of Minnesota Press, p. 42.

Rivera, T. (1992). "Richard Rodriguez's Hunger of Memory as Humanistic Antithesis," in J. Olivares (ed.), *Tomás Rivera: The Complete Works*. Houston, TX: Arte Publico Press, p. 410.

Rosaldo, R. (1993). "After objectivism," in S. During (ed.), *The Cultural Studies Reader*. New York, NY: Routledge, pp. 104–117.

Rowe, W. & V. Schelling. (1991). *Memory and modernity: Popular culture in Latin America*. New York, NY: Verso, p. 109.

Stam, R. (1991). "Bakhtin, polyphony, and ethnic/racial representation," in L. D. Friedman (ed.), *Unspeakable images: Ethnicity and the American cinema*. Chicago, IL: University of Illinois Press, pp. 251–276.

Weedon, C. (1987). *Feminist practice and poststructuralist theory*. New York, NY: Basil Blackwell, p. 23.

Ybarra-Frausto, T. (1991). "The Chicano movement/The movement of Chicano art," in *Exhibiting cultures: The poetics and politics of museum display*. Washington, DC: Smithsonian Institution Press, pp. 133–134.

———. (1989). "Rasquachismo: A Chicano sensibility," in *Chicano aesthetics: Rasquachismo*, catalogue. Phoenix, AZ: MARS [Movimiento Artistico del Rio Salado], Inc., p. 5.

Zuno, J. G. (1967). *Orozco y la ironía plástica*, cited in *Historia de las artes plásticas en la revolución mexicana*, tomo I. Mexico, D.F.: Biblioteca del Instituto Nacional de Estudios Históricos de la Revolución Mexicana, p. 151.

Public Space and Culture: A Critical Response to Conventional and Postmodern Visions of City Life

David R. Diaz

The postmodernist debate on spatial relations currently focuses on three issues: the appropriation and social reproduction of space by development interests, increasing government intervention in and the restriction of public use of space, and political controversy in reaction to the destruction of community space caused by constant growth. How different cultures organize and utilize space in postmodern society is an area that has been ignored by most current theorists. Cultural theorists have adopted either a middle-class or elitist paradigm defining how spatial relations influence society (Pfeil, 1990; Best & Kellner, 1991).

For instance, a recent book edited by Michael Sorkin (1992) addressed the private sector and the government's role in restricting space, the creation of malls and other consumerist meccas, and the increase in gated urban developments. The analysis of different spatial relations in various cities, as well as the perspective developed by the contributors to Sorkin's text, reflects a serious diminution of the vibrant street life and daily social networking occurring in most cities with significant culturally diverse populaces. A primary focus of this genre is of elite and upper-class centers of consumerism and commerce that indicate a "redefinition" of the form and content of modern culture. This logic purports "to close off the past by saying that history is finished" (Hall, 1986). Postmodernists (Jameson, 1984; Jencks, 1977; Sorkin, 1992) appear oblivious to the existence of a bicultural street milieu, based on walking to, socializing, and communing within dated commercial spaces. The implication is that this type of activity possesses scant social meaning. Postmodernists are locked into a mind-set that undervalues cultural and historical social patterns in bicultural communities in which active street life is an essential component of daily life.

Postmodern literature focusing on public space bemoans private capital's structurally imposed limitations on social encounters and the attempts of middle-class culture to shield itself from Third World people and cultures that have immigrated into advanced capitalist societies. This perspective is problematic in that those very cultures have introduced new ways of knowing and have also reappropriated social space. These new cultural influences, which Henri Lefebvre (1991a; 1991b) has theorized, work to redefine social relations both internally and externally from their bounded communities.

Everyday space has significantly different meaning when viewed from various cultural vantage points (Young, 1990). In fact, a vibrant, spatially oriented cultural milieu characterizes most ethnic communities in their everyday experiences. Space on a human scale is celebrated and actively integrated into daily life patterns. This difference in the cultural realism of spatial relations indicates that postmodern theorists' myopia within staid "Western" middle class paradigms (Hall, 1986) has failed to acknowledge the transformative influence of bicultural communities on everyday spatial relations. Through the lens of the social reproduction of spatial relations, a reunited cultural realm is redefining urban society in most major urban centers. Within the crossroads of everyday space, the concept of diversity possesses its most profound meaning in a transforming cultural order which is significantly impacting the terrain of popular culture.

The recent attention to the fabric of everyday spatial relations and coinciding political, social, cultural, and economic considerations mirrors the theoretical explorations developed by Lefebvre in a series of publications between 1940 and 1980.[1] Lefebvre focused his writings on political theory in terms of political conflict over everyday space and how cultural and social transformation is linked to the reconstruction of space. His work is an attempt to celebrate the liberation of space by daily consumers within localized spatial situations. His vision of a spatial theory of conflict within the built environment was structured to validate the importance of everyday life in the reconstruction of both civic and political society. By turning to the dynamics of the street and its evolving culture, a culture created and recreated by local social actors, Lefebvre developed the conceptual framework for a transformative politics based on the reappropriation of space from the state and the private sector, thus returning control over spatial relations to those actors establishing a new social and political dialectic in defense of localized cultural and social networks.

Lefebvre's theoretical explorations exhibit an anticipation of the current cultural metamorphosis occurring in Western culture with the predominance of Third World influences integrating themselves into everyday life in England, France, Germany, Italy, and the United States. The culture shock of a new era of acculturation, grounded in a vibrant street scene in which the street has been reappropriated as a prime focus of social and economic interaction, has been attacked by a revisionist and nativist conservative backlash.

The whole concept of the "other" in society is openly reviled as a threat to a set of social and cultural norms that are socially produced to protect the existing moral and economic order (Lefebvre, 1991b).

The fact that a renewed social order based on close personal interaction has an intrinsic transformative power is of scant interest to either centrist analysts (Rieff, 1991; Garreau, 1991)[2] intent on building physical and literal bridges against any type of new social relations, or progressive "postmodernists" (Jencks, 1977; Sorkin, 1992; Crawford, 1992) who focus solely on a staid analytical attachment to a narrowly defined political economy. Neither conceptual framework limits any tangible assessment of the transformative power of bicultural influences within the urban environment nor reflects the reality of a new urban culture which focuses outward into everyday life. Both centrists and progressives appear mesmerized by a sedate and myopic fascination with an introverted and decaying middle class living in stark fear of its own existence (and its assumption that other cultures want to overtake and disrupt it). The street culture of the current era is the antithesis to this introverted vision of social relations.

STREET CULTURE IN OLD AND NEW ETHNIC COMMUNITIES

The streets act as an important social and economic arena in bicultural neighborhoods in communities throughout the Southwest. Los Angeles, in particular, exhibits a long history which combines social and economic activity centered on everyday relations. A historic cultural center, *Calle Olvera*, in which *puestos* (small booths) are a main feature, symbolizes a deep attachment to street culture. In this setting the sociocultural function is of equal importance to the physical form and daily commerce which coincides with the ambience of the street.

In numerous Latino neighborhoods, daily consumers of time and space interact on a number of dimensions. The essence of human scale (a bygone relic of the past in the view of postmodernists) is found in:

• Walking, or time spent meandering at an unencumbered pace;

• Meeting and conversing with friends and strangers in chance situations which have a fluidity that is strikingly normal in a city that is supposed to fear anything strange and new or an experience outside of the confines of a car; and

• Children walking to the market on an errand (an unforgivable sin in suburbia) throughout the day and early evening.

The purchase of daily necessities, consumption that is ageless, is only limited by the weight tolerable for the traverse back home. The most important dimension is freedom, the freedom to be human in an urban milieu designed to discourage meaningful personal interaction.

In several Southern California neighborhoods—East Los Angeles, South

Central, Pacoima, Long Beach, the mid-Wilshire corridor, and other newly established Latino and Asian neighborhoods—the pace of everyday life is reflected by the avid use of space. Seniors congregate at favorite cafes or park benches to share gossip and discuss local events, politics, and personal scandals. Teenagers meet openly in a friendly arena of interaction sanctioned by family and community. Children tag along with parents hoping for a treat, a *paleta*, *fruta*, or *churo* as payment for their obedience or to placate their fatigue. Adults wander through various commercial areas for specific purchases, chance sales, and bumping into family and friends. The streets themselves are the center of attention.

In these ethnic communities there is rarely special reconstruction or reincarnation of physical form. They have transformed aging and mundane commercial corridors into active and vibrant public space. Occasional efforts to improve the condition of commercial buildings and local streets or add a few benches pale in comparison to the tens of millions of dollars thrown away in ridiculous attempts to satisfy elitist demands for "public culture" in redeveloped civic centers.

Cultural patterning in the streets is a special mixture of necessity and pleasure. Daily shopping chores merge into visual and social encounters with acquaintances and close friends. A trip is readily extended by a conversation with a neighbor or the local grocer who's heard the latest gossip. The walk itself is a liberating release from home life and cars. Extended trips requiring buses and transfers are major events for children lucky enough to join their parents or older siblings. While the bus system in this city is in horrible condition, it remains a vital component of street culture. In fact, many street vendors prefer setting up shop close to intersections and bus benches, knowing that a steady stream of customers will traverse the locale during the day (Beyette, 1990).

On weekends, streets are filled with people: women with strollers and children in tow, teenagers, adults walking to the market or the liquor store, youths riding bikes, religious workers, drug addicts, and kids calling out for the ice cream truck to stop at their home. This kaleidoscope of humanity is a normal pattern of daily life, a reflective zone of reaction and absorption anticipating and internalizing what is occurring on the streets.

Southern California's car-mad culture has difficulty acknowledging a pace of life grounded in pedestrian activity. Conversely, bicultural communities exhibit an integration of both aspects of local travel, with a rooted attachment to street level activity. The cultural gulf that exists between differing interpretations of daily life is exemplified by shopping zones that have developed with the pedestrian as the main component in the evolution of bicultural neighborhoods. Cars and parking lots are not the main functional design criteria. In fact, finding parking in most ethnic shopping areas is a pain.

The street scene, however physically attractive or unattractive, is recreated by people. Streams of people penetrate streets much like streams feeding into rivers. Walking is a process that is anticipated with pleasure and ease, a period to absorb the local social world at a leisurely pace. Interaction with fellow travelers reinforces the intrinsic value of life in a nonmechanized scale. Personal presence (in space and time) is of paramount importance. Seeing space at its most normative level is the foundation of the diversity of this evolving region. On the streets, people acknowledge one another within the shared experience of community, a community that constantly interacts with itself.

THE PARANOID VISION: LEFT AND CENTER

The soul of a bicultural community is found in the interaction taking place throughout the day. All factions of the locale carve out a functional public existence that is celebrated and tolerated in a rapport with mundane daily activity. This fact, a continual, intensive use of space, is a key element in the growing nativist and racist attack on the "others" in this society (Martinez, 1991). In a sense the anti-Third World xenophobia is not defined solely in a dry demographic exercise of numbers crunching; it is a reaction to what has become alien to "postmodern society"—a high visibility and presence of people in the streets.

A new era of cultural patterning is taking place, in which the high priests of culture and economic power have little concrete control. Fear of these "growing" ethnic enclaves indicates that the most visible forms of current popular culture are in fact being dominated by bicultural communities which historically were degraded for their lack of sophisticated social graces. An entire region is rapidly being redefined by street vendors, Korean entrepreneurs, Asian business signage, and people of color fully utilizing public space. The simple act of walking to the market creates a mystique within mainstream Euro-American cultural critics and defenders alike about the shock of everyday life being experienced in its most basic fashion. As a consequence, centrist critics attempt to devalue such cultural patterns, while leftist cultural sages, by focusing solely on malls and other symbolic middle-class zones of daily commerce, tend to romanticize or ignore the existence of ethnic communities.

Ironically, liberal cultural critics have engaged in a rigid dialectic which patronizes the very middle-class symbolism they purport to criticize (Young, 1990). This reified vision is reflected in various essays in Sorkin's text (1992) which grandly and blithely declares "the end of public space." Here, leftist theorists attempt to bash the idea of public encounters at a human scale. The postmodern city is described as being little more than a conspiratorial network of artificial consumption artifacts. The authors collectively fall into a self-imposed trap of viewing the world from a middle-class lens that nostalgically reaches back to the city culture of the past, in which people actually interacted with one another in a vibrant fashion.

While looking toward the past to recreate the present has some merit, there are a number of gaps inherent in this logic. A major problem is that people of color were prevented from entering the sacred social spaces of previous cityscapes that are glowingly alluded to in the text. In fact, in some instances the authors are simply incorrect. The most glaring example of this is Mike Davis' (1992) article, which alludes to photos of downtown Los Angeles as the basis to imply racial integration in the city during the 1940s. These images are in reality "spillovers of World War II propaganda, fantasies constructed by the Popular Front imagination" (Berman, 1992).[3] This era was characterized by a civic center ruled by a strictly enforced apartheid hierarchy.[4] Such examples of a "fabricated and idealistic" past are reflective of how the reality of bicultural social experience is incorrectly visualized by cultural critics.

In a harsh critique of suburban malls, Margaret Crawford (1992) fails to conceptualize how the bicultural others in postmodern society conduct daily shopping excursions. An assumption that the shopping mall "has become the world" simply reifies a false societal premise that malls are the only form of daily commerce. While decrying the stultifying effect of a "commodified world," she fails to define the limits of that world, specifically in terms of social sectors that do not frequent malls or that have different patterns of daily commerce. By rigidly connecting "the mall" to the totality of urban consumer culture, the whole issue of "other" consumers and their growing influence on everyday popular culture is completely negated.

The critical debate on the value (or lack of value) of these edifices is based on an assumption that an entire culture is sitting in wait for a mall to dramatically appear in their neighborhood. In Los Angeles, numerous examples of regionally-based shopping dominated by Third World consumers offer a significantly different perspective on consumer patterning centered on reuse of older spaces which have experienced dramatic transformations due to the reappropriation of everyday space, space without mega-parking lots, roofs, or elevators. Santee Alley (Central Los Angeles), the old Uniroyal Tire Plant (City of Commerce), the Pico-Union community (west of downtown Los Angeles), and Pacific Avenue (Huntington Park) are examples of people-driven reconstruction of spatial relations in which ethnically influenced patterns of street culture have infused a new life, commercial and social, into the urban milieu of the region.

In bicultural communities, malls are not the main focal point of daily commerce. In fact, malls serve as the antithesis of the vibrant social interaction occurring in conjunction with personal consumer habits. This aspect of a dramatically changing urban society appears unimportant in the analysis of the role of malls, in which bicultural communities are "crowded" into a narrow homogeneous niche which simply does not accurately reflect an entirely different form of daily commerce.

While leftist cultural critics continually hammer away at the spatial dilemmas of postmodern society, centrist analysts tend to both extol growth in all its new manifestations and devalue the lived experiences of bicultural communities. The most perturbing aspect of bicultural spatial relations for centrists is the strong presence of various ethnic communities in the streets all hours of the normal day. In particular, the virulent opposition to street vending has become the metaphor of a racist reaction to the cultural transformation currently evolving within the region's popular culture (Martinez, 1991; Clifford, 1992). The specter of a permanent, multiethnic society, in the vanguard of a renewal of an integral street culture dominating everyday interpersonal relations, sends shivers down the spine of the defenders of the past (Rieff, 1991). The past that is vehemently being defended was a social construction of a monoethnic, self-satisfied suburban society created to spur demand for a hegemony based on unrestricted growth (Gottdiener, 1985). This suburban ideology, initially constructed at the turn of the century, started to become a spatial reality for a burgeoning middle class during the 1950s. This era of white homogeneity lasted for approximately thirty years. Since the 1980s, this pristine concept of the postmodern city is no longer credible.

Two recent books, *Edge City* (Garreau, 1991) and *Los Angeles: Capital of the Third World* (Rieff, 1991), are intent upon raising the fear level of social traditionalists, Euro-Americans who claim sole rights for the maintenance of "cultural norms" in the region. A new ethnically diverse city is viewed with disdain and arrogance. Both books sound alarms that the cultural and spatial relations which were assumed permanent—a car culture, strict adherence to middle-class values, city streets devoid of pedestrians, and an introverted built environment—are being structurally ruptured. The problem is that in numerous ethnically diverse neighborhoods people are reclaiming local social space in which the conduct of everyday life requires an interactive street scene.

The visual imagery of a culture based on a realistic interpretation of society's historic past and daily commerce conducted through interpersonal communication is deemed alien and illogical to a society which has lost touch with itself (Lefebvre, 1991a; de Certeau, 1984). These two books reinforce the notion that an insulated and alienated middle-class lifestyle is the only appropriate communal form of existence. Defense of isolation, fear of new "others," and the way in which these bicultural others interact are all ample cause for a reactive opposition to change. The irony of these centrists' logic is that they purport to defend the free operation of the liberal marketplace, which demands constant spatial transformation to ensure its existence (Mishan, 1977). That this transformation is apparently permanent and economically subservient to the constituents of these centrist critics is of minimal importance in their dire assessment of the future of culturally diverse society.

What leftist and centrist cultural critics tend to share is a limited comprehension of the spatial contributions of bicultural communities within a transforming regional popular culture. Each vantage point mimics the other in a conceptual race to define, positively and negatively, the influence of urban spaces dedicated to middle-class symbolism. The debate over space has in fact become a debate on the value of "fabricated space"—malls, redevelopment areas attempting to reconstruct "street culture," and gated communities—a totality which is compressed into a judgmental assessment of suburban enclave consciousness.

The left frequently centers an analysis of spatial relations within the realm of high culture or a romanticism with gangs. This avenue of analysis tends to ignore the majority of bicultural social actors, who proceed through a daily routine that is creating a new urban culture. Meanwhile, centrists extol the benefits of the liberal marketplace and decry the loss of culture to an invasion of bicultural heathens. Within this framework, attention to spatial relations in ethnic communities is situated in a negative and secondary strata that completely diminishes the renewal and active utilization of urban streets.

POSTMODERNISM'S MYOPIA WITH A MIDDLE-CLASS PARADIGM

The predisposition of postmodernist cultural critics toward a middle-class paradigm of spatial relations begs the question, "Do people of color exist?" Onion-skin, high-rise design, mini-midi-maxi malls, renaissance redevelopment, Haussmanesque urban destruction, office plazas, and reconstructed street culture have anchored postmodern logic within the historical construction of middle-class cultural symbolism. High culture is situated as the sole forum from which an exposition of critical conceptualization of everyday social relations can be "properly" redefined. This elitist vision continues the despicable tradition in academia of excluding the "others" in a society increasingly defined and influenced by cultural diversity. Cultural change in the symbolic patterning of the built environment conversely (yet not surprisingly) remains the purview of what is the latest style being built by elites for an amorphous middle class. Only social actors totally immersed in the car culture of Americana are considered fair game for criticism of the perversions in popular culture. The whole context of change is predicated on analyzing and criticizing new buildings and new urban complexes normally located in the midst of regional financial centers or suburban enclaves. From the complexities of new structures, postmodernists situate themselves firmly in comfortable territory, physically and literally the social construction of European-oriented middle-class ideology (Best & Kellner, 1991; Pfeil, 1990).

While high culture is doted upon in terms of new trends and the latest fads, it does exhibit a distinct aversion to risk when the issue is exploring a changing urban world. Wandering into bicultural neighborhoods unattended and directionless is beyond the parameters of tolerable behavior. The safety net of recognizable styles, prominent names, architects, places, and "controversies" is adequate fodder from which to judge the nuances of popular culture. Thus, the postmodern vision of everyday space and social relations has become a sterile exercise in defining a narrow and antiseptic window of cultural patterning.[5]

In similar fashion to the social construction of suburbia in the late 1800s and early 1900s, postmodernist logic proceeds along a path wedded to an idealized concept of pristine social relations. What is occurring in bicultural neighborhoods is a meaningless aberration to a normative middle-class grail. The influence of bicultural communities in the reconstruction of everyday spatial relations and its impact on new cultural patterning is relegated to a minor blip on the screen of the postmodern world vision. Where Geraldine Finn (1993) asks, "Why are there no great women postmodernists?" minority theorists would ask, "Why are there are no bicultural neighborhoods deemed important within the body of postmodern logic?"

One of the most active street scenes in the Los Angeles region exists around the intersection of Brooklyn Avenue and Soto Street in East Los Angeles. This site has experienced the entire drama of a multicultural urban evolution since the turn of the century. Currently, this commercial district is a self-contained example of the reappropriation and acculturation of urban space. The cultural patterning of an entire community is defined by the social networking conducted in public space (Diaz, 1993). If postmodernity is to have any tangible meaning, it will have to refocus attention away from its structures of choice, which are stagnant artifacts, to the transformation of popular culture encompassing this region.

For example, when cultural and physical change is assessed, the vision of "City Walk," an exclusive and artificial street (located within Universal Studios, Los Angeles), is given absolute attention by the denizens of postmodern criticism and mainstream media while actual street culture (that does not require a hoard of PR boosters or a cadre of shiny-toed and high-heeled investors) is of no consequence.

When Charles Jencks (1977) called for a "pluralistic language," his conceptual focus was in the way "the actual messages (are) sent" (pp. 96–97). However, this step toward architectural pluralism was also directly influenced by ideological preconditions. It is those preconditions—building for multinational corporations, wealthy clients, elites demanding an egotistical, high-skyline civic identity—all symbolic of the modern movement, that remain the client base of postmodern logic. Within this framework, the conceptualists of postmodern space, while meekly groping to escape the requisite spatial boundaries of clients, remain locked into a narrow vision of everyday space. Designing homes in isolated canyons and hillsides, or hidden from the street behind barricaded walls, is light years removed from a pluralistic design framework. Incorporating plazas at the base of unsightly office structures, where parking costs average twenty dollars or more a day, challenges any claim to a new spatial design vision that "speak(s) to various groups, to the whole spectrum of society rather than just one of its elites" (Jencks, 1977, p. 101).

The basis of postmodernism as a challenge to the barren condition of the modern movement is a questionable proposition (King, 1992). Furthermore, the ideological basis of the challenge implicit in the language of pluralism has not been reflected in the reconstruction of a built environment which has failed to significantly influence the everyday culture of bicultural communities. In fact postmodernism, in function and language, is replicating the critique of modernism, a physical form shielding elites and high culture from popular culture. Thus the term postmodern, which acts as vehicle for a new dialogue in theory and space, is caught looking at its own reflection on the fortieth floor, mirrored in a modernist ideological stranglehold (King, 1992).

Space is more than a reinterpretation of traditional symbols or an eclectic approach to assembling bricks, glass, steel, and mortar. Postmodern design and its implied spatial relations remain anchored to a middle-class symbolism and elite ideology characteristic of the modern movement. The design function continues to look away from the pluralism Jencks attempted to infuse into the debate on spatial relations by habitually producing structures which fail to acknowledge the changing cultural patterns in cities (Wilson, 1991, chap. 9). As exemplified by the creation of City Walk within the Universal Studios complex, the "postmodern architectural language" is in reality a fabrication and exaggeration of pedestrian-oriented everyday space. It is an experience which requires a high exclusionary price of admission, socially and culturally.

Conversely, the intersection of Brooklyn and Soto is a metaphor for numerous culturally defined areas where social actors, by their constant presence, have forged a spatial pluralism and redefined the physical environment. Postmodernism has no response to the contradiction of fabricated space versus the vibrancy of everyday space forged by bicultural consumers and citizens reestablishing place based and socially grounded urban networks which are free of charge. The contradiction between Brooklyn and Soto and City Walk captures the stark differences between culturally organic use of urban space in ethnic communities and space redefined for a middle class that is increasingly reluctant to engage directly with people residing within their immediate neighborhood. Postmodern spatial symbolism accommodates this spatial revisionism, in which the only "real" people space is designed to keep a pluralistic society at its doorstep. Whereas the Brooklyn and Soto neighborhood celebrates spatial freedom and localized social interaction, City Walk reinforces (and reenforces) urban alienation and postmodernist spatial segregation. The difference between these two areas provides an example of the cultural segregation that postmodernist logic has failed to penetrate.

STREET VENDORS: THE BATTLE OVER CULTURAL INTERPRETATION

The recent controversy regarding street vending in Los Angeles has become a flash point for racist anti-immigrant sentiment (Martinez, 1991; Moffat, 1991). The underlying issue of street vending is not the most important aspect of this raging debate. The key concern focuses on the future of the city and who will control urban cultural patterning in Los Angeles. Street vending has been conducted throughout the city's history. Vendors have sold various types of products since the city's early history (Martinez, 1991). As this community was transformed into a Latino enclave, the practice of street vending remained a mainstay of everyday life. Vendors, shop owners, and consumers coexisted in a social relationship that viewed each as part of a whole.

When U.S. Cold War policies influenced the civil wars in Central America, Los Angeles became the *de facto* second city of Nicaragua, El Salvador, and other nations. Refugees fleeing persecution entered the city anticipating a certain level of opportunity and job security (Lopez-Garza, 1989). What existed was a region in the initial phase of deindustrialization experiencing a decimation of low-wage jobs. Many immigrants had few options from poverty and low-wage injustice. A number of Central Americans joined immigrant Mexicans and established street vending as a major component of the city's informal economy. The result, by the mid-1980s, was a burgeoning street culture dominated by Latinos—vendors and consumers—which was dramatically transforming the cultural landscape of Los Angeles.

The elite barons of culture and white suburbanites initiated a vehement opposition to the looming transition of urban Los Angeles into a city with a vibrant street culture dominated by bicultural communities (Lopez, 1993). The independent-minded street vendors became the most visible target to those social and economic sectors aghast at the cultural changes occurring in everyday life, changes over which they had minimal control or understanding. Los Angeles became a cultural target of both internal and external critics decrying the transition from a European-dominated society into a culturally diverse city increasingly characterized by a constant street culture that Euro-Americans had abandoned for the suburbs two decades earlier (Rieff, 1991).

The battle to eliminate street vendors is in reality a site of confrontation to regain control over areas that suburbanites had ignored and avoided for years (Moffat, 1991). The downtown establishment, appalled by their apparent lack of control over what was occurring below their high rise offices, joined in this attempt to reinstitute a suburbanite symbolism to city streets. Why they wanted to regain political control had more to do with their revulsion to a new spatial transformation manifested in street culture than any challenge to the independent and free-market spirit of the street vendors (Beyette, 1990). Thus, the real battle over spatial relations in Los Angeles and other cities is over who will control new cultural patterns and new cultural groups.

The active intervention of a mass of social actors connected to everyday space is being characterized as a social phenomenon to be feared and eliminated (Martinez, 1991). The power elite have spent a small fortune in a foolish assumption that money can buy street culture and a civic center filled with active street users. When ethnically diverse daily consumers of space appeared and the streets were reincarnated as essential components of a ethnically diverse city, revisionists raged with disdain. The "wrong people" were transforming the streets. The massive redevelopment subsidies had failed to reinvent a middle-class urban civic center. Something had to be done to reverse the flow of users of space (predominately Latino, Asian, and African

American) in defense of middle-class cultural symbolism and economic power. When the street vendors ask, "What's wrong with selling *fruta, aguas, maize,* or a *paleta?*", the answer is, "Nothing is wrong with the concept, it's just all those people" who are constantly on the street creating the demand. The street vendors have become the target of a strategy designed to reverse the infusion of a new and vibrant street culture that is controlled by everyday people of the city. Street vending is not a problem; people walking is not a problem. The racialization of the people involved in this liberating activity is at the crux of the controversy.

CROSSROADS OF EVERYDAY SPACE

Street culture is free. There is no price of admission. Yet, the elites of the city view free space in sterile economic terms and how daily consumers fit a socioeconomic profile conforming to a specified function of the built environment (Gottdiener, 1986). In downtown Los Angeles, the vertical expansion of the financial center was programmed to be mirrored by a horizontal expansion of white-collar professionals. Built on an assumption that function follows form, the city invested millions to attract steel and glass towers, with an expectation that it would be followed by people with high expendable incomes. Tax subsidies and super economic zones were established in part to "recreate" urban culture. Los Angeles' self-image was deficient in comparison to London, New York, Paris, and Tokyo. There was a perceived dearth of people and activity in the financial district. When this economic catalyst worked to attract a new immigrant populace during the 1980s, the streets of the city were transformed. However, bicultural communities tended to patronize neighborhood space and carefree zones of daily consumption. East Los Angeles, Westlake, Chinatown, Santee Alley in the garment district, and selected suburban thoroughfares patronized by Latinos assumed a character reflective of this emerging street culture. The city's streets became a site of experimentation in which new interpretations of old world traditions of street culture reconstructed daily life (Roseman & Vigil, 1993). While ethnic communities engaged in liberating social public space, an "alienated" car culture hurriedly rolled up its collective windows and stepped on the gas pedal.

The social landscape of the city is in the process of a permanent transformation directed by bicultural communities intent on retaining patterns of cultural interaction transferred from previous life experiences onto the city's existing social milieu. The "Crossroads of Space" (Rieff, 1991) are being redefined through the simple act of walking as a major form of daily commerce and social networking. In a real sense, "the street and the demonstration (are the) primary symbols of modern life" (Berman, 1984). The irony of this renewed period of the social reconstruction of spatial relations is that the physical form of Los Angeles is horribly ill-suited for a high level of pedestrian activity. Sidewalks are narrow; there are few public plazas; the city caters to cars, not people; the city's elite has destroyed much public park space; and open air cafes are a nouveau (1980s) development. In spite of this city's regressive history of planning for concrete and steel in abeyance of the needs of daily social actors, the streets have come alive in the last ten years. In diverse geographic districts, urban and suburban, the use of public space has dramatically intensified. The rebirth of the historic Broadway commercial zone is among the most notable examples of how immigrant Latinos have reintroduced an active street culture into a built environment which had remained obdurate since the 1920s and 1930s (Roseman & Vigil, 1993). The reappropriation of public space by bicultural communities now is the most influential signifier of urban culture in this city.

In this era of new interpretations of older cultural traditions, the reconstruction of a new civic culture has refocused attention on who is appropriating and reappropriating urban space. The focus on *who* are the users of public space—not the fact that use of this space is a desirable attribute or characteristic—has become the political battleground of the 1990s. What is occurring is a desperate attempt to superimpose a revisionist value system, reflective of a disappeared past, designed to restore an illusionary cultural hegemony (Lefebvre, 1991a; de Certeau, 1984, p. 201). Instead of celebrating users of space, the dominant culture decries the loss of cultural control and their lack of power to force-feed a narrow interpretation of culture into an economically driven self-concept of daily social life.

Having abandoned the inner city and ignoring its decline for decades, a nervous middle class is demanding a revisionist reincarnation of its value system to be superimposed on bicultural neighborhoods (McDonnell & Jacobs, 1993). Apparently, economic and political hegemony has proven an insufficient advantage in the contest over the future of cultural and spatial relations. The raging controversy concerning immigrants is not solely how laws should be interpreted or enforced, it is how to limit the infusion of different cultural symbols and practices that influence public space and everyday life.

Unfortunately, postmodern cultural critics focus on middle-class spatial considerations which render an imagery of a social world constructed only for Euro-Americans with high expendable incomes. In lieu of advancing the critical debate over spatial relations and the transformation of urban culture, both postmodernists and revisionists are locked into competing camps judging the value of middle-class-dominated urban semiotics. The challenge to this postmodern theoretical lineage is to advance beyond a narrow definition of the social construction of cultural relations by determining just what is "postmodern" about racism, sexism, and elitism in the 1990s. Until these issues are addressed, the postmodern debate over the state of urban culture is notable only for its reluctance to situate bicultural communities within the center of the controversial transformation of everyday life.

Social transformation is inherently connected to the creative capacity of everyday life, language, and space which serve to reconstruct social relations

(Lefebvre, 1991b). Within this framework, reappropriation of space is understood as a fundamental challenge to the cultural hegemony of Euro-Americans.
Space is political; it is not a scientific object removed from ideology or politics;
it has always been political and strategic (Lefebvre, 1976). The influence of
bicultural communities on urban culture extends into both the economic and
political arenas. In the midst of contemporary controversy and racist reactions
against bicultural communities, new actors and new struggles are taking shape
in which social conflicts and cultural achievements are reconstructing social
life (Touraine, 1981). A reflected view from the barrio to the high rises crys-
tallizes the basic contention over who is really experiencing everyday life.

At the level of everyday street culture, a new urban culture has already
arrived. What has not been resolved is the avoidance and detachment from
daily life of a middle-class ideology based on social consumption in which the
consumer is the one who is consumed (Lefebvre, 1971). Active street culture
directly contradicts this middle-class social construction of urban space. Bicultural communities, in reestablishing the streets as the focus of everyday
life, are returning a basic political and social function to social actors, and are
thereby gaining control over their lives.

"Casual time . . . is the actual discourse of the city" (de Certeau, 1984, p.
203). Indeterminate interaction within places and random social practices articulate the fabric of community. Space, in a growing number of neighborhoods dominated by bicultural actors, is becoming liberated on a human scale
and in celebration of community. Walking down the street, touching people,
seeing neighbors, feeling communal space is a liberating experience. That's
an alienating thought in a "postmodern" society.

NOTES

1. The foreword in *Critique of Everyday Life* (1991a) is a synthesis of how Lefebvre's
conceptualization of the theory of space was refined during a period in which he broke
from doctrinaire Marxism, intertwining socialist theory with a critical analysis of modernism. He grounded his theoretical analysis in the context of existing social practice
and cultural patterns. Lefebvre's lifelong project experienced renewed interest within
American social theory after the publication of *The Social Production of Urban Space*
(Gottdiener, 1985). Gottdiener's interpretation of Lefebvre acknowledges the importance of the theory of space in modern social theory and within the context of transformative social change.

2. The use of the term centrist within this context presumes the fact that a wide
range of Euro-American culture is in opposition to the existence of bicultural communities in this society. In this regressive era, a return to overt racist politics encom-
passes an array of "conservative and liberal" social actors into a broadly defined centrist
position on the issue of a bicultural society. This period is characterized by a strong
nativist demeanor toward non–Euro-American communities.

3. Berman (1992) in a critical book review of *Variations of a Theme Park* is the
source for this point of information. Berman's critique focuses on the ideological rigid-

ity of the articles and the negation of existing cultural patterns that the authors collectively, in his view, devalue existing street culture. In his analysis of the Mike Davis article, Berman contends that Davis is groping for a symbolic image that could serve as a basis for a harmonious integration which did not exist during this era. The use of fabricated scenes is a grievous error for a leftist social historian in attempting to make a leap of faith that 1940 Los Angeles was less racist than in the current era.

4. Oral histories of minorities who experienced the unspoken apartheid practices of the era clearly document the fallacy of the images contained in the propaganda photos. On Broadway, the region's main commercial district, African Americans and Mexicans were openly harassed if they attempted to traverse this zone through the early 1930s. After this period, minorities continued to experience covert and overt discrimination into the 1950s. The era which includes the infamous Zoot Suit riots can hardly be considered a period of racial harmony in Los Angeles.

5. The deconstruction of "new forms and styles" would encounter serious problems if analyzed along with communities that continue to thrive socially and culturally without the assistance of new physical form. In focusing attention on high culture, the concept of everyday culture within bicultural communities is subsumed into a broad matrix defined by middle-class ideology, which is a simplification of dubious merit in contemporary society.

REFERENCES

Berman, M. (1984). "The signs and the street." *New Left Review* (144) (March-April).
———. (1992). "Hitting the streets." *Los Angeles Times*, book review of Michael Sorkin (ed.), *Variations on a theme park*. New York, NY: Hill and Wang (March 29).
Best, S. & D. Kellner. (1991). *Postmodern theory*. New York, NY: Guilford Press.
Beyette, B. (1990). "Vendors vs. the law." *Los Angeles Times* (June 27).
Clifford, F. (1992). "Immigrant Rights Heats Up. Mayoral Debate." *Los Angeles Times* (December 6).
Crawford, M. (1992). "The world in a shopping mall," in Michael Sorkin (ed.), *Variations on a theme park*. New York, NY: Hill and Wang.
Davis, M. (1992). "Fortress Los Angeles: The militarization of urban space," in Michael Sorkin (ed.), *Variations on a theme park*. New York, NY: Hill and Wang.
de Certeau, M. (1984). *The practice of everyday life*. Berkeley, CA: University of California Press.
Diaz, D. (1993). "La vide libre: Cultura de la calle en Los Angeles este." *Places*, 8(3).
Finn, G. (1993). "Why are there no great women postmodernists?" in V. Blundell, J. Shepard & I. Taylor (eds.), *Relocating cultural studies*. New York, NY: Routledge.
Garreau, J. (1991). *Edge city*. New York, NY: Doubleday.
Gottdiener, M. (1985). *The social production of urban space*. Austin, TX: University of Texas Press.
———. (1986). "Culture, ideology, and the sign of the city," in M. Gottdiener & A. P. Lagopoulos (eds.), *The city and the sign*. New York, NY: Columbia University Press.
Hall, S. (1986). "On postmodern and articulation." *Journal of Communication Inquiry*, 10(2) (Summer).

Jameson, F. (1984). "Postmodernism or the cultural logic of late capitalism." *New Left Review* (146) (July-August).

Jencks, C. (1977). *The language of post-modern architecture.* New York, NY: Rizzoli.

King, A. D. (1992). "The times and spaces of modernity." Paper presented at the conference on "A New Urban and Regional Hierarchy," International Sociological Association, UCLA, Los Angeles, CA (April 23–25).

Lefebvre, H. (1971). *Everyday life in the modern world.* London, England: Allen Lane.

———. (1976). "Reflections on the politics of space." *Antipode, 8*(2).

———. (1991a). *Critique of everyday life.* London, England: Verso.

———. (1991b). *The production of space.* Oxford, England: Basil Blackwell.

Lopez, R. J. (1993). "Pushcart power." *Los Angeles Times* (July 25).

Lopez-Garza, M. (1989). "Immigration and economic restructuring: Introduction." *California Sociologist, 12*(2).

Martinez, R. (1991). "Sidewalk wars: Why LA's street vendors won't be swept away." *LA Weekly* (December 6–12).

McDonnell, P. J. & P. Jacobs. (1993). "FAIR at forefront of push to reduce immigration." *Los Angeles Times* (November 24).

Mishan, E. J. (1977). *The economic growth debate.* London, England: Allen and Unwin.

Moffat, S. (1991). "Vendors bring new way of life to Los Angeles streets." *Los Angeles Times* (December 25).

Pfeil, F. (1990). *Another tale to tell.* London, England: Verso.

Rieff, D. (1991). *Los Angeles: Capital of the third world.* New York, NY: Simon and Schuster.

Roseman, C. C. & J. D. Vigil. (1993). "From Broadway to Latinoway." *Places, 8*(3).

Sorkin, M. (ed.). (1992). *Variations on a theme park.* New York, NY: Hill and Wang.

Touraine, A. (1981). *The voice and the eye.* Cambridge, MA: Cambridge University Press.

Wilson, E. (1991). *The Sphinx in the city.* Berkeley, CA: University of California Press.

Young, I. M. (1990). *Justice and the politics of difference.* Princeton, NJ: Princeton University Press.

The Idea of *Mestizaje* and the "Race" Problematic: Racialized Media Discourse in a Post-Fordist Landscape

Victor Valle and Rodolfo D. Torres

The flurry of print articles and television news coverage of the Los Angeles uprising of April 1992 shared a common theme. Whether victim, bystander, or hero, the media portrayed the residents of the riot zones as actors in a great melodrama of "race relations." Both local and national media promoted a discourse that employed "race" as the operative narrative and analytical category.[1] For audience convenience, it seemed, the cast was color-coded.

The following examples of post-riot coverage illustrate the pattern. Stressing racial harmony over economics, one *Los Angeles Times* poll question asked, "Do you think race relations in Los Angeles are getting better or worse?" ("Understanding the Riots, Part I," p. 4). With predictable pessimism, 84 percent of the respondents answered that race relations had either deteriorated or stagnated. No doubt the responses to the poll reflected the anxieties of a public which had just witnessed the alarming spectacle of a televised riot sparked by the acquittal of the police officers who had beaten Rodney King, with the deed captured on videotape. From the public's perspective, the televised images of burning and looting were firmly linked to video replays of the King beating. *The Times* poll merely reaffirmed what its readership had accepted as true.

Ted Koppel's post-riot forays into South Central Los Angeles reinforced the image of the dangerous black male by turning over his "Nightline" interviews to African-American gang members. There was only one problem. An analysis of court records conducted by the *Times* revealed that only one in ten of those arrested had gang affiliations. Moreover, the records revealed that the rioters were united more by lives of chronic poverty, incarceration, and homelessness than by race (Lieberman & O'Reilly, 1993).

Koppel's post-riot specials conformed so easily to the race relations discourse because of the coverage that had preceded it. Through sheer force of televised repetition, King's beating at the hands of white LAPD officers, and white truck driver Reginald Denny's beating by young black males, the riot had been framed between the horrifying bookends of white-on-black and then black-on-white violence.

In each case, the confusion is revealing. The "two societies, one black, one white—separate and unequal" dichotomy made famous by the Kerner Commission could not contain a "multicultural" riot in which villains and victims defied racial type casting. Cornel West (1993), who calls for a new language on race, concludes the following from the riot's contradictions:

What happened in Los Angeles in April of 1992 was neither a race riot nor a class rebellion. Rather, this monumental upheaval was a multiracial, trans-class, and largely male display of justified social rage. What we witnessed in Los Angeles was the consequence of a lethal linkage of economic decline, cultural decay, and political lethargy in American life. Race was the visible catalyst, not the underlying cause (p. 1).

Thus, the field of chaotic forces from which the riot emerged frustrated the media's ability to assert its narrative authority, revealing the profound distance between the media's racialized portrayal of inner city life, and the racial, cultural, linguistic, political ambiguities implicit in Latino and other non-Anglo lived experience. It is this paper's intent, therefore, to draw out from the riot coverage the special role racialized discourse played in reinforcing the status quo, and then to reveal by means of a critical cultural analysis the categories of meaning obscured by the riot coverage. It is further assumed that, although none of what is presented here is empirically grounded, this essay may offer new strategies for conceptualizing future studies of Latino media and audiences, and, in a more general sense, inner city media coverage.

CATEGORY BLINDNESS

Although racism created and led up to the conditions that sparked the Watts Riot of 1965, it did not play the same role in the Los Angeles riot of 1992. The causes of social pathology had changed. The structural changes associated with the emergence of post-industrial economy had somehow reconfigured the city's social relations in ways that were not fully evident during the Watts Riot. The most obvious difference between these disturbances were the Latinos who appeared on the television screen as looters in the second and third days of the riot coverage. Later, studies of the arrest records and economic losses confirmed the riot's new demography. About half of those arrested were Latinos. And of those Latinos, nearly 80 percent were recently arrived immigrants. Only a third of those arrested were employed, most often as low-paid casual laborers, while nearly two-thirds of those arrested were high school dropouts (Lieberman, 1992; Lieberman & O'Reilly, 1993). Nor were those arrested during the riot driven to lawlessness because they were angered by the Rodney King verdict. Instead, chronic poverty and simple opportunity appeared to be the motivating factors for rioting.

To the extent the media's riot coverage focused on Latinos at all, it did so by stressing their "foreignness." Local television broadcasts, for example, juxtaposed images of Latinos loaded down with loot with voice-overs of television anchors speculating on their status as "illegal aliens." The frame of illegality was also hung over Latino riot victims. Television reporters, in attempting to dramatize the plight of families who had escaped burning apartment buildings, reminded viewers that the newly homeless also feared deportation. The reporting on this last point was factual. Federal agents were indeed deporting Latinos arrested for alleged curfew violations. However, the repetition of this theme, to the exclusion of other types of coverage, again reconfirmed the image of Latinos as outsiders. In the 1930s, to cite one historical example, the local Los Angeles media helped to legitimize "Operation Wetback," the quasi-official campaign to deport Mexicans by effectively portraying them as excludable foreigners undeserving of civil rights protection (Hoffman, 1974). The 1992 riot merely provided a new opportunity for the media to reenact a semantic obfuscation. The obfuscation stems, in part, from the Latino community's perceived lack of "racial" clarity.

Latinos, Los Angeles County's majority population, cannot be strictly categorized as a race, a nationality, or an ethnic grouping since it constitutes a cross section of Latin American immigrants, most of whom are racially mixed Mexicans and Central Americans. Latinos, as a mixed or mestizo people, are woven from indigenous, African, Iberian, and European, as well as Asian strands. Culture, language, gender, and history, in addition to class, must be accounted for when attempting to grasp multiple, overlapping Latino identities. During the riot, however, the media's reliance upon a racialized language precluded the use of alternative explanatory categories. Like the new virus which the body's immune system has not yet learned to recognize, the media lacked a semantic category with which to identify and conceptualize Latino ambiguity. The Latin American word for that ambiguity is *mestizaje*—the continent's unfinished business of cultural hybridization. In Latin America, the genetic and cultural dialogue between the descendants of Europe, Africa, Asia, and the hemisphere's indigenous populations has been expressed in discourses reflecting and responding to a host of concrete national circumstances. In some cases, *mestizaje* has risen to the level of a truly critical counter-discourse of revolutionary aspirations, while at other times it has been co-opted by the state.

In the United States, however, neither the media nor its audiences have created a language with which to fully reveal the nation's equally heterodox ensemble of racialized ethnicities and cultures. Rather, the suppression of this cultural dialogue has been institutionalized. The Census Bureau, for example, has had a very difficult time trying to figure out how to classify Latinos by color. In the 1940 Census, Latinos were classified as "black" or a racial non-white group. In 1950 and 1960, the term "white person of Spanish surname" was used. In 1970, the classification was changed to "white person of Spanish surname and Spanish mother tongue." Then in 1980, Mexican Americans, Puerto Ricans, and other Central and Latin Americans of diverse national origin were reclassified as "non-white Hispanic." Latinos were back to square one. Because the Census uses a white/black paradigm to classify its citizens, it has shuttled Latinos back and forth between these two extremes. In each case, the organizing principle behind the labels is the perceived presence or absence of color.

DISCOURSE DISCIPLINE

While the media covered the riot, it also reported the national debate over multiculturalism. The confluence of the riot and the multicultural polemic provided the media an opportunity to conflate two categories. The riot, because the media portrayed it as "race debate," provided fresh evidence that multiculturalism, whatever it meant, could now be blamed for fueling racial conflict. By linking the multicultural debate to the race debate, the media had re-energized the race relations discourse, and thus its service to the status quo.

Thomas S. McCoy (1993) provides a useful approach for revealing the linkages between media discourses and state power. Drawing together the analyses of Stuart Hall and Michel Foucalt, McCoy argues that the media establishes discourse dominance through its control over the means of information production, and from its tight-knit relations to the state's ensemble of mutually empowering institutions.

The relationship of power and public discourse begins with the media's ability to make its version of the social order appear natural, and thus transparent. By rendering the cultural and ideological assumptions of journalistic "facts" invisible, the audience is encouraged to adopt these facts as public knowledge. The media performs this sleight of hand by making its facts appear objectively true, and thus normal and beyond disputation. It is in this way that the media's version of the social order acquires verisimilitude when, in fact, it is actually disseminating ideology normalized and commodified in discrete units of consumption, otherwise called news.

In time, the media's enculturation of its audiences to news consumption produces a disciplinary effect. Cultivational analysis of television viewing appears to confirm McCoy's assertions (Gerbner & Gross, 1976; Postman, 1985). Heavy television viewers exposed to recurring portrayals of television violence begin to feel that the world is more dangerous than it actually is. As fear turns into chronic insecurity, the viewer withdraws from the world, magnifying feelings of isolation and political impotence (Gerbner, Gross, Morgan, & Signorielli, 1982). Again, the cultivation of chronic insecurity serves a dual purpose of discourse discipline and normalization. First, the heavy television viewer is conditioned to remain vulnerable to the media's productive methods (i.e. cultivating fearfulness to increase viewership). Second, the cultivation of insecurity normalizes the heavy television viewer to the dominant social and political order by legitimating the need for more police and the suspension of civil liberties in the name of internal security.

The media, however, cannot completely suppress all competing knowledge systems or anticipate all epistemological challenges. The media must therefore reiterate its semantic victories to maintain its narrative authority, and thus the exchange value of its news commodities. The disciplinary effect flows from the media's mode of producing public knowledge, and from its reiteration of the dominant social order. Each of these functions is enabled by a single software, as it were—the mass media's "codes of meaning" which shape both the content and the structure of the information that will be allowed to enter the realm of public knowledge (McCoy, 1993). As McCoy explains:

Mass media order society's discourses by structuring the thresholds of thought, knowledge, and communication. [Media] institutions strategically, if unintentionally, collude with corporate and governmental interests in the pursuit of policies that maximize control over populations, as well as individual members of society (p. 141).

Collusion occurs as the media "normalizes" information for the purpose of dissemination. In a sense, the normalizing act can be viewed as a process by which information is socialized to the dominant discourses. The news media does not render its services for free—thus commodification. It helps the forces of hegemony inscribe their version of the social order as long as it can maintain its control of the means of producing public knowledge.

But a problem arises. The media has the power to filter out information or interpretations that contradict the dominant discourses. In the news media, oppositional or alternative views are filtered through various screens, including agenda-setting, the application of "professional" or "objective" news values to establish hierarchies of news worthiness, and the reliance upon narrative conventions that are believed to be especially entertaining. The alternative or oppositional views that manage to pass through such a filtering process are usually disconnected from the political, social, or cultural contexts that produced them. Whether excluded or shattered into harmless fragments, the news media's filtering power effectively subordinates those discourses that interfere with the maintenance of the hegemonic order (McCoy, 1993, p. 143). The degree to which the news media can sustain the illusion that it disseminates information in the general interest enhances its narrative authority while obscuring the means by which the hegemonic order uses news discourse to inscribe its vision of social reality.

By directing the various means of production, semantic and economic, the hegemonic leadership plays out social reality for the subordinate cultures. The inscription of the social universe confirms the political legitimation of the State and forms the hegemonic enterprise (McCoy, 1993, p. 144).

Yet it would be wrong to view McCoy's analysis as deterministic. As the Los Angeles riot demonstrated, chaos can often destabilize the hegemonic order by offering scenes it cannot quickly normalize. At such moments of discourse disequilibrium, the media's discourse reflex becomes most detectable. The media's linkages to the larger institutional ensemble become detectable. Power that had seemed anonymous, self-generative, and systematic suddenly becomes visible when mobilized to reassert its authority over the production of public knowledge. The more violent the social upheaval, the more aggressively the media reasserts its narrative authority. The first hours of televised rioting show the media's reactive discourse reflexes in action. Shielded and socially removed from the streets, television anchors quickly resorted to calling the rioters "hooligans" when it became clear that the violence filmed from helicopters would not be contained by the police.

For example, the despairing commentary of broadcasters such as Paul Moyers, then at KABC, expressed more than moral revulsion. It expressed a crisis of inscription when his reporting could not normalize the rioting as it flamed out of control. Lacking a perspective with which to render the scene meaningful, Moyers had no choice but to fill the void by attempting to uphold the values of the status quo. By running out of journalistic language, as it were, he broke the normalizing quality of his television persona, which is usually affable, paternalistic, and jocular. His lapse of professional composure thus undermined his efforts to reiterate the "morality" of the status quo. For that brief moment his normalizing reassurances could not hide his journalistic impotence, and that of his medium. Pragmatism thus dictates that the media's service to the social order be momentarily suspended in order to re-establish its narrative authority.

When viewed in real time, a crisis of signification can be brief. Within hours of the first evidence of rioting, the media had mobilized to regain its narrative authority by reiterating two mutually empowering discourses—the riot as racial conflict and the riot as spectacle of law and order, a theme which could be further subdivided. Some law-and-order coverage focused on police maneuvers and plans for imposing marshal law and deporting "illegal aliens"; another focused on damage to property; and then later, efforts to repair or rebuild the city's smoldering businesses.

Taken together, each thematic response reinforced the desirability of the status quo by intensifying social anxieties in a manipulative reaction Stuart Hall and his colleagues refer to as "moral panic" (1978). After all, television stations and newspapers function in local landscapes. News coverage that frightened residents of the riot zone into respecting the police, stopping destruction of private property, and participating in rebuilding efforts also recommitted them to the values of the dominant social order. The image of

Hollywood actor Edward James Olmos sweeping up the glass of shattered shop windows perfectly illustrated the media's complicity in the fabrication of hope. The media seized upon his brigade of sweepers as evidence of a populace heroically recommitted to the social order.

But the media did not deliberately conspire to racialize and criminalize the rioters or ennoble the sweepers. Its responses to the crisis of signification were instead mediated by two other factors. First, because journalists feel more comfortable when speaking the language of their traditional news sources, they often become transmitters for the discourses of power. Second, the media reiterates the dominant discourse in an attempt to revalidate its own narrative authority, a strategic reflex that protects the media organization's immediate self-interest. Over time, however, repeated discourse mobilizations produce long-term effects. By emphasizing the need for racial harmony, law and order, and "rebuilding" efforts, the local media, in effect, ignored or minimized the social inequities/unequal power relatons that contributed to the riot. Notions of causation were thus filtered from the grammar of coverage.

The media's version of 1992 riot drama bore a striking resemblance to its coverage of the 1965 Watts Riot. In 1967, the Kerner Commission's report criticized the media's failure to explain the underlying social and economic causes of the rioting that had just swept through the nation's major cities two years earlier. In 1992, however, the media repeated this mistake, but in a different form.

The Watts Riot of 1965 marked the beginning of the demise of the city's former economic order. That order was dominated by corporate land development, the movie and television industry, light and medium-sized manufacturing, warehousing and distribution, and weapons and aerospace production.

However, key sectors of this economic order began to undergo a dramatic transformation. Large corporate entitites based upon industrial mass or Fordist production began to falter in the face of a domestic and offshore manufacturing regime some have characterized as post-Fordist. In contrast to Fordist manufacturing, which uses mass efficiencies of scale to reduce the cost of production, post-Fordist manufacturing is based on a decentralized, or a flexible craft-based production system dedicated to small-batch outputs (Scott & Paul, 1990). Although Japanese manufacturing would later be recognized as the preeminent center of flexible manufacturing, a significant portion of Southern California manufacturing had already begun to emerge under the Post-Fordist regime.

As Mike Davis (1992) recounts, the plant closures that resulted from "economic restructuring" hit those Fordist industries which had only recently begun to employ African Americans in significant numbers. These plant closures, in turn, set in motion a chain of demographic events that radically transformed Los Angeles' urban landscape:

This outward seepage of the Anglo population in the 1960s (−36,510) became an exodus in the 1970s (−123,812) and the 1980's (−43,734). Racial hysteria, abetted by "block-busting" in the city of Lynwood, was followed by a second wave of plant closings in the late 1970s. Much of the trucking industry, escaping gridlock and land inflation, migrated to new industrial zones in the Inland Empire, fifty miles east of L.A. And disastrously, within the short space of the "Volker recession," local heavy industry—including the entirety of the auto-tire-steel complex—collapsed in the face of relentless Japanese and Korean competition. In most cases, plant closure followed within a few years of watershed black . . . breakthroughs in shop-floor seniority and local union leadership. While white workers for the most part were able to retire or follow their jobs to the suburban periphery, nonwhites were stranded in an economy that was suddenly minus 50,000 high-wage manufacturing and trucking jobs (p. 57).

The second round of plant closures triggered the flight of as many as 75,000 working and middle-class African Americans from South Central during the 1970s and 1980s (Corwin, 1992). Like their white counterparts, they abandoned neighborhoods for jobs in San Bernardino and Riverside Counties, or moved to southern hometowns their parents had migrated from during and after World War II, when they sought jobs in burgeoning defense industries. The exodus was further destabilizing since it undercut the financial viability of South Central's once thriving small-business community. Left behind were those segments of the African American community with the least social resources or work skills (Hubler, 1992). Without effective intervention, the Watts riot made the exodus of small black-owned businesses irreversible, thus setting the stage for April's riot.

To be fair, some elements of the media tried to retrace the economic chronology that linked Watts to Rodney King and the arson and looting on the afternoon of April 29. The *Times*, for example, in a series that ran two weeks after the riot, attempted to summarize the history connecting the Watts riots to the "Rodney King" riots ("Understanding the Riots, Part I," 1992; Hubler, 1992). Although the special section noted the riot's "fundamental causes," which included demographic change, chronic unemployment, police brutality, poor schooling, and the delay in sending in the National Guard, the public policy failures and global economic forces that had produced these symptoms were not addressed. The most direct acknowledgment of post-industrial decline the series could muster were three one-sentence captions that noted the closure of plants that had employed South Central residents. The series also reported in its chronology the publicly financed redevelopment of the downtown cityscape of high-rise banks and hotels, but did not connect this diversion of local tax dollars to the historic neglect of South and Central Los Angeles by the city's economic and political elites.

Still, the series went far beyond the explanatory efforts of other media, which settled for law-and-order and personalized race relations coverage. Instead, the media's habit of seeking the "human interest" angle in its riot coverage effectively framed the race relations discourse in the language of popular racism. In contrast to elite or institutional racism, popular racism is a belief system held and expressed by individuals (Van Dijk, 1993). It is by nature diffuse, ubiquitous, reactive, and not the expression of a deliberate corporate or government policy or program. The coverage that played upon Rodney King's "Can we all get along?" plea illustrates one way the riot was personalized for media audiences (Wallace & Chavez, 1992).

Though compelling, the media's habit of explaining the riot as the consequence of popular racism freed the audience to either ignore or accept blame for the disaster. The riot's human interest stories, because they reduced complex events to the scale of individual emotions, avoided asking if certain social classes were disproportionately responsible for the rioting. The atomizing power of the race relations discourse thus reinforced the hegemonic order by extricating social institutions or elites from the crime scene.

Cultural experience or indeed every cultural form is radically, quintessentially hybrid, and if it has been the practice of the West since Immanuel Kant to isolate cultural and aesthetic realms from the worldly domain, it is now time to rejoin them (Said, 1993, p. 58).

For the Latinos of Los Angeles, the media's reiteration of the race relations discourse can be appreciated in two ways. It reframed inner-city life as a competition in which the contenders were defined by means of racial taxonomy. And, through reiteration, it continued to dominate the cultural space of competing interpretations, ideas, and perspectives required to evolve into counter-discourses.

Stated another way, the race relations discourse functions in a universe of boundaries, one which mirrors the now-fading classical concept of culture. Renato Rosaldo (1989) writes that classical anthropology's obsession for studying "pure" or "traditional" cultures was premised on static and bounded conceptions of human conduct, a view of the human condition made problematic as migration, global commerce, and instant communications have blurred the demarcations between nations and cultures.

In this context, the fiction of the uniformly shared culture increasingly seems more tenuous than useful. Although most metropolitan typifications continue to suppress border zones, human cultures are neither necessarily coherent nor always homogenous. More often than we usually care to think, our everyday lives are crisscrossed by border zones, pockets, and eruptions of all kinds (p. 207).

The Latinos who reside in the Southwestern borderlands occupy one of the world's richest zones of "creative cultural production" which, unfortunately, the dominant discourse renders as transitional and empty (Rosaldo, 1989).

Similarly, the borders between nations, classes, and cultures were endowed with a curious kind of hybrid invisibility. They seemed to be a little of this and a little of that, and not quite one or the other. Movements between such seemingly fixed entities as nations or social classes were relegated to the analytical dustbin of cultural invisibility. Immigrants and socially mobile individuals appeared culturally invisible because they were no longer what they once were, and not yet what they could become (p. 209).

In many ways, the journalist's non-responsiveness to multiple Latino identities resembles the classical social analyst's attitude toward border regions. Academic institutions maintain "fields" of social science the way the media inscribes the race relations discourse—by creating and maintaining boundaries that validate institutional and discursive authority.

Under such circumstances, *mestizaje* survives as an outlaw discourse, acknowledged by Latino intellectuals and lived by the Latino community, but ignored by the nation's dominant institutions. Marginalization, however, does not imply the absence of a documented history. At the end of the nineteenth century, Latin American writers and intellectuals such as José Martí began the process of translating lived *mestizaje* into written discourse.

Although Latino *mestizaje* in the United States has its antecedents in Mexican and Latin American history, its lived experience changes in the United States. On this side of the border, immigration accelerates the process through which Latinos encounter the First World, as well as other Third World immigrants they would have been less likely to meet at home. On this side, its meaning and experience have also evolved beyond the bounds of official ideology, such as Mexico's ruling Partido Revolucionario Independiente (PRI), which invokes the term to maintain the hegemony of a one-party state. Where in Mexico, the term has been co-opted to legitimize and integrate the nation's mestizo middle class and peripheral regional cultures, here in the United States its lived experience occurs beyond official sanction.

Mestizaje on this side of the border thus expresses a refusal to prefer one language, one national heritage, or culture at the *expense* of others. Culturally speaking, then, *mestizaje* is radically inclusive. At other times, it takes the form of a deliberate transgression of political borders. These transgressions, however, are not overtly ideological, but adaptive and strategic. Stated in economic terms, the globalization of capital, with its power to penetrate and dominate regional markets and undermine native economies, obliges the Mexican peasant or Guatemalan worker to ignore state boundaries to survive. Sentimental loyalty to a particular nation-state, and by extension, the traditional culture idealized by that state, become impoverishing luxuries. To this extent, then, the lived transcultural experience of *mestizaje* must also be considered transnational, and potentially post-national, a notion that emerges again and again in Pan-Latin American discourse since Bolívar.

The border-crosser thus becomes a kind of cultural "cross dresser" who willfully blurs political, racial, or cultural borders in order to better adapt to the world as it is actually constructed. Latinos have simply developed a tradition of juggling languages, music, clothing styles, foods, gender—anything, in short, with which to fashion a more meaningful cultural coherency.

Yet the lived experience of *mestizaje* is not schizoid, nor does it lack the capacity to produce identity. Instead, mestizo culture coheres, acquires integrity and patterning from its mode of construction, which is essentially strategic in its orientation to the world. Over time, these strategies take on the appearance of what some would call tradition, but which could just as appropriately be called an aesthetic or a style.

Whatever the terminology, the styles of mestizo cultural construction are not entirely defined by material conditions or their historic genealogies. Chicanos have known this instinctively when they acknowledge their cultural differences and similarities to Mexicans or other Latinos. To this degree, then, the mestizo cultural strategy is adaptive in the sense that other cultural strategies are. It changes, and is changed by, the world as it is encountered. Internal consistency through time is derived from the culture's repertoire of strategic responses as it interacts with the dynamic elements of a specific landscape.

As it turns out, *mestizaje* is one of many transcultural styles of border crossing.

"All of us," Rosaldo (1989) writes, "inhabit an interdependent late-twentieth century world marked by borrowing and lending across porous national and cultural boundaries that are saturated with inequality, power, and domination" (p. 217).

However, *mestizaje*, as one of many strategic responses to the decline of the imperial West, does not make cultural border crossing any less threatening. Rather, the border crosser *que se amestiza* in the act of transgression, inevitably undermines the discourses of the nation-state while, paradoxically, contributing to the same state's economic well-being by providing cheap surplus labor. Perhaps that's why the media image of the tattered immigrant scrambling under barbed wire is so potent in its ambiguities. That's why both Republican and Democratic demagogues have manipulated the media image of the Latino immigrant in pre-election scapegoating gambits. The unfounded claims that Latinos are a drain on local welfare and educational institutions are represented as threats against the state. A people who violate boundaries of "race," language, and culture thus upset myths of a democratic nation-state based on borders and exclusions. From the exclusionist's perspective, Latino immigrants actively disregard the sacred boundaries and categories that sustain idealized notions of national integrity (Giroux, 1991).

But the exclusionist misinterprets the immigrant's transgressions. The economic and political processes that have precipitated the cultural implosion of the Imperial West will continue to create transitional border zones where the so-called First and Third Worlds will collide or coexist. And because Latino immigrants must transgress political and cultural borders to survive, recurring crises of discourse discipline remain endemic to the border zone. As Said (1993) observes, the lived cultural experience of more and more people occurs outside the boundaries of the idealized state, despite efforts to "reassert old authorities and canons" (p. 58).

[We] have never been as aware as we are now of how oddly hybrid historical and cultural experiences are, of how they partake of many often contradictory experiences and domains, cross national boundaries, defy the police action of simple dogma and loud patriotism (p. 15).

Cultural *mestizaje*'s aggressive disregard for boundaries and unexpected in-clusions should therefore be appreciated in a context of global transformations.

The unequal development resulting from the emergence of post-industrial society, with its concomitant transition to an information society based upon a post-Fordist industrial regime, will continue to produce massive economic and social dislocations at home and abroad. The complex dialectics of capital, markets, and resources in the developing world will continue to make cities such as Los Angeles a diaspora of choice for Latin American immigrants. Technological innovation will continue to facilitate the breakup of mass media audiences into smaller segments and, at the same time, promote the emer-gence of an information elite whose job it will be to create the information and cultural commodities to service the information superhighway (Rustin, 1989). The information elites will emerge as a dominant economic class of a social regime based upon post-Fordist production, leaving behind those cul-tural and social sectors still affiliated with Fordist and pre-Fordist modes of production. Under post-Fordism, where information industries emerge as the dominant productive force, the winners will either own or control the pro-duction of information. Everyone else, writes Michael Rustin (1989), stands to lose social prestige. "Insofar as mental labor does become more central to the production process, it is not surprising that those who live by it gain in social power, just as the depopulation of the countryside earlier had its con-sequences for class relations" (p. 66).

How the Latino community will fare during the ensuing transition to an information-based society is impossible to predict. But Latinos—both as mem-bers of a working and owning class—who remain tied to inefficient Fordist and post-Fordist industries cannot expect to participate in, let alone gain con-trol of, the dominant culture-creating industries. That role is reserved for the information elites that serve at the pleasure of post-Fordist capital.

Some may take heart in knowing that the *maquiladoras* along the North Mexican border and the suburbs of the nation's major cities employ huge numbers of Latinos in post-Fordist industries. Yet most of these highly de-centralized industries employ Latinos at the lowest skill levels, offering them the lowest pay and social benefits. Their present affiliation with post-Fordist production does not appear to promise greater cultural visibility since, up to now, they are excluded from the means of mental production. In this regard, long-term social movements that lead to educational and professional empowerment can prepare Latino workers to participate in the culture industries that produce cultural commodities for the emerging information order. But the value of this approach must not be exaggerated since these industries enculturate professional values that effectively validate the organization's methods of producing public knowledge. So far, efforts to increase the minority presence in the news media have altered the means of discourse production only in modest ways. Still, professional groupings such as the National Hispanic News Media Association may hold out some opportunities for providing logistical and technical support to Latino community groups involved in counter-discourse development. Umbrella organizations such as Responsible Immigration Debate and Education (RIDE), a coalition of Latino groups seeking to counter political scapegoating of immigrants, embodies another route for the development of a Latino counter-discourse. Already, the coalition has invited other ethnic groups to join its campaign against immigrant bashing. The coalition could eventually turn its attention to cultural strategy by translating *mestizaje*, or the discourse of border crossing, into terms comprehensible to the nation's emerging immigrant pluralities. The expansion of this discourse beyond the Latino community may thus help to inhibit the media's tendency to marginalize what it considers exotic or aberrant.

At the same time, however, it also appears that the hegemonic order will continue to face crises of signification. Some will be triggered by social upheavals caused by the growing disparities of late post-industrial capitalism, while others will result from the multicultural crises powered by migration, demographic change, and increased communication between the developing and developed worlds. The blurring distinction between media programming and computer software will also continue to produce periods of discourse disequilibrium, as will the continuing decline of mass (Fordist) media and emerging dis-massed/dispersed/fragmented/dismantled (post-Fordist) information industries. And as the cultural benefits of the information superhighway become more widely available, the emerging ethnic pluralities in the nation's image-making cities, both as consumers and workers, may acquire the tools with which to undermine or challenge the media's discourse dominance, but only with a deliberate strategy for exploiting the opportunities that arise with each "moral panic." Under such circumstances, the Latino community's success at advancing a counter-discourse on *mestizaje* can take on crucial strategic significance, both for the community itself and for other communities "disappeared" by the dominant media discourses. Any counter-discourse based upon inclusions, that renders ambiguity meaningful and which undermines the hegemony of isolating boundaries, will provide a nation as heterodox as the United States with tools to defend itself against the media's marginalizing discourses. To the degree a discourse of cultural *mestizaje* is not touted as a basis for a new orthodoxy, it can contribute to a richer understanding of what presently passes for multiculturalism, and can also lead to the realization that a majority of Americans are mestizos under the skin—a far more aggressive cultural position from which to counter the resurgence of what Edward Said (1993) has called "embattled patriotism" (p. 58).

NOTE

1. For a trenchant critique of the idea of race and the race relations paradigm, see *Racism After "Race Relations"* (Miles, 1993). Miles asserts, "The use of 'race' (and 'race relations') as analytical concepts disguises the social construction of difference, presenting it as somewhat inherent in the empirical reality of observable or imagined biological difference" (p. 48). According to Miles, racism is a meaningful analytical category, and should be the object of study and understood in terms of the specific historical and material conditions which gave rise to it through the process of racialization.

REFERENCES

Corwin, M. (1992). "L.A.'s loss: 'Black flight.' " *Los Angeles Times* (August 13).

Davis, M. (1992). "The empty quarter," in D. Reid (ed.), *Sex, death, and God in L.A.* New York, N.Y.: Pantheon Books.

Gerbner, G. & L. Gross. (1976). "Living with television: The violence profile." *Journal of Communication*, 32(2), pp. 172–199.

Gerbner, G., L. Gross, M. Morgan, & N. Signorielli. (1982). "Charting the mainstream: Television's contributions to political orientations." *Journal of Communication*, 28(3), pp. 176–201.

Giroux, H. A. (1991). "Postmodernism as border pedagogy: Redefining the boundaries of race and ethnicity," in H. A. Giroux (ed.), *Postmodernism, feminism, and cultural politics*. Albany: State University of New York Press.

Hall, S. et al. (1978). *Policing the crisis: Mugging, the State, and law and order*. London, England: Macmillan.

Hoffman, A. (1974). *Unwanted Mexican Americans in the great depression*. Tucson, AZ: University of Arizona Press.

Hubler, S. (1992). "South L.A.'s poverty rate worse in '65." *Los Angeles Times* (May 11).

Lieberman, P. (1992). "Fifty-one percent of riot arrests were Latino, study says." *Los Angeles Times* (June 18), p. 3.

Lieberman, P. & R. O'Reilly. (1993). "Most looters endured lives of crime, poverty." *Los Angeles Times* (May 2), p. 1.

McCoy, T. S. (1993). *Voices of difference: Studies in critical philosophy and mass communication*. Cresskill, NJ: The Hampton Press, Inc.

Miles, R. (1993). *Racism after "race relations."* New York: Routledge.

Postman, N. (1985). *Amusing ourselves to death: Public discourse in the age of show business*. New York, NY: Penguin.

Rosaldo, R. (1989). *Culture & truth: The remaking of social analysis*. Boston, MA: Beacon Press.

Rustin, M. (1989). "The politics of post-Fordism: Or, the trouble with 'new times.'" *New Left Review* (175) (May/June), pp. 64–66.

Said, E. W. (1993). *Culture and Imperialism*. New York, NY: Alfred A. Knopf, Inc.

Scott, J. & A. S. Paul. (1990). "Industrial development in Southern California, 1970–1987," in J. F. Hart (ed.), *Our Changing Cities*. Baltimore: The John Hopkins Press.

"Understanding the riots, part I: Path to fury." (1992). *Los Angeles Times* (May 11), pp. 2–12.

"Understanding the riots—six months later. Separate lives: Dealing with race in L.A." (1992). *Los Angeles Times* (November 16), p. 4.

Valle, V. (1993). "A Chicano reporter in 'Hispanic Hollywood': Editorial agendas and the culture of professional journalism," in Chon Noriega (ed.), *Chicanos and film: Essays on Chicano representation and resistance*. St. Paul, MN: University of Minnesota Press.

Van Dijk, T. A. (1993). *Elite discourse and racism*. Sage Series on Race and Ethnic Relations, vol. 6. Newbury Park, CA: Sage Publications.

Wallace, A. & S. Chavez. (1992). "Can we all get along?" *Los Angeles Times* (November 16), pp. 1–3.

West, C. (1993). *Race matters*. Boston, MA: Beacon Press.

Working with Gay/Homosexual Latinos with HIV Disease: Spiritual Emergencies and Culturally Based Psycho-Therapeutic Treatments

Lourdes Arguelles and Anne Rivero

Voices

They come thinking they are being punished by God. They want to be cleansed.
—Ignacio Aguilar, Clinical Director, Proyecto Amanecer,
Bellflower, Southern California

I want to die looking young and looking at palm trees. I was born with my young mother looking at palm trees. It is only reasonable that I should die that way.
—Ricardo, Cuban PWA, died February 1991

AIDS is the force that pushes us through the opening and into the world that never ends.
—Rene, Chicano PWA, died July 1987

Dying of AIDS is dying religiously, martyred.
—Jorge, Nicaraguan PWA

I know I have been hexed. I know who did it and when. That is why I have AIDS.
—Carlos, Mexican PWA

AIDS has contributed to the change in Afro-Caribbean healing practices in the United States. And so has the increased visibility of gays and lesbians in our communities.
—Chief Alade, North American Yoruba Society

It is a punishment, and so it is only God who can cure me. I go to church all the time. I'm very afraid to die.
—Anonymous, Mexican PWA

The time of an HIV-positive diagnosis is a time of great crisis and can be a time to reconnect with la cultura.

—David Marquez, former Clinical Director,
Milagros AIDS Project, East Los Angeles

For many men, women, and children diagnosed with a deadly disease, the diagnosis and the subsequent unfolding of an illness process can help precipitate a spiritual emergency or a state of profound psychological transformation that involves the individual's entire being. Spiritual emergencies often take the form of states of consciousness of a non-ordinary nature and involve very intense emotions that may lead to new philosophical insights. These experiences tend to revolve around spiritual themes and can include sequences of psychological death and rebirth, feelings of oneness with the universe, and encounters with several mythological beings (Grof & Grof, 1990). Several investigators (Bragdon, 1988; Grof, 1985, 1988, & 1992; Grof & Grof, 1990; Hood, 1986) have explored the healing potential of spiritual emergencies and have mapped out the kinds of circumstances and psychotherapeutic techniques that tend to make these experiences beneficial for the individual and for those closest to him or her. The investigators have also been careful to differentiate between spiritual emergencies and mental states such as psychosis or other serious pathology. These alternative pioneer researchers have encouraged clinicians to deal with certain non-ordinary states such as visions and recall of past lives as difficult stages in a natural developmental process rather than as evidence of disease. Working in this way, some clinicians have felt the need to establish referral and consultation links with traditional and alternative healers and advisors (Achterberg, 1985; Krippner & Villoldo, 1986; Torrey, 1972). Among the positive results of these linkages has been an expansion of options for individuals seeking assistance in coping with their problems and/or further developing their emotional and spiritual lives.

One critique of consciousness research and the non–pathology-oriented treatment of spiritual emergencies in the United States is that there is negligible impact made by this kind of research and clinical work among bicultural communities. What is often overlooked, however, is that from within these populations certain indigenous traditional and alternative practices have been drawn upon and modified to fit very new circumstances by creative clinicians, researchers, healers, and clients. Such culture-based approaches may parallel in process and effectiveness some of the techniques developed by alternative consciousness researchers.

This chapter describes the various spiritual emergencies faced by some Latino gay/homosexual men living and dying with the HIV disease and the psychospiritual strategies that they and some of their clinicians, traditional healers, and other helpers have accessed or developed. The types of experiences and struggles reported by clients and clinicians have resulted in a broadening of the term "spiritual emergency" to include less acute manifestations and culture-bound syndromes such that the lines are somewhat less sharply drawn between the Grofs' designations of "spiritual emergence" versus "spiritual emergency" (Grof & Grof, 1990). This chapter also illustrates some changes which have taken place in conventional mental health treatment and traditional and alternative healing practices in various Latino communities in the context of the AIDS pandemic as gay/homosexual HIV sufferers have become more visible in communities of color. It is based on many years of clinical and prevention education experiences with people with HIV/AIDS as well as ongoing conversations with therapists and healers who approach the spiritual emergencies and spiritual searches catalyzed by the experience of AIDS using an eclectic combination of culturally sanctioned healing models and more conventional psychotherapeutic strategies. It is about work in progress.

MESO-AMERICAN/CHICANO SPIRITUALITY-BASED TREATMENT STRATEGIES

Upon witnessing the spiritual struggles interwoven in coping with HIV infection/AIDS, the first thing that struck us was that the degree and type of spiritual emergency escalates in accordance with the types of causal attributions made about the illness. This was illustrated in a substantial sample of HIV-infected Latino men served by the Milagros AIDS Project in East Los Angeles. David Marquez, a clinical social worker and the former clinical director of the project, reports that more than 90 percent of the approximately three hundred HIV-infected Latino men that the project served between 1988 and 1990 believed that their illness was a punishment from God or that they had been hexed (Marquez, personal communications, 1988–1992). The men, who were primarily recent immigrants from Mexico and Central America, had come to the project for both material and emotional assistance. They were having extreme difficulty dealing with the HIV/AIDS diagnosis that they had been given, with the symptoms of the disease process, and with the social stigma surrounding AIDS. Their sense of hopelessness and helplessness was exacerbated by their beliefs in hexes, spells, or God's punishment as explanations for their current and anticipated suffering with AIDS. Hexes and spells were associated with the notion that people who were full of envy and hatred had made them sick. God's punishment as a causal explanation for suffering was associated with a rather simple moral causal ontology full of references to transgression and sin with same-sex eroticism as its centerpiece. Many of these men reported having previously sought help from *curanderos* and *curanderas* (Latin American traditional spiritual healers) in their local area and as far away as Tijuana, Mexico to deal with the fear and guilt that resulted from being hexed or punished by God. The men believed that these healers could dispel hexes and intercede with God. The reported results from these contacts were mixed. A small number stated that they had received valuable assistance, though some felt that the local healers were not as effective as those they had known growing up in their countries of origin. The majority, however, reported having felt mistreated because of their homosexual behavior and/or exploited economically. Still others complained that they were unable to find good *curanderos* who were accessible in their area, or that they were too ill or lacking in the resources and documentation necessary for crossing the U.S.–Mexico border. These reports are in agreement with prior investigations of *curanderismo* networks which report a decline of practitioners and of usage in large metropolitan areas as well as distortions of traditional practices in the hands of transplanted or new practitioners (Edgarton, Kamo, & Fernandez, 1970; Padilla, Cados, & Keefe, 1976).

These immigrant HIV sufferers were left then, as a last resort, with community AIDS projects, mental health and social service agencies, and conventional medicine. Given that their illness was experienced as a supernatural/ spiritual event, these secular approaches could not be seen by them as very helpful. Compliance with treatment or self-care practices was perceived as useless if the hex or divine punishment was still in place. Thus, the first item of the clinical agenda for Marquez and his staff of Latino therapists was to help these clients eliminate the effects of the hexes and the notion of God's punishment as a causal explanation for their HIV/AIDS diagnosis and symptomatology. Unlike many clinicians, Marquez never thought that suppressive medication was the first answer to these men's predicaments. Having grown up in a culture in which attributions made to the direct actions of God and spirits as well as the practice of hexing were everyday occurrences, Marquez knew that he had to deal with these men's attributions partially in the context of their received culture. As a gay-identified therapist, however, he also felt the need to ensure that the heterosexist assumptions embedded in some of the cultural practices in these men's lives were not reinforced as their cultural connection was strengthened through a culturally based therapeutic intervention. Marquez also understood that the men no longer lived in the context of an intact Meso/Central American received culture but in a setting of overlapping co-cultures and that the culture crossings in which they and their therapists engaged as a matter of routine had important clinical implications.

Predictably, then, Marquez set out to intervene therapeutically in a culturally-based, albeit hybrid and eclectic fashion. He used approaches drawn from a combination of Mexican/Chicano healing practices, conventional clinical techniques, and from his therapeutic experiences assisting gay men in coping with emotional and social stresses. In addition to his childhood and adolescent experiences, Marquez had gained familiarity with traditional Mexican/Chicano healing practices in the context of an organization named Calmecac which stands, in Nahuatl, for sacred school. This organization, the brainchild of U.S.–trained Mexican psychiatrist and shaman apprentice Arnaldo Solis, drew together in the late 1970s and throughout the 1980s some of the best-known

Chicano clinicians in the Los Angeles area to study and to experiment with a variety of traditional healing practices in the context of their conventional therapeutic work with Latinos. At least two of the members of this small group were openly gay, and it seems that their sexual orientation was not construed as problematic. Solis was also to later become well known for his work with gay Latinos with AIDS in the San Francisco Bay area. Calmecac, which operated between 1978 and 1990, represented a setting of alternative Latino consciousness research and spiritual emergency clinical practice which partially transformed and in turn was transformed by the rapid growth of the HIV epidemic in the Latino community.

Among the therapeutic healing practices effectively utilized by Marquez, and partially developed within the Calmecac collective, was the practice of *conocimiento* (knowing or becoming acquainted with). This exercise was designed to reconnect the client with his received culture and his ancestors by helping him remember where he came from and allowing him to share that personal history within a group therapy context. Another practice was that of encouraging the client to seek ancestor guidance and assistance with the illness. Such connection with deceased ancestors is carried out in the Mexican tradition within the context of the celebration of the Days of the Dead and the building and maintenance of altars both in the home and in work settings. In a riveting video exploration of the meanings of the Days of the Dead for contemporary Mexicans and Chicanos on both sides of the border, Portillo and Muñoz (1989) documented the transformations of this celebration and altar-making tradition among the gay Latino community in the San Francisco area. The theme of AIDS and the photographs of lovers and friends lost to the fatal disease as well as the use of such modern items as neon statues and VCRs in the altars in the Portillo-Muñoz video vividly and publicly illustrate some of the types of practices employed by Marquez and his staff and clients in the privacy of the Milagros AIDS Project.

Rene, a former client of the first author, related his feelings when he saw his friend Ramon put the photograph of his deceased lover in an altar made specifically for the November celebration of the dead in the Logan Heights Latino district of San Diego.

I felt very strange because in my family's altars we only had pictures of the "blood family" like dead parents, grandparents, and so on. But when Ramon said that our lovers and our friends who had died of AIDS were the "true blood brothers" it made sense. I feel very good thinking that one day many of my friends will have me in their altars and that I will be invited to come back and help them with their problems. I need to prepare in this life to do just that. I need to recenter. AIDS and my friends have given my life a spiritual focus. At first it was difficult because I had to go on living as before, working and shopping while knowing that I am dying. But the altar reminds me that the change is real. It reminds me of where I will be next year, in the spirit world.

A year after Rene's death, Ramon contacted the first author to invite her to visit the altar he had prepared for that year's Days of the Dead celebrations and mentioned that Rene's picture was in a place of honor.

Marquez reports that the majority of his clients were able to deal more constructively with their illness after months of culturally-based therapeutic interventions. These interventions included, in addition to *conocimientos* and altar-making practices, *limpias* (cleansings of body, mind, and spirit) as well as group therapy where issues of internal and external homophobia were carefully addressed. He reports that the men began to take better care of their bodies through conventional medical care and with the assistance of *sobadores* (traditional masseuses), *herberos* (herbalists), and acupuncturists. He reports, however, that a few who had made considerable progress in cognitively restructuring their views of the etiology of HIV infection away from attributing it to hexing or punishment, or who had alternatively dealt with the purported hexing through a *limpia* or cleansing, tended to regress in their therapeutic progress and in their ability to cope emotionally and physically with their illness when they joined Christian fundamentalist churches. These churches were not tolerant of their sexual orientation and overtly or covertly emphasized the view of AIDS as punishment of God for having transgressed morally. In some studies, membership in these and other institutionalized religions have been found to be highly correlated with fear of death among people with AIDS (Templer, Cappelletty, & Kauffman, 1990–1991).

When asked why he thought the men had joined fundamentalist Christian churches, Marquez stated that though the work at the Milagros project gave them a sense of reintegration with their culture and involved them in spiritual practices, it seemed that the men saw their involvement with the fundamentalist churches as a natural progression in their spiritual development in the absence of other institutional structures. Marquez added that the role of these churches in outreach and material assistance to the most disenfranchised groups of the population and the concomitant decline in influence of the Roman Catholic Church among Latinos cannot be overlooked.

Another clinician working to help heal the misattributions of AIDS and other physical and mental disorders to hexing and punishment is Ignacio Aguilar, the director of a Latino mental health project called Amanecer (Dawn), located in the heavily Latino area of Bellflower. In addition to being a clinical social worker, Aguilar is reputedly an accomplished *curandero*. His approach differs somewhat from that of Marquez in that he seems less direct in his views on sexuality and in his dealings with internal and external homophobia. In his work the guilt and self-blame, specific or nonspecific, appear to be simply material to be worked through. He approaches the clinical agenda for persons with AIDS, including gay/homosexual men, with a focus on the primary task of assisting in the cleansing of body, mind, and soul, and he adjusts his cleansing methodology according to the geographical and cultural origin of the client. He has found that for the majority of Mexican clients, water (signifying purity) is a good cleansing agent. Caribbean clients, primarily Cubans, need to be cleansed using the *santos/orishas* or spiritual beings represented as Catholic saints which in fact mask African spirits or deities in the Afro-Cuban santeria (Afro-Cuban syncretic religion) tradition (Cabrera, 1980; Canizares, 1993; Sanchez, 1978; Sandoval, 1975). This is more challenging for Aguilar, who is not a *santero* (official practitioner of *santeria*). Aguilar has observed in people living with AIDS or with other terminal or severe chronic illnesses a pattern consisting of a series of crises which he believes are related to strong spiritual longings that have been repressed (Aguilar, personal communications, 1992). These spiritual longings may lead people to search for their "root" spiritualities or spiritual practices with which they became familiar as children but with which they lost contact due to migration, culture blending, or other factors. Others may become attracted to traditional and alternative spiritual traditions when they feel that everything else has failed them. They look for spiritual homes where they can find comfort and answers to the questions arising in the spiritual emergencies that manifest during their times of crisis. Aguilar has also noted that some Latino parents who have remained involved in *curanderismo* practices throughout their lives may bring in their children in an effort to reconnect them with their "lost spirituality" and their culture.

AFRO-CARIBBEAN-INFLUENCED PSYCHOSPIRITUAL TREATMENT

In the western United States (with the possible exception of Los Angeles), finding a clinician and/or spiritual mentor who can help them reconnect with spiritual roots can be much more difficult for Latinos of other than Mexican or Central American backgrounds. Ricardo, a Cuban who died of AIDS complications in 1991, commented on the difficulties of Caribbean gay men in securing psychospiritual assistance at a time of emotional and spiritual crisis. He noted that most of the non-conventional healing performed in the San Francisco Bay area was derived from Mexican and Central American origins, as seems to be the case in southern California. Though he found *curanderismo* and other Meso–American-based syncretic practices interesting, and at times sought assistance from various *curanderos*, Ricardo felt that he needed someone experienced in African-oriented spiritual practices to assist him with the overwhelming influx of experiences that he judged to be spiritual.

Talks with Ricardo revealed a dramatic change in his view of himself and the world, such that things which had seemed very important before his AIDS diagnosis no longer seemed so. He also became aware of a free-floating terror that no one could assuage and which he interpreted as a premonition. He reported believing that beings he had never seen but intuited were *orishas* (ancestors deified after death and appearing as an immaterial force) would come to visit him and tell him about other worlds better than the one he was about to leave. His dreams had mostly to do with his lost homeland and one of its sacred trees, the royal palm. For him, the *curanderismo* tradition was too Christian, too alien, and too bland. The Christian influences in the practices of the *curanderos* bothered him as a gay man given the homophobia embedded in Christianity both historically and in contemporary settings. He felt at times that *curanderismo* was more Christian than pre-Columbian. He explained that though the *santos* of the Afro-Caribbean traditions to which he felt he belonged were borrowed from the Christian tradition, they actually represented African orishas who often had two genders (Arguelles & Rivero, forthcoming). As such, the *orishas* engaged in sexual relations with both sexes and danced, played, and laughed. He felt that gay men like himself, as well as transgendered people, could identify with these spiritual beings much better than with the serious and austere saints and the celibate Christ of the Christian traditions. He also felt that more openly gay people were involved in the practice of *santeria* than of *curanderismo*, although he recognized that homophobia was by no means absent in the "houses" of *santeria* (Ricardo, personal communications, 1988–1990). Though the *curanderismo* that Ricardo found in California did draw upon certain Native American traditions and influences, it did not seem to include any influences from certain native groups which considered sacred those individuals and practices involved with gender-blending or same-sex eroticism (Guerra, 1971; Lame Deer & Erdoes Lame Deer, 1973; Williams, 1986).

Had Ricardo been living in the East Coast area, access to the African-based healing he was seeking would have been much easier. One such source is Chief Alade, born Mercer Ashby of a family originally from Barbados. He describes himself as a bisexual chief in the North American Yoruba Society, and his practice is based in Manhattan but extends as far as the Carolinas and Florida. His practice partner, a lesbian clinical psychologist who prefers to remain anonymous, has also recently been confirmed as a chief in the North American Yoruba tradition. Together they have constituted a house called *Abale-Alade-Onise-gun* (royal community which deals with medicine) where a great number of gay men, lesbians, and bisexual men and women, whom Alade and his partner consider their godchildren, have found spiritual sanctuary and assistance with their problems.

The AIDS pandemic in the United States and in Africa, according to Chief Alade and his partner, has brought about considerable change in his practice of traditional African religion and healing and in the types of practitioners with whom he works. The chief believes that the four most important changes are (1) the increase in the number of referrals of people with HIV disease to traditional healers, (2) a partial resolution of long-standing rivalries among such healers, (3) the restoration of long-suppressed androgynous or transgendered *orishas* to their rightful importance, and (4) the adaptation and further development of ancient "blood rituals" for the treatment of AIDS (Ashby, personal communication, November 6, 1992).

Chief Alade reports that in the last five years, with the rise in the perceived and actual threat of AIDS in communities of color, the number of referrals by conventional clinicians to traditional healers has increased exponentially. The number of clinicians, including his partner, who have sought out apprenticeships in traditional healing, or who have begun to incorporate the philosophies and practices of African religions into their conventional mental health practice, has also greatly increased. A new generation of Afro-Caribbean healers in the United States has also become more interested in relationships with conventional caregivers. Chief Alade himself maintains close relationships with members of the Black Psychologists Association in New York for mutual consultation purposes. Unlike the *curanderos*, clients, and clinicians on the West Coast to whom we have talked, Chief Alade has not found that the majority of those who come to him with an HIV diagnosis believe that their illness results from a hex or from divine retribution. He believes that this difference in attribution may have to do with the fact that many of the people who reach him already believe that they know what to do to counteract hexing. They are likely to have taken care to remove any ordinary spells or hexes before approaching the chief for "higher order" healing. He reports that the concept of divine retribution is something he does not often encounter. He suggests that this may be so because believers in African traditions do not tend to experience their gods as punitive and condemning in the way that Christians do.

People seek out Chief Alade, or are referred to him, as they would search for a specialist after having exhausted their other resources. Referrals come from traditional, alternative, and conventional practitioners working with a variety of people who have a link to African religions by ancestry, socialization, marriage, or personal choice. According to the chief, this is a significant change from the situation ten years ago when the Afro-Cuban santeros who dominated the African healing scene on the East Coast would isolate practitioners like himself and Oba Adefunmi, the founder of the North American Yoruba Society. The reason for the ostracism was their being too "fundamentalist African" and not having strong connections with the powerful *santeros* in Cuba and the diasporic religious practices of Caribbean people.

According to Chief Alade, one consequence of this earlier divisiveness and suppression was that few openly gay or lesbian individuals were able to find a comfortable home in the practices connected with the diasporic African religions. He feels that the overlay of Christianity in Afro-Caribbean *santeria* exacerbated any existing homophobia of *santeros* and practitioners alike. As a result, gays and lesbians involved in these practices tended for the most part to remain in the closet or to be fairly discrete about their sexuality. This reported discomfort with varieties of sexuality on the part of transplanted *santeros* appears to be in contrast to what was observed by the first author within the confines of Cuba in earlier decades (Arguelles, 1993; Arguelles & Rich, 1984).

An additional problem, distinct from the issues of sexuality, was that in earlier times in the East Coast area most of the ceremonies were conducted in Spanish. The language use excluded from serious practice anyone not fluent in Spanish, including many second generation Latinos.

More currently, Chief Alade has observed changes which he considers very positive. The return to some African fundamentalist spiritual practices, primarily of Yoruba origin, the rise in the numbers of visible gay, lesbian, and bisexual people in communities of color, and the diminished influence of aging homophobic Cuban *santeros* have combined to bring about more cooperation and cross-referrals between various African-oriented healers and between their houses. There has also been a proliferation of bilingual ceremonies giving more access to people of varied linguistic backgrounds. A new generation of gay, lesbian, bisexual, and transgendered people with African roots or connections, some of whom call themselves the New Wave Orishas, are indicative of the trend of cooperation as well as of a return to some fundamental Yoruba beliefs divested of the homophobic Christian overlay of santeria and other Afro-Caribbean diasporic traditions.

Another positive development is the resurrection of some forgotten or neglected *orishas*. An example is the *orisha* Inle which, as Alade theorizes, may have been neglected due to the influence of Christian homophobia. Inle may not have been totally acceptable to the Christian component of the syncretic Afro-Caribbean spiritual blend because of its clearly androgynous nature. The study of the *orisha* Inle has become extraordinarily important for Chief Alade and those who practice with him in his house. Inle has also become very important for people living with HIV, for it is a medicine *orisha*. Associated with Archangel Raphael in the Catholic tradition, Inle has become the patron *orisha* of many gay and lesbian Latinos involved in African healing practices. His/Her feast on October 24 has become a growing gay religious festival in New York. Also important has been the initiation and confirmation of openly gay, lesbian, and bisexual chiefs, such as Alade and his partner, in various African diasporic healing traditions in the United States. These men and women believe that their sexuality imbues them with special gifts to understand and heal, gifts which may be unavailable to those living exclusively as heterosexuals.

A final important change articulated by Chief Alade is that of the adaptation of certain medicinal rituals involving the use of blood, such as those rituals connected with the *orisha* Ogun, for work with people living with HIV disease. The Chief was not at liberty to delineate the details of this and similar rituals, nor to be specific regarding particular changes or adaptations that have taken place. He did note, however, that the use of the *orisha* Inle in these particular rituals was something new and important. These rituals, which have become meaningful among HIV-infected people as part of their spiritual healing practices, involve actual and metaphoric transfer of fresh blood. Chief Alade allays the fears of contagion by assuring that tremendous care is taken to insure that HIV-infected blood is not circulated in the rituals.

In the experience of the authors, as well as of the healers and clinicians with whom we have been in dialogue, the tradition-based healing and spiritual practices mentioned in this chapter do not seem to be pulling HIV-infected Latinos away from conventional medical treatment. On the contrary, it has been observed that the benefits derived from participation in these practices seem to put individuals in a more positive frame of mind and enhance their willingness to accept help from more mainstream medical providers.

There are some problems, however, as well as benefits for those who return to root spiritualities and/or traditional healing practices. The first problem may arise with those few traditional healers who are not educated in or accepting of the advantages of conventional medical treatment. They may overtly or covertly discourage clients from seeking the most optimal range of treatment. Additional vulnerability to such discouragement may exist in persons already experiencing exclusion from mainstream medicine because of economic deprivation or lack of legal documentation. A more intractable problem arises from the opposite direction, that is, from conventional medical practitioners' ignorance and lack of acceptance of traditional and alternative healing practices. Ricardo shared his experience of this phenomenon. He was aware that his San Francisco Anglo gay physician, with whom he felt extremely comfortable and to whom he was grateful for excellent medical treatment, would have been appalled if he had known that Ricardo was also seeking the help of *santeros*. He had in fact heard his doctor make derogatory comments about traditional healers and "folk superstitions." Ricardo would occasionally speculate about trying to switch to a Latino physician who might be more understanding of his faith in traditional beliefs and healing practices, but feared that he might then encounter much more homophobia. He once said, "If you have to be Latino, gay, and with AIDS, don't add another stigma to your life with santeria practice."

PSYCHOSPIRITUAL PRACTICES AND HIV/AIDS PREVENTION EDUCATION

The use of traditional psychospiritual practices in work with the Latino population and HIV infection has not been confined to clinicians and traditional healers. The AIDS prevention work of some Latino educators has also been influenced by these spiritualities. Pino and Arguelles (1987) developed a prevention education program framed within Meso-American traditional spiritualities for use with recent Mexican immigrant women. The format included the use of opening and closing cleansing ceremonies as well as suggestions for follow-up spiritual practice. The program drew freely from the work of the aforementioned Calmeeac collective. In addition, the late Daniel Lara (former head of Latino programs at AIDS Project Los Angeles APLA), Yolanda Ronquillo (an AIDS educator formerly with the American Red Cross), and Milagros Davila (San Diego County Public Health Department) are all

well known for their use of these spiritual traditions in AIDS prevention education. Educators such as these, who have wanted to integrate spiritual concerns into their work, have reported frustration that these concerns have been
often ignored or pushed aside in the context of the despiritualization endemic
in mainstream agencies and organizations in which they were working. In
spite of the resistance in these types of settings, dedicated educators have
found ways to make possible some introduction of traditional psychospiritual
frames of reference into AIDS prevention education targeted to Latino communities. This has largely taken place through less conventional venues.
Within some of the community-based agencies in which a culturalist orientation is more prone to see traditional spirituality as an integral part of Latino
culture, it was sometimes possible to find more acceptance for these approaches. AIDS prevention thus became, in the work of some educators, another avenue for reconnecting with root spiritualities as elements of Latino
culture that were felt to have healing potential. Introduced in the context of
these programs, where participants were not yet overwhelmed by the emergencies brought about by an HIV diagnosis, some ritual spiritual practices
were seen as effective and often pre-conscious means to reduce fear and isolation, premised as they were in views of death as a natural, non-threatening
part of life and on the importance of healing the soul as well as the body.

In introducing or reawakening these concepts, it was found necessary to
take great care to not confuse healing of the soul and the resultant inner peace
with an otherworldly and fatalistic orientation. Interwoven with the spiritual
work was much emphasis on empowerment and the development of knowledge and skills to be utilized by participants in their struggles, both individual
and collective, against the pandemic. Spirituality could thus become another
tool to help in the work of overcoming fear, numbness, helplessness, fatalism,
and individual and collective irresponsibility.

For Latinos struggling with HIV, discovery of or return to root spiritualities
has not been their exclusive choice in dealing with spiritual struggles or spiritual emergencies. Some have found comfort or transformation in following
other pathways. A few have sought a place, albeit a very marginal one, within
the institutional structure of the Roman Catholic Church, while some have
sought similar accommodations within the context of other Christian
traditions. Others have found their way into specifically gay-oriented churches
such as the Metropolitan Community Church or the New Life Ministry. Still
other gay Latinos have found resonance with non-Western and New Age spiritualities. In so doing they may have established links to previously alien aspects of Anglo or Asian experience and broadened, enriched, and rebalanced
their culture blending. Indeed, as some have found spiritual healing in a return to cultural roots, others seem to have facilitated transformation by step-
ping into (for them) radically new realms.

The complex forces of spiritual path selection among HIV-infected gay/
homosexual Latinos have yet to be clearly conceptualized, but the importance

of the spiritual dimension for this and other bicultural populations cannot be overestimated. A recognition of that importance and an understanding of possible options in addressing spiritual crises are critical in the development of an optimal interrelationship between conventional mental health care and alternative or traditional psychospiritual interventions. It is hoped that our observations, and those of other clinicians and researchers such as those mentioned here, will add to a growing body of knowledge necessary for implementing the most comprehensive and compassionate responses to the psychospiritual needs of gay/homosexual Latinos and gays/homosexuals of other ethnicities and cultures as they struggle with the challenge of HIV.

REFERENCES

Achterberg, J. (1985). *Imagery in healing: Shamanism and modern medicine.* Boston, MA: Shambhala.

Arguelles, L. (1993). "Crazy wisdom: Notes from a Cuban queer," in A. Stein (ed.), *Beyond the lesbian nation.* New York, NY: E. P. Dutton.

———, & A. M. Rivero. "Same-sex eroticism and spirituality: Crosscultural perspectives," forthcoming.

Arguelles, L., & B. R. Rich. (1984). "Homosexuality, homophobia and revolution: Notes toward an understanding of the Cuban lesbian and gay male experience." *Signs, A Journal of Women in Culture and Society,* 9(4) (Summer), pp. 51–71.

Bragdon, E. A. (1988). *Sourcebook for helping people in spiritual emergency.* Los Altos, CA: Lightening Up Press.

Cabrera, L. (1980). *Yemaya y Ochun.* Miami, FL: Ediciones Universal.

Canizares, R. (1993). *Walking with the night: The Afro-Cuban world of Santeria.* Rochester, VT: Destiny Books.

Edgarton, R. B., M. S. Karno, & I. Fernandez. (1970). "Curanderismo in the metropolis." *American Journal of Psychotherapy,* 24, pp. 124–134.

Grof, S. (1992). *The holotropic mind: The three levels of human consciousness and how they shape our lives.* San Francisco, CA: HarperSanFrancisco.

———. (1988). *The adventure of self discovery.* Albany, NY: State University of New York Press.

———. (1985). *Beyond the brain: Birth, death, and transcendence in psychotherapy.* Albany, NY: State University of New York Press.

Grof, C. & S. Grof. (1990). *The stormy search for self.* Los Angeles, CA: Jeremy P. Torcher.

Guerra, F. (1971). *The pre-Columbian mind.* London, England: Seminar Press.

Hood, B. L. (1986). "Transpersonal cases: Understanding spiritual emergencies." Ph.D. dissertation, University of Massachusetts, Boston.

Krippner, S. & A. Villoldo. (1986). *The realms of healing,* 3d ed. Berkeley, CA: Celestial Arts.

Lame Deer, J. F., & R. Erdoes Lame Deer. (1973). *Seeker of visions.* New York, NY: Simon and Schuster.

Padilla, A. M., M. L. Cados, & S. E. Keefe. (1976). "Mental health service utilization by Mexican-Americans," in M. R. Miranda (ed.), *Psychotherapy with the Spanish speaking: Issues in research and service delivery.* Monograph 3. Los Angeles, CA: Spanish Speaking Mental Health Research Center, University of California, Los Angeles.

Pino, N. & L. Arguelles. (1987). *Flor de Vida: An AIDS prevention education project.* Los Angeles, CA: California State University.

Portillo, L. & S. Munoz (Directors & Producers). (1989). *La Ofrenda* (Videotape recording). The American Film Institute.

Sanchez, J. (1978). *La religion de los Orichas.* Hato Rey, Puerto Rico: Coleccion Estudios Afrocadbenos.

Sandoval, M. C. (1975). *La religion Afro-Cubana.* Madrid, Spain: Playor.

Templer, D. I., G. Cappelletty, & I. Kauffman. (1990–1991). "Exploration of death anxiety as a function of religious variables in gay men with and without AIDS." *Omega,* 22(1), pp. 43–50.

Torrey, E. F. (1972). "What Western psychotherapists can learn from witch doctors." *American Journal of Orthopsychiatry,* 42(1), pp. 69–76.

Williams, W. L. (1986). *The spirit and the flesh: Sexual diversity in American Indian culture.* Boston, MA: Beacon.

African Americans, Gender, and Religiosity

Daphne C. Wiggins

The dawn of the twentieth century brought fresh challenges to American Prot-estantism. Previous splits fostered by abolition debates in mainline religious bodies still remained intact. The influence of the Enlightenment and Darwin-ism still wielded a significant impact upon the "faithful." The battle between Fundamentalists and Liberals gained momentum, churches experienced a de-creasing influence in public and private domains of life, and became further "domesticated," as evidenced by a decline in men entering the clergy, a de-crease in financial support for the church, and an increasing absence of men from congregational participation (Douglas, 1977).

These forces impacted black and white Christians differently. As white Prot-estantism bemoaned an increasing secularization and apparent decline in the importance of religion, the centrality of the black church among African Amer-icans appeared unthreatened. Whether North and South, the church was the constant meeting place for African Americans to worship God, have their hu-man worth and dignity reaffirmed, release their frustrations, and amass strength to survive in an oppressive world. Black Methodism experienced an influx of members as African Americans retreated from or were pushed out of white congregations. Black Baptists and Pentecostals exhibited racial and ecclesiastical autonomy by establishing denominations. There was a significant increase in black church attendance between 1890 and 1906 (Woodson, 1972) and continuing into the 1930s (Mays & Nicholson, 1933). Amidst this influx, two patterns of African-American Protestantism remained consistent: (1) the clergy was overwhelmingly male, and (2) the supporters predominantly female. It is this second phenomenon, a female-dominated religious context among African Americans, that commands our attention.

This chapter is a theoretical exploration of gender disparities in religiosity among African Americans. The term "gender" is used interchangeably with "sex" (which distinguishes biologically maleness and femaleness) rather than in a more technical sense to designate psychological, social, and cultural constructions of maleness and femaleness. I begin with the premise that this present gender disparity has historic roots in American religion at least since the eighteenth century and in African American religion since Reconstruction. This premise emerges from the historical analysis of New England Christianity presented in Douglas' (1977) *The Feminization of American Culture*, DeBerg's (1990) *Ungodly Women*, and Mays and Nicholson's (1933) *The Negro's Church*. This discussion will proceed with a literature review followed by a synthesis of the scholarship and critique of existent theories. The review of the literature will be twofold: (1) a discussion of the concept of religiosity and its development with attention to gender and African Americans, and (2) a summation of the most relevant bodies of theory which attempt to interpret the variation in male/female religiosity. In the critique section, I will also identify the limitations of previous scholarship, and suggest promising directions for future research.

DEVELOPMENT OF RELIGIOSITY

The term "religiosity" is used interchangeably with religious involvement, religious commitment, and religiousness. No singular definition captures the phenomenon social researchers have labeled religiosity, nor is there agreement as to its content. Applications of the term range from narrow to broad. Perhaps a word about what it is not may be instructive. Religiosity can not be confined to a measuring of adherence to a Christian Orthodoxy scale, although orthodoxy may be one aspect included if sampling those who profess allegiance to the Christian faith (Hunsberger, 1989). It can not be determined solely by church membership[1] or frequency of prayer or self-reported importance of religion in one's life. Nor can it be determined by an amalgam of church attendance, financial support, and reading the Bible.

Taylor (1988a) suggests religiosity is the interfacing of three factors: frequency of church attendance, church membership, and frequency of participation on an index of activities related to devotionalism.[2] Alternatively, Roof (1979) defines religiosity as "an individual's beliefs and behavior in relation to the supernatural or ultimate intensity values." This definition may seem too encompassing for scholars analyzing "church-type" religious commitment; however, the deemphasis upon a deity or doctrinal orthodoxy is intentional, allowing for the study of adherents to American "civil religion,"[3] "invisible religion,"[4] and alternative meaning systems.[5] I will partially appropriate Roof's and Taylor's definitions for my purposes. Throughout this chapter, religiosity will be used to denote a social phenomenon describing one's beliefs and behaviors in relation to the supernatural, which is evidenced by a matrix of religious actions and attitudes.

The empirical study of religiosity gained ascendancy in the early 1950s. Joseph Fichter's research on Catholicism paved the way. "He distinguished between [differences in religiosity among] Catholics based on frequency of attendance at Mass and an overall level of involvement in the life of the parish" (Roberts, 1990, p. 15). His research resulted in a fourfold typology and shifted the understanding of religiosity from one-dimensional to multidimensional. Scholars building upon this shift sought to verify the internal coherence of various dimensions. Lenski (1963) and Fukuyama (cited in Roof 1979) were two of the earliest. Lenski identified four dimensions of "church type" religious commitment; two related to group involvement—associational versus communal involvement—and two related to religious orientation—doctrinal orthodoxy versus devotionalism.[6] Fukuyama also developed a different four-tier schemata which described ways that persons are religious: cognitive, cultic, creedal, and devotional. He examined the correlation of these dimensions to basic demographic indicators and discovered the dimensions "were related differently to one another and varied in relation to basic social and demographic correlates such as sex, age, education and social class" (Roof, 1979, p. 21).

Another stage of development has been to identify facets of religion which presumably are universal. Glock and Stark's first attempt at this resulted in five core dimensions, which have since undergone greater refinement and revision with the final creation of eight dimensions: experiential, ritualistic, devotional, belief, knowledge, consequential, communal, and particularistic.[7] Lenski's four were incorporated into this model. Davidson and Knudsen took the universalizing tendency a step further, creating two umbrella categories, religious orientation and religious commitment. The first dimension is further subdivided into five components: specific beliefs, tendencies to particularism, religious knowledge, communal orientation, and ethical application of beliefs to one's life. And the second dimension is divided into two: religious consciousness—the extent to which religion is part of one's sense of identity—and religious participation (Roberts, 1990, p. 18). They argued the second dimension, religious commitment, was the more valid measure of religiosity. This differed from other studies by giving more credence to an individual's personal assessment of the impact of religion, and less importance to religious content and knowledge.

In summation, the study of religiosity has moved from doctrinal and unifocal to more synthetic ones. The shift has required new theories, empirical testing, and continued redefinition and refinement. Assumptions of multidimensionality are held by most, and particularity of populations are more closely regarded.[8] Generally, researchers appear to have focused on correlations among dimensions more than on exploring the content and meaning of the dimensions themselves. There is ongoing debate over the generality or specificity of the instruments and how they are utilized. Yet no approach can be judged inappropriate outright, since the instrument is dependent upon the intended purpose and level of analysis the researcher seeks to investigate.

AFRICAN AMERICAN RELIGIOSITY

The single most consistent measure of religiosity has been church attendance. Among African Americans, we find that as early as 1903, the black church was deemed the "social center of Negro life" and membership was considered normative for the black community. In regard to southern Negroes, Du Bois (1903) concluded:

Practically every American Negro is a church member. Some, to be sure, are not regularly enrolled, and a few do not habitually attend services, but practically, a proscribed people must have a social center, and that center for this people is the Negro church. The census of 1890 showed nearly 24,000 Negro churches in the country, with a total enrolled membership of over 2.5 million, or ten actual church members to every 28 persons, and in some Southern states one in every two persons (p. 215).

In *The Negro Church,* Mays and Nicholson (1933) provide some of the earliest confirmation of differences in male-female attendance rates. Though not totally reliable, church membership statistics combined with observations were sufficiently accurate for them to confidently report that women outnumbered men at worship services nearly two to one. The pastors in the study were in agreement "that there are more women members than men, and that women do more of the church work" (p. 101).

In a 1955 study of a mill town named Kent, Lewis (1971) found that 90 percent of the black population had been affiliated with some church at one time or another, and nearly 60 percent were presently considered active or on church rolls, with 33 percent of that membership in attendance on a given Sunday. Admittedly these are low attendance rates, but Lewis suggests they should not be regarded as the sole indicator of the church's impact in the community. He points us to other social and cultural determinants which influence black religiosity.

In the first place, going to church is highly approved behavior and even the chronic non church goer will indicate that he should go more often—and goes occasionally; in the second place, there are special church events such as the "annual meeting," communion and homecoming which are more fully attended and which loom large in the anticipation and memory of most people (p. 101).

Similar to other black church scholars, Lewis (1971) noted a distinct disparity in male/female attendance (women were more frequent worshippers), the leadership was male-dominated, yet women exerted formidable influence in the affairs of the church.

Prevalent stereotypes of black religiosity have stated that blacks are more emotional in their religion, more otherworldly in their theological orientation and more churched than whites.[9] Several studies have tested these assumptions. In one of the first, Lenski (1963) found that blacks score higher than whites only on the measure for "devotionalism." Examination of attendance differences among blacks and whites yield mixed conclusions. Lenski ranked black church attendance between white Catholics and white Protestants. Norval Glenn (1964) found no difference in attendance between white and non-white Protestants,[10] while Bernard Lazerwitz (1961) found higher rates of attendance for blacks when comparing black and white Baptists.[11] An analysis of Gallup data available from the late 1950s through the 1960s by Nelsen and his associates (1971) revealed that Catholics have the highest attendance rates and white and non-white Protestants reverse positions in various years. The latest poll year included in their analysis, 1969, supported Glenn's findings.

Emotional religious expression and theological conservatism among African Americans was the focus of another study by Nelsen and Nelsen (1975). They analyzed Gallup data on four dimensions: experiential, ideological, ritualistic, and intellectual. The first significant finding was a slightly higher incidence of "a mystical or religious experience" among whites than blacks, and region (north versus south) was inversely related to experiential religiosity for both. Southerners overall reported more direct religious experiences. Secondly, black and white Protestants scored similarly on the ideological measurement, with sectarianism being more prevalent among lower educated southerners from small communities. Frequency of and reliance upon prayer was one of two measures of the ritualistic component. Rather than racial differences surfacing, frequency of prayer was positively associated with age and inversely associated with sex, showing females more likely to turn to prayer. On the other component of the ritualistic dimension, church attendance, there was a greater attendance among blacks, and was positively correlated to age, education, occupation, and inversely related to sex (greater for females), region (greater for the south), and residential size. There were no significant cultural differences in the level of religious knowledge. Nelsen suggests "the stereotype that blacks are otherworldly and thus not concerned with temporal problems must be rejected" (p. 81).

In recent years, religious research has expanded to include a core of studies specifically focusing on African Americans. Taylor's (1988a) finding confirmed the same characteristics of African American church attendance as the Gallup data.

Women, older respondents, those with more education, and persons with higher occupational status all reported attending church more frequently than their counterparts. Region and urbanicity were not significantly related to church attendance. Respondents with fewer years of education and those who resided in the South were more likely than their counterparts to report having had a mystical or religious experience (p. 115).[12]

Taylor also found married persons participate in religious activities more frequently than never married persons; and nearly 80 percent of the respondents reported praying daily. The study did not give credence to the general belief that lower socioeconomic blacks are more involved in religious activities.

Studies of black non-affiliated persons has been another focus of religiosity scholarship among African Americans. I will briefly mention three pertinent studies. Welch (1978) studied black "non-affiliates,[13] Catholics, and Protestants. His findings revealed non-affiliation was characteristic of younger blacks and decreased with age, a higher percentage of males identify as non-affiliates than females, and socioeconomic status was not impacted by religious affiliation (p. 292). In light of the importance usually attributed to the black church as a religiosociopolitical center of the black community, these findings invite new attention to African Americans for whom affiliation with organized religion is not primary. Welch suggests,

the study of non-affiliation might at least provide suggestive evidence about how well those black Americans have fared who choose not to receive the benefits or burdens church membership confers, evidence which has relevance for the continuing debate over the functionality of the black church for the black community (p. 289).

Nelsen (1988) uses cross-sectional data from the Gallup Unchurched American Study of 1978 in his study of unchurched black Americans. His designation of "churched" is more specific than Welch's and distinguishes between those with nominal church preferences, but who are not members or rarely attend, from those who are actively more religious in a formal way. "Churched" describes "a person who is both a member of a church or synagogue and who has attended church or synagogue in the last six months, apart from weddings, funerals, or special holidays" (p. 398). He found that while blacks have a higher rate of church membership than whites, they are also exhibiting an increasing growth rate of "no religious preference"[14] and the unchurched largely reside in metropolitan areas.

A third study found one in ten African Americans were not presently religiously affiliated, and nearly 10 percent reported they had never attended a religious service as an adult except for a funeral or wedding. It is not clear to what extent these two classifications, non-attenders and non-affiliated, coincide. However, confirming previous findings, non-affiliates are more apt to be younger males residing outside the South. Non-attenders likewise were more likely to be young men with lower levels of income and education. Widows ranked highest among non-attenders, followed by those never married. Married people are most likely to be attenders. This study also found high percentages of non-affiliated and non-attenders who report praying every day, respectively 40.9 percent and 48.2 percent. Perhaps equally startling was evidence that nearly 50 percent of non-affiliated and over 50 percent of non-attenders assessed themselves as very or fairly religious (Taylor, 1988b, pp.

126–139). Considering the past emphasis applied to church attendance as a measurement of religiosity, this study suggests traditional definitions of religiosity may need some reconstruction, to take into account self-reporting of religiosity in the absence of a communal context.

FEMALE RELIGIOSITY

Sociological studies have identified that women's dominant image of God as "healer" is positively related to church attendance;[15] religiosity has a limited impact on sex-role attitudes; and sex predicts closeness to God.[16] Attempts to explain generational transmission of religious participation has also been studied, often from the perspective of formative experiences and socialization. In families where both parents are Protestant, Catholic, or non-religious, the majority of the children will emulate their parents' patterns of religious behavior. In instances of mixed Protestant marriages or Protestant/Catholic unions, the children are more apt to follow the mother's patterns and beliefs (Nelsen, 1990).

Given these descriptors of female religiosity, can one explain women's constant predilection for religious participation? Explanations have generally fallen into three larger categories: (1) psychological theories, (2) socialization theory, and (3) structural location theory.[17] Psychological theories suggest women are naturally inclined toward religion, women experience guilt at greater levels than men and use religion as a relief agent, and God is imagined and functions as a male father figure. Socialization theories (Mol, 1984; Thompson, 1991) give prominence to the role of culture. They account for the religiosity of women by analyzing early childhood experiences and female socialization, which has emphasized appropriate female attributes such as submissive and nurturing—qualities which are considered consonant with a religious environment.[18] Structural location theory has been operationalized in various ways, but generally it emphasizes three aspects of women's location in society: (1) child rearing responsibilities of females;[19] (2) rates of labor force participation among females;[20] and (3) women's attitudes toward work and its relationship to one's valuation of family.[21]

To my knowledge, no studies specifically address African-American religiosity with attention to the gender differences in participation. The religiousness of blacks has generally been compared with their white counterparts, in particular concerning church attendance rates. Isolation and appraisal of this variable, along with a discussion of urbanization's impact on the black church in the twentieth century, will enhance our understanding of black religiosity.

As early as the 1930s, Mays and Nicholson (1933) expressed concern that greater opportunities for blacks, a result of urbanization, would effect the choice of ministry as a vocation for black men. Recognizing that there was only one professional domain with unbarred access to African-American men, religion, greater opportunities would be a positive racial gain. However, they were concerned about a potential decline in church leadership. Mays and Nicholson do not suggest what the consequences of similar economic and professional access for black women would mean for the life of the church or female participation in it.

Frazier (1964) predicted different consequences from greater economic access among African Americans. The upward mobility of blacks, and a decrease in the social control of the church over their lives, would be a positive and necessary step toward full integration of blacks into mainstream America. He did not bemoan the potential loss to clergy or of the centrality of the church in the black community. Rather it was an institution which would have outlived its utility once blacks had become less marginalized in American society. Since Frazier first predicted the demise of the black church, nearly forty years have passed and neither urbanization nor secularizing forces have brought about the extinction of the black church. Increased social integration, desegregation in public accommodations and education, gains in black political participation, and the legislative legacy of the civil rights movement, which has benefited Americans in general and African Americans especially, have not preempted the necessity nor the desire for the black church. Nowhere is this more evident than in the persistent participation of upwardly mobile black women in church life.

Vitality, activism, and prophetic proclamations are frequently cited characteristics of the black church. As the historic social center of the black community the church has addressed economic empowerment and educational achievement; provided a base for political and leadership training; combatted racial injustice and discrimination; and created and sustained a cultural heritage. As a consequence, one can assume African Americans have expectations of this institution. Johnstone (1988) suggests that if or when the black church fails to "offer a response to injustice when the problems are perceived as changeable, people are encouraged toward 'secular' rather than sacred resources" (p. 230). The results would not be a mass exodus from the church; rather the disenchantment would result in a shift in the attraction and reasons for its viability to the community. In other words, persons would still attend but with different expectations. The communal associations, habitual attendance, and the historic centrality of the black church will function to maintain the social group and ward off the radical personal disjuncture that disaffiliation would create. This seems to be particularly true for black women in the church.

Throughout much of the history of the black church, women have been refused ordination to the clerical position. However, some women preached anyhow and others agitated for official recognition. Lobbying on the part of women resulted in a structural change in the AME church in the creation of the office of deaconess in 1900. In the mid-twentieth century black Methodism began to accept women into full ordination. The Progressive National Baptist Convention now ordains women. And although the National Baptist Convention, USA, Inc., National Baptist Convention, Unincorporated and The Church of God in Christ do not have an official policy prohibiting ordination of women, in practice the ordination of female clergy is a rare occurance.

Absent from religious scholarship are inquires into the allegiance of women to the black religious tradition. Black women have functioned in a variety of roles and tasks, most of which would be deemed "supportive" and/or secondary leadership roles.[22] In the past and present, they have labored as ushers, choir members, Sunday School teachers, cooks, deaconesses, and so on. They are lauded as spiritual mothers, missionaries, and visionaries, considered the "glue" or "backbone" of the congregation, and often rewarded with great respect. Outside the church, they have engaged in community organizing and political initiatives. Black church women have been significantly involved in woman's suffrage, anti-lynching campaigns, establishment of the Atlanta Baptist Female Seminary (now Spelman College), the social gospel movement, and the civil rights movement. Providing support for the NAACP, campaigning against negative stereotypes of blacks in the media, and working collaboratively with white religious groups should also be recognized as part of their service. The creation and vitality of women's auxiliaries and conventions provide further evidence of black women's commitment to (1) their religious heritage; (2) addressing the specific needs of black women; (3) institutional autonomy; and (4) self-governance.[23] Still their experiences remain absent from academic inquiry and their voices muted.

CRITIQUE AND CONCLUSIONS

A vast body of material has been presented in this chapter. A brief recapitulation of the salient features will help focus these concluding remarks. The study of religiosity initially relied upon one-dimensional measures, concentrated primarily on Christianity, and compiled consequent demographics and determinants of a particular group's religiosity (i.e., white rural Southerners). It has advanced to include multivariate scales, the study of non-traditional religions, the study of the religiously affiliated and non-affiliated, and distinctions within the black religious community. In general, since the mid-1960s there has been no clear evidence to indicate that white or black Protestants are more religious than the other. What is distinctive is Catholics consistently outrank other religious groups in America on scales of religiosity. Whites and blacks rank second or third depending on the variables and the year. There were no racial distinctions in levels of religious knowledge between whites and blacks. Whites report having slightly more mystical, experiential encounters with God than blacks, while blacks score higher on measures of devotionalism.

A constant finding irrespective of race has been that women are more religious than men, and attend church more often. The most likely participants in a black church are women, older people, married persons, and those with advanced education and higher occupational status. The least likely are young males who live in the metropolitan North. It has been established that disaffiliation decreases with age, and one's socioeconomic status is not affected by church involvement. The literature also reflects an increasing growth rate of black persons claiming "no preference."

The absence of studies that closely examine the allegiance of women to black religious tradition suggests several future directions of inquiry. First, a more definite formulation of religiosity is necessary. Second, theories discussed in this chapter are among seminal attempts to break the mystery surrounding the greater religiosity of women. All three bodies—psychological, socialization theories, and structural location theory—are limited. There may be partial answers in all of these assessments, but alone neither provide an adequate interpretation of black female church attendance. This is in part due to the inattention to race specificity when describing and interpreting female religious experience. The impact of race in black women's lives, coupled with the different socioeconomic realities, family structure, cultural norms, and so on, are sufficient to indicate that other factors may influence black church women's attendance in distinction from the determinants of white female attenders in "mainline" congregations. While convenient, it is inadequate to assume that gender socialization and the social or psychological needs of black women parallel those of white females in America. Nor can one assume similar behaviors (i.e., attending church) are generated by the same forces and carry the same significance for black women without investigation. Such a posture would run the danger of giving tacit support to the concept of female essentialism.

A void in black church scholarship is the lack of an interpretation of the gender disparities. Admittedly scholars cannot investigate every query that results from their research. However, given the historical reality of attendance, participation, and fidelity of women to the black church, disregard for the particularities of the African-American women's religious experience is unacceptable and handicaps all. Without rigorous and critical analysis of black men's and women's religiosity, one cannot determine whether the secularization of the church pushed men out and propelled more women in; whether women who have left the church express similar sentiments as men; if there is a social bias in the black community which allows males to circumvent or rebel against religious instruction; or what the rates of disaffiliation for women actually are.

There is a paucity of fundamental data on the religiosity of African-American women. The present emphasis in many congregations on the black male and "why men aren't in the church" has allowed presumption and speculation to answer "why women are" or assume she always will be the "backbone" of the church. What are her perceptions, attitudes, likes/dislikes of the black church? Does the imbalance of black men in the church impact the worship atmosphere or her "sense of wholeness"? What does it mean to be the majority in the pew and the minority in the pulpit, and other focal leadership roles in the church? Do black women hear the exigencies of their existential situation addressed?

In addition to the limitations of research on female religiosity, major studies on the black church have depended upon written documentation and church records, the perspective and/or recounting of the pastor or clergy (usually male) to interpret the contributions and activities of the black church, or either focuses upon the clergy as the object of study. The findings are often generalized not to the specific population but to the black church at large. Several limitations inherent in such a methodology come to mind: (1) possible embellishment, (2) the fallacy of equating the leader's perception with the membership's, (3) the possible bias of official institutional documentation to record predominantly the voices and actions of the official "leadership," which is male-dominated in black churches, and (4) the muting of black women's voices as agents and interpreters of the church.

Another possible approach to analyzing the intersections of religiosity and gender among African Americans could be rooted in comparative analysis or alternative expressions of black religiosity outside of Protestantism, namely the American Muslim Mission, the Nation of Islam, and the Jehovah Witnesses. In most urban centers these three groups are fixtures in the black community. The Islamic groups have a high percentage of black men, while the Jehovah Witnesses contain a significant number of family units, including the black male. It might be instructive to black Protestantism to understand the ability of these religious faiths to attract and retain black females and males. How the identities and lives of religious women in these traditions are similar or distinct from African-American women in the black church tradition is an obvious point of departure.

Finally, the study of African-American women's lives is warranted for the contribution this makes to our understanding of Protestantism in America. Much of the historical and sociological studies of American religion have relied and focused upon the trends, contributions, and theologies of "mainline" (white) denominations. Such dominance of religious scholarship lends support to the perception of white religious experience as the normative standard for evaluating religion's impact on American culture, politics, and values. This majority/minority dichotomization must be deconstructed and a more inclusive rendering of American religious life and practice depicted. Black religious culture should not be regarded as marginal to the religious landscape, neither as a simple replication or an abridgement of white Protestantism. Examination of shifts in Protestant piety, increases and declines in attendance, the church's support of family values, and the influence of "gender equality" and feminism upon parishioners are just a sampling of issues which can be enriched by incorporating dynamics of African-American Protestant culture and particularly the perspectives of those who participate most consistently, African-American women.

NOTES

1. Previous usage of this sole criteria of religiosity has yielded some profitable research at the broadest levels, such as church members versus non-church members in terms of divorce rates, racial attitudes, and so on. The limitations of this "uni-dimension" are numerous. It ignores those who have an unconventional faith or meaning system, assumes that a single index will be an accurate predictor of other religious behavior, and does not take into account that "different churches emphasize different behaviors as signs of faithfulness." See Keith A. Roberts, *Religion in Sociological Perspective*, 2d ed. (Belmont, CA: Wadsworth Publishing Co., 1990), p. 14.

2. This third factor intends to assess non-organizational religious involvement in contrast to the other two. This variable included four questions: (1) "How often do you read religious materials?" (2) "How often do you watch or listen to religious programs on television or radio?" (3) "How often do you pray?" and (4) "How often do you ask someone to pray for you?" See Robert J. Taylor, "Structural Determinants of Religious Participation Among Black Americans," *Review of Religious Research, 30* (1988a), p. 117.

3. Persons in this school include Will Herberg, Lloyd Warner, Phillip Hammond, and Robert Bellah. According to Bellah its characteristics include "certain common elements of religious orientation that the great majority of Americans share. These . . . provide a religious dimension for the whole fabric of American life, including the political sphere. This public religious dimension is expressed in a set of beliefs, symbols and rituals" which have their focus in public political events, not worship centers; it is manifest in national crises, holidays, and presidential inaugurations. Empirical research on civil religion is still in its formative stages (Roof, 1979, p. 29).

4. Thomas Luckman and Milton J. Yinger are prominent investigators of this type of religiosity. Invisible religion examines people's ultimate concerns that have no institutional religious forms. The aim of the researcher is to answer, "How is the person religious?" rather than "How religious is the person?" For instance, Yinger's work among students is deliberately nondoctrinal, and sensitive to "privatized religious meaning systems" that get at "awareness of and interest in the continuing recurrent, permanent problems of human existence" (Roof, 1979, p. 31).

5. Religion as alternative meaning systems goes beyond examining people's expression of ultimate concern to the "symbolic constructions used in defining and ordering reality." Roof (1979) writes that central to the inquiry is "how people interpret experiences and events in their lives that call for some kind of judgement about the nature of reality." Robert Wuthnow, as cited by Roof, has identified four types of meaning systems: theism, individualism, social science, and mysticism, each distinguished by one "primary force governing life" (p. 33).

6. "Associational involvement refers to frequency of attendance at church services and participation in the workings of the institution. Communal involvement is a measure of how many of one's close friends and relatives were members of the same religious group . . . . Doctrinal orthodoxy refers to agreeement with the central beliefs set forth by that denomination. Devotionalism refers to a sense of personal contact with God" (Roberts, 1990, p. 15). For a complete account of the study see Gerhard Lenski, *The Religious Factor* (New York, NY: Anchor Books, 1963).

7. More is not always desirable however, especially if when operationalized the

dimensions are constrained by traditional conceptions of religion. For instance, a very devout Congregationalist could score low on the belief scale, which asks, "do you believe that a child is born into the world already guilty of sin?" and yet be faithful to the teachings of their church. This sort of internal bias seems to impose a definition of religion that would make one Christian denomination more devout than another. For a description of each dimension see Roberts (1990), pp. 15–17.

8. In a series of studies implemented by Morton King and Richard Hunt to test the multidimensionality hypothesis, it was shown that their sample manifested even more dimensions (13) and there were subtle delineations in the dimensions. These new dimensions had gone undetected in prior studies heavily reliant on student populations. Hunt & King's data base were actual church members from several denominations in Texas (Roof, 1979, p. 29).

9. E. T. Kruger surmised in 1932 that "religion is to the Negro what music and poetry are to the white man." Cited in Hart Nelsen, Raytha Yokley, and Anne K. Nelsen, *The Black Church in America* (New York, NY: Basic Books, 1971), p. 9.

10. Glenn found no difference in church attendance between blacks and whites based on the Gallup polls of 1957. However, he says the polls should be regarded as the most general of interpretations and other factors support a greater religiosity hypothesis: more non-whites watch or listen to religious services on television or radio than whites; non-whites perceive a decrease in the influence of religion in American life; and Negroes tend to be traditional, fundamentalist Christians. See Norval Glenn, "Negro Religion and Negro Status in the United States," in Louis Schneider, ed., *Religion, Culture and Society* (New York, NY: Wiley, 1964), p. 625.

11. These findings were the results of two surveys, one conducted in 1957 and the other in 1958 by The Survey Research Center of the University of Michigan. Lazerwitz reports that 84 percent of Negro Baptists responded they attend church regularly or often, in contrast to 69 percent of white Baptists. He implies from these proportions that church attendance for blacks in general is higher than for whites, especially since Blacks are overwhelmingly Baptist and Baptists attend church more than other Protestant groups. Since Baptists comprise less than 20 percent of the sample, it would have been informative to have an analysis of church attendance between white and black Protestants as a whole. See Bernard Lazerwitz, "Some Factors Associated with Variations in Church Attendance," *Social Forces*, 39 (1961), p. 304.

12. A complete documentation of the study can be found in Taylor, "Structural Determinants of Religious Participation Among Black Americans."

13. The total data pool was 18,182. There were 1,516 black respondents (1,316 black Protestants, 121 black Catholics, and 79 black non-affiliates). Churched blacks were distinguished from their unchurched counterparts by their answers to the question, "What is your religious preference?" found in Michael R. Welch, "The Unchurched: Black Religious Non-Affiliates," *Journal for the Scientific Study of Religion*, 17 (1978), pp. 289–293.

14. In 1983, blacks had a church membership rate of 76 percent, and whites were members at a rate of 69 percent. In 1957 whites and blacks differed less than one percent in rates of "no religious preference," 2.6 percent and 3.5 percent respectively. By 1983 there was a 3 percent difference, 9 percent among whites to 12 percent among blacks. See Hart M. Nelsen, "Unchurched Black Americans: Patterns of Religiosity and Affiliations," *Review of Religious Research*, 30(2), pp. 114–125.

15. Nelsen, Cheek, and Au found that women more often than men imagine God

as "healer" rather than "King" or as relational. All the images, however, were positively related to church attendance. See Hart M. Nelsen, Neil H. Cheek Jr., and Paul Au, "Gender Differences in Images of God," *Journal for the Scientific Study of Religion,* 24 (4) (1985), pp. 396–402.

16. Kathryn Feltey and Margaret Poloma found that sex is a predictor of reported closeness to God. However, while there is a gender difference in perceived closeness to God, they also discovered that variance in most dimensions of religiosity (between men and women) can be accounted for by "gender ideology." See "From Sex Differences to Gender Role Beliefs: Exploring Effects on Six Dimensions of Religiosity," *Sex Roles,* 25 (3/4) (1991), pp. 181–193.

17. A thorough summation of these three frameworks can be found in David DeVaus and Ian McAllister's "Gender Differences in Religion: A Test of the Structural Location Theory," *American Sociological Review,* 52 (August 1987), pp. 472–484.

18. Hans Mol's socialization theory centers on the cultural reinforcement of sex-typed behaviors which maintain the gender disparity in measures of religiousity. He states, "religious orientations aid conflict-resolving, emotionally healing, integrating functions with [which] both religion and women are traditionally occupied." On the other hand, drive and aggressiveness characterize male behaviors, which find reinforcement in the larger society. Hans Mol, "The Domestication of the Church," *St. Mark's Review,* 119 (1984), pp. 3–12. A similar position is argued by Thompson, who rejects the biological basis of intrinsic differences between male and female religiosity. He concludes that religiosity of men and women is attributable to "feminine" and "masculine" orientations (world views), not innate religious predispositions. For further discussion, see Edward H. Thompson, Jr., "Beneath the Status Characteristic: Gender Variations in Religiousness," *Journal for the Scientific Study of Religion,* 30 (1991), pp. 381–394.

19. Studies have found that children's participation in Sunday School has drawn mothers into the church; the child-rearing role of females leads to social isolation, of which church involvement is a mechanism to overcome isolation; primary child providers who don't work outside the home have the available time to be active in church; and children discourage religious involvement because of the time-consuming task of child rearing (DeVaus and McAllister, 1987, p. 473).

20. It is suggested that workforce participation militates against religious commitment; provides alternative sources of identity, values, legitimation, and commitments; and provides adequate opportunities for social interaction to alleviate isolation. Ibid., p. 473.

21. Theories in this framework rely on the other structural location emphases. There is an assumption that women will value family over workforce participation (a male priority). This priority combined with a sense of deprivation (generated by the status of non-workforce participation) may produce an interest in religion. Religion serves to affirm family values and provides psychic comfort for the child care provider. Ibid., p. 474.

22. For a discussion of several prominent clergywomen of the 19th century see Jualynne Dodson, "Nineteenth Century A.M.E. Preaching Women," in Hilhah F. Thomas and Rosemary Skinner Keller, eds., *Women in New Worlds* (Nashville, TN: Abingdon Press, 1981), and William L. Andrews, *Sisters of the Spirit* (Bloomington, IN: Indiana University Press, 1986).

23. Extensive discussion of the activism and initiatives of Baptist women in the early

twentieth century can be found in Higginbotham's *Righteous Discontent: The Women's Movement in the Black Baptist Church, 1880–1920* (Cambridge, MA: Harvard University Press, 1993), and the role of the church women in the civil rights movement in David Garrow, ed., *The Montgomery Bus Boycott and the Women Who Started It: The Memoir of Jo Ann Gibson Robinson* (Knoxville, TN: University of Tennessee Press, 1987). Sanctified traditions have not been without their active church and community workers. See Cheryl Townsend Gilkes, "The Roles of Church and Community Mothers: Ambivalent American Sexism or Fragmented African Familyhood" in *Journal of Feminist Studies in Religion,* 2 (Spring 1986), pp. 41–59, and Jualynne E. Dodson and Cheryl Townsend Gilkes, "Something Within: Social Change and Collective Endurance in the Sacred World of Black Christian Women," in Rosemary Ruether and Rosemary S. Keller, *Women and Religion in America,* vol. 3 (New York, NY: Harper & Row, 1987), pp. 80–130.

REFERENCES

Andrews, W. L. (1986). *Sisters of the spirit.* Bloomington, IN: Indiana University Press.

DeBerg, B. (1990). *Ungodly women.* Minneapolis: Fortress Press.

DeVaus, D. & I. McAllister. (1987). "Gender Differences in Religion: A Test of the Structural Location Theory." *American Sociological Review,* 52 (August), pp. 472–484.

Dodson, J. E. (1981). "Nineteenth century A.M.E. preaching women," in H. F. Thomas and R. Skinner Keller (eds.), *Women in new worlds.* Nashville, TN: Abingdon Press.

Dodson, J. E., & C. Townsend Gilkes. (1987). "Something within: Social change and collective endurance in the sacred world of black Christian women," in R. Ruether and R. S. Keller, *Women and Religion in America,* vol. 3. New York, NY: Harper & Row.

Douglas, A. (1977). *The feminization of American culture.* New York, NY: Doubleday.

Du Bois, W.E.B. (1903, 1982). *The souls of black folk.* New York, NY: American Library.

Feltey, K. & M. Poloma. (1991). "From sex differences to gender role beliefs: Exploring effects on six dimensions of religiosity." *Sex Roles,* 25(3/4), pp. 181–193.

Frazier, E. F. (1964). *The Negro church in America.* New York, NY: Schocken Books.

Garrow, D. (ed.). (1987). *The Montgomery bus boycott and the women who started it: The memoir of Jo Ann Gibson Robinson.* Knoxville, TN: University of Tennessee Press.

Gilkes, C. T. (1986). "The roles of church and community mothers: Ambivalent American sexism or fragmented African familyhood." *Journal of Feminist Studies in Religion,* 2, pp. 41–59.

Glenn, N. (1964). "Negro religion and Negro status in the United States," in L. Schneider (ed.), *Religion, Culture and Society.* New York, NY: Wiley.

Higginbotham, E. B. (1993). *Righteous discontent: The women's movement in the black Baptist church, 1880–1920.* Cambridge, MA: Harvard University Press.

Hunsberger, B. (1989). "A short version of the Christian orthodoxy scale." *Journal for the Scientific Study of Religion,* 28, pp. 360–365.

Johnstone, R. L. (1988). *Religion in society: A sociology of religion,* 3d ed. Englewood Cliffs, New Jersey: Prentice-Hall.

Lazerwitz, B. (1961). "Some factors associated with variations in church attendance." *Social Forces, 39*, pp. 301–308.

Lenski, G. (1963). *The religious factor.* New York, NY: Anchor Books.

Lewis, H. (1971). "Blackways of Kent: Religion and salvation," in H. M. Nelsen, R. C. Yokley, & A. K. Nelsen (eds.), *The black church in America.* New York, NY: Basic Books.

Mays, B. & J. W. Nicholson. (1933). *The Negro's Church.* New York, NY: Institute of Social and Religious Research.

Mol, H. (1984). "The domestication of the church." *St. Mark's Review, 119*, pp. 3–12.

Nelsen, H. (1988). "Unchurched black Americans: Patterns of religiosity and affiliation." *Review of Religious Research, 29*(4), pp. 398–412.

———. (1990). "The religious identification of children in interfaith marriages." *Review of Religious Research, 32*, pp. 122–134.

Nelsen, H., & A. K. Nelsen. (1975). *The Black church in the sixties.* Lexington, KY: University of Kentucky Press.

Nelsen, H., N. H. Cheek, Jr., & Paul Au. (1985). "Gender differences in images of God." *Journal for the Scientific Study of Religion, 24*(4), pp. 396–402.

Nelsen, H., R. Yokley, & A. K. Nelsen. (1971). *The black church in America.* New York, NY: Basic Books.

Roberts, K. A. (1990). *Religion in sociological perspective,* 2d ed. Belmont, CA: Wadsworth Publishing Co.

Roof, W. C. (1979). "Concepts and indicators of religious commitment: A critical review," in R. Wuthnow (ed.), *The religious dimension.* New York, NY: Academic Press.

Taylor, R. J. (1988a). "Structural determinants of religious participation among black Americans." *Review of Religious Research, 30*(2), pp. 114–125.

———. (1988b). "Correlates of religious non-involvement among black Americans." *Review of Religious Research, 30*(2), pp. 126–139.

Thompson, E. H. (1991). "Beneath the status characteristic: Gender variations in religiousness." *Journal for the Scientific Study of Religion, 30*, pp. 381–394.

Welch, M. R. (1978). "The unchurched: Black religious non-affiliates." *Journal for the Scientific Study of Religion, 17*, pp. 289–293.

Woodson, C. G. (1972). *The history of the Negro church,* 3d ed. Washington, DC: Associated Publishers.

Voice and Empowerment:
The Struggle for Poetic Expression

Luis J. Rodriguez

Gee, it feels like dancing!

—Statement by three-year-old girl after drinking
sparkling water for the first time

Listen to children: the way they speak, using poetry without a command of language; the way they find connections to feelings, to concepts, to things; their use of metaphor. Making metaphor is one of the basic building blocks of human communication. Children embody this, as do many cultures. Among Guatemala's Quiche Indians, for example, there is no word for spouse. One's love/sexual companion is known as "the keeper of my eyes."[1]

What does a revolutionary Marxist poet have to say about this in the time of the so-called "end of Communism?" Plenty. The rapidly evolving electronics revolution is transforming every aspect of industrial society, including those socialist governments formed on the basis of mechanical productive energy.

The growth of the present technology also spells the end of capitalist social relations as we know them. The development of the microchip means that the social productive capability can be accessible for all. Why shouldn't the producer be owner of the product? If one can ask the question, then the possibility of an answer already exists. While communism appears to have lost its political potency, it is being reborn in the productive forces metamorphosing as we speak. American revolutionary Nelson Peery (1993) expounds:

Scientists and engineers are developing instruments that eventually could expand our mental capabilities as much as the industrial revolution expanded our physical capabilities. More than that, we stand at the threshold of eliminating mental as well as physical labor (p. 5).

Since politics is the expression of economics, a social revolution is inevitable. The 1992 Los Angeles riots are reflective of this process. People sense, if they don't quite understand, that there's no need for hunger, homelessness, and illiteracy with the vast technological resources and wealth this country possesses.

More so, these fundamental changes should be the basis for the greatest unleashing of human creative energy the world has yet known. Here is the crux of the crisis: the liberation of social creativity is blocked by the outmoded relations of capitalist society, which depended on backbreaking menial work or highly skilled mechanical work, both of which required a relatively subservient and culturally fettered labor force.

This is the truth of our age. And this is also reflected at the most basic levels of language expression.

POETRY AS BIRTHRIGHT

All people, by virtue of their innate creative and communicative capabilities, are born poets (not that they all will be, but that they all can be). Still, the power relations of this society, based on the present economic system, are the biggest impediment to the nurturing of the poet in each of us.

By poetry I mean the complex word shaping that conveys the intimate life (in all stages of its development) of a human being. It is how information, images, sounds, and feelings find countenance through poetic structure. The poet becomes a prism from which the myriad light rays of the natural world are refracted into a singular dimension—the poem through the body of the poet. The quality that best conveys what a person brings out of a poem is called "voice," which, although linked, is more than what comes out of the vocal chords.

Anne Schultz (1992), of the "Writing from the Source" program at the Chicago Teachers' Center, said this about voice discovery in a child:

We have a momentary glimpse of the writer . . . certainly tiny, easy not to notice because it is so small. But there is the beginning of voice here, and of a sense of audience that is real, however, small; and if we listen and let this piece of writing stand, we are helping the writer to embark on a journey of discovery of his voice and his stories that will also be a discovery of the world around him and his place in it (p. 2).

What children invoke in schoolyards may not be considered poems; at best, they are only trying to get over fractured concepts, based on their real and imaginative life experiences. But this can and should be a strong foundation for poetic expression or, as Robert E. Peterson (1991) writes,

Children's learning should be centered in their own experience, language, and culture. For this to happen, the classroom environment should be "language rich," allowing the children to develop their language and thinking abilities in as natural a setting as possible (p. 159).

Instead, what I find in North American schools is the forced reduction of poetry, or any written expression, to lines, to rules, to syntax, to grammar—to the static miens of language construction.

The result, I believe, is that most children are denied their natural impulses for poetry. They are so often defeated on such things as spelling that they turn away from writing as a vital means of expression or empowerment. Or, if they learn their lessons well, some students become good writers, all t's crossed and all i's dotted, but end up concealing with "proper" language what should otherwise be honestly revealed.

Educator Patrick L. Courts (1991) puts it clearly: "Language is not simply a system of phonemes; it is not simply a set of surface structures . . . language is the possibility of making meaning of and in the world" (p. 7). The current classroom, however, is the governance of the static, the conceptual, the abstract over the living, vibrant, breathing artist in everyone.

Lesson plans, grade systems, tests, tracking, and authoritative teachers continue to be the main aspects of U.S. schooling (although based on the needs of a dying, industrial-based society). The main aspect instead should be the intrinsic powers each student brings to the class. Here's Donald Oliver (1989) on the subject:

The crude assumption that specialization and hierarchy are indicators of a progressive culture and society has been transformed into conventional wisdom. We expect modern societies to be differentiated into economic, political, legal, cultural, and health care systems, each run by a pyramidal management structure. Modern schools and universities which prepare people for life and work are commonly organized around these categories (p. 12).

Victory is the strongest mortar for building artists in any field. My seventeen-year-old daughter Andrea recently clarified this point for me. Two years ago, Andrea had skipped out about thirty times from one of her classes. I asked her why. "I'm tired of being defeated every day in that class," she responded. So Andrea preferred not to show up at all, even if it meant failing the class. Dictated from above, the issue for her was not whether she attended class or not (an issue for the teacher, perhaps), but that she could not participate in a relationship in which she was constantly on the losing end.

Once she began to connect learning with her own self-interest (tied to a sense of validation as a person, not just as a student) and to envision pathways toward victory, she not only attended classes, but excelled in them.

Although this is true for all students, so-called minority youth have to contend with issues of "race" and cultural dominance (and often class) that most non-minority youth don't address. In response, "the cultural experience of minorities in the United States requires they become not only marginal persons but also bicultural ones, capable of demonstrating competence both in the larger society and within their own ethnic community" (Spencer, et al., 1991). Unfortunately, when minority students insist on expressing their cultural difference as a way to mediate their identity and existence in an Anglo-dominated society, their activity is often linked to "cultural deviance" (p. 367).

In my visits to a number of suburban Chicago schools, I found that where there has been a growth in the number of African and Latino students, there has been an increase in the use of "gang lists," expulsions, and extra-security responses based on manner of dress (for example, hip-hop clothes), talk, and demeanor. I've talked to many such youth who feel they are being "judged" by aspects not related to their abilities, their desires to learn, or actual achievements.

[T]he tensions which surface as a consequence of cultural conflicts must be recognized as a source of major stress for students of color. Cultural conflicts result from differences in the manner of which cultural groups prioritize core values and interact with their environments. When these differences collide or clash, individuals experience heightened stress and dissonance which causes a sense of frustration and disorientation. This experience of disorientation is far greater for those students who come from subordinate cultures, since their values and beliefs are not institutionalized and readily reinforced within the greater society (Darder, 1992, p. 14).

It's important to point out that the greatest social energy for learning in a classroom is not the teacher, the lesson plans, or the administration (or the "institution," as is often the case)—although they all play an important role. It is the student's own natural capacity for learning; their own willpower, creativity and intellect. As Lisa D. Delpit (1988) says, "The teacher cannot be the only expert in the classroom. To deny students their own expert knowledge *is* to disempower them" (p. 288).

Of course, all students need structural parameters for this learning to be facilitated. It's not simply an issue of "process-oriented versus skills-oriented" writing instruction.

Many liberal educators hold that the primary goal for education is for children to become autonomous, to develop fully who they are in the classroom setting without having arbitrary, outside standards forced upon them. This is a very reasonable goal for people whose children are already participants in the culture of power and who have internalized its codes. But parents who don't function within that culture often want something else. It's not that they disagree with the former aim, it's just that they want something more. They want to ensure that the school provides their children with discourse patterns, interactional styles, and spoken and written language codes that will allow them *success* [emphasis added] in the larger society (Delpit, p. 285).

In my case, despite "language" difficulties as a child, I became a successful and award-winning poet, journalist, and critic as an adult. I could not have done this solely within a "process" approach (which didn't exist when I attended school). "Product" was also important. To reach my goal of writing clearly, eloquently, and as masterfully as I could, I had to learn "how" to write, not just to "want" to write.

My point is there has to be a proper tension and balance between the concepts of process and skills; the key, however, is the direct engagement of the student's innate curiosities, interests, and cultural values.

One of the greatest barriers to any "child-centered" approach is the imposition of "outside" values, based on political, social, or economic determinants, or the dominant culture's need to "break" the cultural "deviance" of non-Anglo students. (Conversely, there are "whites" who accept and push the "otherness" and "diversity" of a classroom in order to deal with their own identity/culture dilemmas which surface for them as members of a dominant group.)

Instead of being formed by the absolute movement of becoming, the child is formed by the relativity of the past, battered by premature judgments (mostly determined by the politics of color, nationality and class, and often, gender) of form, but, more dangerously, of content. Often this constitutes the first major step in his or her social estrangement. And when the artist within dies, the good "citizen" is conceived. Welcome to the New School of the New Order!

THE BILINGUAL/BICULTURAL PARADIGM

In 1992, I did a six-week poetry residency at Gail Elementary School in the Chicago neighborhood of Rogers Park. The neighborhood is one of the most culturally diverse in the city. I worked with ten- and eleven-year-olds in a bilingual program; most of the students were Spanish-speaking immigrants from Mexico.

The first day I asked the class, "Who does poetry?" No one would raise their hand. They were too "cool" for this; some were already members of local street gangs and designated as troublemakers.

Later a Puerto Rican teacher asked me to come to his class of nine-year-olds, just recently arrived from Mexico and Central America. I asked them the same question: "Who does poetry?" They all raised their hands. I then asked: "Who wants to recite some poetry?" They all clamored to be the first to recite.

The image of one Mexican girl, with strong Indian features, stays with me. She recited in what is called *declamation*, with her eyes closed, rocking and swaying with the rhythms of the Spanish words. I was deeply moved and heartened by this. Then the teacher told me that in a year or two, these children will be just like the ones I had been working with!

What is it about the schools that takes the poetry out of our children? Here a paradigm of truly empowering bilingual/bicultural instruction is of vital importance. As Carlos Ovando (1990) writes:

[L]anguage is very much more than words, grammar and sounds. It is, as folklorist Cratis Williams writes, "culture expressing itself in sound" (p. 341).

And:

Recent bilingual education research suggests a paradigm shift in the way we think languages are acquired and how they ought to be used in private and public life (p. 342).

And further:

Because of the power of language, bilingual education is more than just a useful pedagogical tool that addresses the learning needs of linguistic-minority students. It also involves complex issues of political power, cultural identity, and social status (p. 341).

In fact, for all children, not just biliterate ones, the power relations of society are learned early in the classroom. There the social class position of the children and, thereby, their relative worth in society is affirmed.

One result of this division of labor is the "exclusive concentration of artistic talent in particular individuals, and its suppression in the broad mass," as Karl Marx and Frederick Engels pointed out in the mid-1800s.[2]

This issue still resonates. In the United States, poetry production, like most art production, becomes marginalized and relegated to the fringes of society—something to be done in galleries and cafes, artists' colonies, or loft communities, under the banner "bohemian," or in the exclusive purview of academic circles. Or, as is often the case, the arts are tied to commercial enterprise, to make products palatable, pleasing, and therefore sellable.

The majority of working-class people are too busy surviving to trouble themselves with artistic endeavor. If working at all, they are driven to become mindless machines, in the drudgery of factory or office work, at the whim of imposed authority. Public education, for the most part, prepares their children for these roles later in life. Even the children of the business owners and professionals are molded into their future life tasks.

Add to this a second-class citizenship based on skin color, nationality, or immigrant status, and we have even more blocks to true, uninhibited human expression. For example, in my youth, Mexican children in Los Angeles were routinely tracked into the lower-division classes. Schools with high percentages of Chicanos, such as Garfield High School or Huntington Park High School, were low in academic achievement but high in industrial arts training (Garfield was known as having the best auto mechanic courses; Huntington

Park had the best welding classes).[3] In affect, these schools made a "liability out of difference" (Lucas et al., 1990).

The aim of all this is to break the creative spirit, to destroy the poet within, and make every neck ready for one leash. It's about the "control" of students, not their full flowering or realization as vessels of emancipatory human life activity.

[T]he issue of critical pedagogy demands an attentiveness to how students actively construct the categories of meaning that prefigure their production of and response to classroom knowledge. By ignoring the cultural and social forms that are authorized by youth and simultaneously empower or disempower them, educators risk complicitly silencing and negating their students. This is unwittingly accomplished by refusing to recognize the importance of those sites and social practices outside of schools that actively shape student experiences and through which students often define and construct their sense of identity, politics, and culture (Giroux & Simon, 1989, p. 3).

Still, as the saying goes, the "flower cracks through the cement." There are some recent notable developments around this concern. The rise of hip-hop culture from the late 1970s to the present is one of these. Its core expression, rap music, is a highly developed language art that grew out of the rubble of places such as the South Bronx and Compton, largely removed from decent schooling or resources. Here youth conjured up poetry with beats from turntables and amplified with microphones. Aerosol art, so-called graffiti, reached levels never before attained. Dancing and music mixed to create styles such as breaking and New Jack Swing. In a time when social programs were cut across the board in every urban community, when industrial jobs were destroyed by the millions, poetry and other arts continued to flourish.

Notwithstanding the introduction of commercialism to hip-hop culture (record deals, megabuck productions, and worldwide marketing strategies, including the use of Rap in commercials and movies), this is a crucial aspect that proves my point: We are all born poets/artists.

Another is the mid-1980s rise of "Poetry Slams," and variants, born in Chicago, but now spread throughout the country and parts of Europe. Here oral poetic performances are judged, jeered, and cheered in places as unlikely as bars, cafes, festivals, and rock concerts.

But the dynamics of capitalism transform what human beings create, naturally and integrally, with their being (including Rap music and Poetry Slams) into alienated and "unnatural" entities.

In the passage of time in a highly competitive commercial society, the unit of concern is transformed from person into "product." Art, music, peanut butter, drama, science, blood, cancer cures, personalities, business executives, surrogate mothers—all become products (Oliver, 1989, p. 21).[4]

Be that as it may, these cultural developments are critical points where learning interaction can occur. As Giroux and Simon (1989) say:

Popular culture and social difference can be taken up by educators either as a pleasurable form of knowledge/power which allows for more effective individualizing and administration of physical and moral regulation or such practices can be understood as the terrain on which we must meet our students in a critical and empowering pedagogical encounter (p. 25).

I would like to explore another process of language creation (outside of "institutions" and official or commercial intervention) which is also exemplary of U.S. urban experience (the flower and the cement). As a teenager in Los Angeles, like so many Mexican immigrant children, I fell through the cracks of two languages, Spanish and English. At the same time, I participated in creating our own hybrid culture, the principal aspect being the *calo* or street slang we used. It too was poetry. Often our talk included a mixture of Spanish and English words; we also created new words to communicate sentiments not matched by school English. It was a special language among homeboys. An intimate language; a dangerous language: *Trucha. Me la rayo. Alivianate. A la brava. Chale. Con Safos.*[5]

Calo is one of ways we resocialized around our otherness, our outlaw and outsider position, both imposed and accepted. *Calo* was neither Spanish nor English. Of course, talking like this couldn't get you a job or into college or even parental approval. But for many young Chicanos in *barrios* without many options, the one place where this language worked, often to save one's life, was in *la pinta* (prison). This is where it had its stature. Necessity made into mind, made into language.

In effect, some of us became "trilinguals," able to traverse three worlds— the "American" (Anglo-dominant), the Mexican (mostly recent immigrant, with strong ties to the old country), and the *cholo*/homeboy (part Chicano, part African American urban).

For me it meant I could talk to teachers, counselors, and law enforcement representatives; I could deal with my parents and older siblings, who maintained their language and cultural distinctiveness despite being in this country for decades; and finally, I could survive/prevail on the barrio/pinta level.

Some of us involved in the literary aspects of the Chicano culture tried over the years to legitimize the "third" language. Magazines were created in Los Angeles along these lines; they included *Con Safos* and *ChismeArte*, and later *Q-vo*, *Firme*, and *Lowrider*. Dictionaries were researched and published, among them *Barrio Language Dictionary* (El Barrio Publications, 1974), *Pachuco* (University of Arizona Press, 1970), *El Libro de Calo* (Floricanto Press, 1986), *Calo Tapestry* (Justa Publications, 1977), and *Dictionary of Pachuco Terms* (Sierra Printers, 1976).

There have been novels and poetry books written with *calo*, most notably the works of Sacramento's Jose Montoya or Fresno's Juan Felipe Herrera. In 1992, *Puerto del Sol,* a literary and art magazine out of New Mexico, came out with a special issue on *calo,* edited by Jim Sagel.

Even recording artists—from Lalo Guerrero, the 1940s Pachuco songwriter and performer, to Cypress Hill, one of most celebrated rap groups of the 1990s—helped push the *calo* into the larger culture.

But *calo,* like many of these non-institutional inventions, was considered a "vulgar" language, a street slang, relegated to the same place where much of African-American street talk is pushed off, even as key words and phrases become part of the everyday American lexicon ("stay cool," "lighten up," "funk," "right on" and on and on).

Yet it's all poetry to me.

BRAVING THE NEW WORLD

Globalization. Robotics. Computers. As educators Lynda Ann Ewen, Walda Katz-Fishman, and Gloria Slaughter (1990) wrote:

The electronics revolution has dramatically changed the demands on the public school system. Employers need fewer workers and those they need must have new skills. Training today means computer interfaces, computer bulletin boards and computer graphics. Basic skills such as typing and filing are no longer useful. Industrial training no longer requires knowledge of mechanics, electricity, and quality control. Robots monitor themselves; computers monitor the line and the robots. Scanners and uniform pricing codes have replaced warehouse workers and those doing inventory. These are only a few examples of the dramatic ways in which the new technology is affecting all areas of employment (p. 5).

In the midst of this revolution, what becomes of the expressive, salient, and human "voice"—what becomes of the *calo* and jive talk? What becomes of our stories and poetry in the swirling throes of social upheaval? What of the imagination? How can all this survive the worldwide economic and political transformations sweeping governments and social orders alike?

We all tremble before the changes; yet that voice, that singular imaginative power within each person, must not be lost, but liberated; must not be paralyzed, but rescued; must not be trivialized, but must become the axis of any new association of humanity to rise upon the bones and sinew of the new technology.

As Anne Schultz once told me, "the imagination is now the last great frontier for humankind." I would add that the developing modern productive forces are how the human imagination can finally advance, unimpaired and unshackled. The technology is on *our side.* There is now the possibility of a society established on a premise first articulated by Marx: The free and healthy development of each is the condition for the free and healthy development of all. This is what's behind the "post-Communist" communism, as an expression of underlying objective motive forces.

The promise is there. To be realized, it has to be organized. In other words, possibilities only become realities when people struggle to achieve them. This quality of making history belongs only to human beings and is inexorably linked to the creative and poetic impulses from which all human imaginative vision emanates. "Humanity has never relinquished its victories or its dreams. History rushes forward precisely to preserve them" (Peery, 1987).

VALUE AND VOICE

Capitalism only values what it can exploit. Still, the competitive drive for profits forces the introduction of computer-controlled robotics and other labor-replacing devices (as opposed to labor-saving devices, which characterized most electro-mechanical developments up until the present period). This in turn has driven millions of people out of work. Economist Richard Barnet (1993) recently wrote that "between 1979 and 1992, the Fortune 500 companies presented 4.4 million of their employees with pink slips" (p. 47).

This shift in the economy is also behind an astronomical rise in homelessness, which has not been seen since the Great Depression. The Rust Belt; the shuttered mills and boarded-up businesses; the "will work for food" signs at highway exits; the hungry employed working at below minimum wage; the children in shelters, now the fastest rising segment of the homeless; these are the symbols of the present epoch. And those whom the system cannot feed, clothe, or house are considered "expendable."

For some four years, I have been doing writing workshops in Chicago homeless shelters, most of this time at Irene's Women's Shelter in the West Town community. There I confront the so-called expendable people mentioned above. Most of the women are mentally ill and/or substance abusers; a few have lost their children or have been raped. What society says gives them value—having a house, a husband, a job, or a child—has been forcibly taken away from them. In the eyes of their community—and subsequently in their own eyes—the women's worth is rendered to nothing. They begin to believe they have no value; they become stuck in a position of helplessness, victims instead of victors.

One of the women, Dolores, related how she and another homeless woman were sitting on the porch of a night shelter, celebrating the fact that the other woman was leaving the shelter for a place to stay. Soon two men passed by— and then spit on them!

"Why?" Dolores painfully asked. Why indeed!

Under capitalism (of which sexism and racism are essential components), no one is any good unless they are "productive," even though the very nature of the system forces whole communities to have their economic lives pulled out from under them. Even so-called good families, even strong, able-bodied men and women, are embraced by this fact.

In my writing workshops, we prove to the women that they have value by virtue of being human beings. We do this by having them tap into that reservoir of creativity within them, through their own stories and poems, something which cannot be taken away. Once the women access their imagination, which is always there and is inexhaustible, they discover the real source of their personal power. They can begin to feel and act less like victims, and more like women whose strength is in their fingertips.

I have seen the transformation. I've seen it with children. The key for teachers who work with "the other" of marginalized or oppressed communities is to begin with a genuine respect for people's basic humanity, which can't help but be a respect for one's culture, language, creativity, capabilities, and intelligence. For their difference. It means hearing, and often heeding, the "voices," which Giroux (1988) describes as

the principles of dialogue as they are enunciated and enacted within particular social settings. . . . The category of voice, then, refers to the means at our disposal—the discourses available to us—to make ourselves understood and listened to and to define ourselves as active participants in the world (p. 199).

Although I'm all for having more teachers come from out of those communities (to break what Delpit called the "silenced dialogue"), I don't believe it's essential. A teacher may be more effective by having an intimate awareness of the students' needs, but effectiveness is not just predicated on one's race, culture, or background. Again, the bridge to get over is respect. The thing for me now is, how can this happen on a wide-scale basis? And if it did, how would this society respond? Power for the homeless! For "inner-city" youth! Unthinkable—or is it?

MANY WHITMANS

More than a hundred years ago, a similar process was developing in poetry and the arts on this continent, which was to later change the face of poetry around the world. American essayist Ralph Waldo Emerson best expressed the kind of poetry needed then, which he claimed had not been met by any American in his 1845 essay, "The Poet":

I look in vain for the poet whom I describe. . . . We have yet had no genius in America, with tyrannous eye, which knew the value of our incomparable materials. . . . Our log rolling, our stumps and their politics, our fisheries, our Negroes, and Indians, our boats, and our repudiations, the wrath of rogues, and the pusillanimity of honest men, the northern trade, the southern planting, the western clearing, Oregon and Texas, are yet unsung. Yet America is a poem in our eyes; its ample geography dazzles the imagination, and it will not wait long for metres.[6]

Scarcely a decade later, Walt Whitman published the first edition of *Leaves of Grass*. This work embodied what Emerson visualized in "The Poet," and Emerson wrote Whitman to say so.

Walt Whitman was also the product of an epoch of revolution: the transformation from an agriculturally-based society to an industrial one. The most significant result of this economic shift in North America was the Civil War, a revolutionary war if ever there was one.

Whitman himself roamed the battlefields during the war, writing letters, articles, and poems of what he saw and felt. A new society that seemed to emerge unhampered out of the ashes to free the United States from the control of the Slave Power was culled forth in Whitman's poems, such as in this stanza from section 31 of *Leaves of Grass*:

> I believe a leaf of grass is no less than the journey-work of the stars,
> And the pismire is equally perfect, and a grain of sand, and the egg of the wren,
> And the tree-toad is a chef-d'oeuvre for the highest,
> And the running blackberry would adorn the parlors of heaven,
> And the narrowest hinge in my hand puts to scorn all machinery,
> And the cow crunching with depress'd head surpasses any statue,
> And a mouse is miracle enough to stagger sextillions of infidels (Whitman, 1855, p. 72).

Whitman's generous lines—his expansive vision, his notions of love beyond the boundaries of history, nations, sexual politics, of true comradeship and fellowship—all of this stems from the basic shifts in the economy that seemed to make all these things possible—nay, necessary!

Human vision is always strongest at the pinnacle of its achievement, always looking beyond the limitations of what has been before it. What dreams people had when industry broke free from the chains imposed by agricultural society—people like Marx, Thoreau, Emerson and Whitman—can only be fulfilled with the electronics revolution. So now we are no less living within a revolutionary epoch than Whitman lived under one more than a hundred years ago. "The objective factors are in place. Now, humanity must write its own history" (Peery, 1987).

Today, however, is a time for many Whitmans. They may be found inside the stale classrooms of immigrant communities like Rogers Park; in basement hovels with makeshift equipment and a microphone in Bedford-Stuyvesant; in "open mike" readings among the beer suds in a Chicago bar.

Poets, who have led the way for the scientists and soldiers throughout time, can also point the way out of social crisis. The whole country must reclaim its poetry, its soul if you will, starting with our children—to make poetry a life-and-death issue again.

To do otherwise is to allow the natural impulses within us to die; to do otherwise is to kill our ability as a people to transform the world—not just to accept the inevitability of change, but to be empowered and fully competent agents of change. This is what a truly liberating pedagogy is about: to make effective social activists out of those whose lives are shaped and determined by the rule of others, who rule not by conscious consent but because of economics, history, and culture.

This is also why poetry must find its revolutionary place in this discourse. Poets can, unlike other purveyors of the word, explore the power politics of society, and consciously tell the truth of it. This too is social contribution of the most heroic kind. With this, then, I leave the last word to Walt Whitman:

> Poets to come! orators, singers, musicians to come!
> Not to-day is to justify me and answer what I am for.
> But you, in a new brood, native, athletic, continental, greater than before known,
> Arouse! For you must justify me (Whitman, 1855, p. 39).

NOTES

1. The concept is written as *nu guachaxil*, and was related to me by Roberto Mendoza, a professional interpreter and translator based in Chicago. Mendoza, originally from Guatemala, studied the Quiche language after realizing that all his life, despite his Indian heritage, he knew nothing about the culture or the people. In doing so, he discovered that the modern tribal dialects—there are twenty-eight Mayan dialects in his country—consisted almost entirely of metaphors, and is one of the most poetic tongues on earth.

2. From Karl Marx and Frederick Engels, as quoted in Lee Baxandall and Stefan Morawski, eds., *Marx and Engels on Literature and Art* (New York, NY: International General Editions, 1973), p. 71.

3. This information came to my attention when I ran for a Los Angeles School Board seat in the mid-1970s; although I lost, I was one of the first candidates of Mexican descent to attack the class nature of the educational system, and a major advocate of bilingual/bicultural education for all children.

4. A powerful passage related to this concept is the following from Marx, excerpted from Baxandall and Morawski's *Marx and Engels on Literature and Art*:

The less you eat, drink and read books; the less you go to the theatre, the dance hall, the public-house; the less you think, love, theorize, sing, paint, fence, etc. The more you save—the greater becomes your treasure which neither moths nor dust will devour—your capital. The less you are, the more you have; the less you express your own life, the greater is your alienated life—the greater is the store of your estranged being (p. 63).

5. These are a few *calo* terms often used among youth in cities with large Mexican populations. They were part of the genesis of the *pachuco*, originally from El Paso, Texas, but by the 1930s and 1940s linked forever with Los Angeles. The so-called

Zoot Suit Riots of 1943—when U.S. sailors, police, and Anglo citizens beat, stripped and arrested hundreds of zoot-suited *pachucos*—made this also a language born of conflict.

6. From Ralph Waldo Emerson, as quoted in Walter Sutton, *American Free Verse: The Modern Revolution in Poetry* (New York, NY: New Directions, 1973), p. 9. Sutton credits Emerson with some of the first articulated concepts of "the near, the low and the common" being "explored and poeticized." Emerson's most famous quote from "The Poet" is also appropriate here:

For it is not metres, but a metre-making argument, that makes a poem—a thought so passionate and alive that, like the spirit of a plant or animal, it has an architecture of its own, and adorns nature with a new thing (Sutton, 1973, p. 7).

REFERENCES

Barnet, R. (1993). "The End of Jobs." *Harpers Magazine*, pp. 47–52.

Baxandall, L., & S. Morawski. (1973). *Max and Engels on Literature and Art*. New York, NY: International General Editions.

Courts, P. L. (1991). *Literacy and empowerment: The meaning makers*. New York, NY: Bergin & Garvey.

Darder, A. (1992). "Reading the world through different eyes: Toward an emancipatory view of literacy," in Philip Dreyer, ed., *Reading the world*. Claremont, CA: The Claremont Reading Conference.

Delpit, L. D. (1988). "The silenced dialogue: Power and pedagogy in educating other people's children." *Harvard Educational Review*, pp. 280–298.

Ewen, L. A., W. Katz-Fishman, & G. Slaughter. (1990). *Murder of the mind: The attack on our public schools*. Chicago, IL: Workers Press.

Giroux, H. (1988). *Teachers as intellectuals*. New York, NY: Bergin & Garvey.

Giroux, H., & R. I. Simon. (1989). *Popular culture, schooling, and everyday life*. New York, NY: Bergin & Garvey.

Lucas, T., R. Henze, & R. Donato. (1990). "Promoting the success of Latino language-minority students: An exploratory study of six high schools." *Harvard Educational Review*, pp. 315–339.

Oliver, D. W. (1989). *Education, modernity, and fractured meaning*. Albany, NY: State University of New York Press.

Ovando, C. J. (1990). "Politics and pedagogy: History, politics, theory, and practice." *Harvard Educational Review*, pp. 341–356.

Peery, N. (1993). *Entering an epoch of social revolution*. Chicago, IL: Workers Press.

———. (1987). "The future of the world revolutionary and Marxist movement." *Proletariat Magazine*, pp. 8–9.

Peterson, R. E. (1991). "Teaching how to read the world and change it: Critical pedagogy in the intermediate grades," in Catherine E. Walsh, ed., *Literacy as praxis: Culture, language, and pedagogy*. Norwood, NJ: Ablex Publishing Corporation.

Schultz, A. (1992). "Writing from the source: A content approach to teaching writing." A paper from the Chicago Teachers' Center.

Spencer, M. B., D. P. Swanson, & M. Cunningham. (1991). "Ethnicity, ethnic identity,

and competence formation: Adolescent transition and cultural transformation."
Journal of Negro Education, pp. 366–387.

Sutton, W. (1973). *American free verse: The modern revolution in poetry*. New York, NY: New Directions.

Whitman, W. (1855, 1980). *Leaves of grass*. New York, NY: Signet Classic Edition.

Bicultural Strengths and Struggles of Southeast Asian Americans in School

Peter Nien-chu Kiang

"Mai's not acting like herself lately," a student mentioned to me after class one day. I noticed it, too. Mai had been quiet and unengaged in class all week long. She was usually one of the most dynamic students in the room—voicing ideas and experiences more readily than others who shared her background as a Vietnamese refugee. Later, when I asked Mai privately how she was doing, she revealed with a mixture of sadness, frustration, and anger: "My family's car was burned, right on the street in front of our house! I don't know why. But I couldn't study. Just keep thinking about it. So depressed. . . . I didn't tell anybody."

As she disclosed her story in greater detail, I realized that she had felt helpless *as a new immigrant* after the incident because she did not know how to handle it—how to call or communicate with the police or fire department at the time. She had internalized the problem *as a Vietnamese*—not telling people outside the family about what had happened. Furthermore, the actual arson of the car had triggered memories of the war in Vietnam, which depressed her even more—reflecting her experience *as a refugee*. Yet, whether or not she realized it, the source of the problem was racial conflict in the neighborhood—reflecting her reality *as a racial minority*.

Recognizing each of these distinct dimensions of Mai's identity enabled me to understand more clearly why her participation had changed in class, and, more importantly, how I could better respond to her situation. Viewing her as "not acting like herself" was wrong. In fact, Mai *was* being herself—a fully bicultural individual within a complex, multifaceted social context. We needed to see who she really was.

Inspired by Mai's story and informed by qualitative research,[1] this chapter presents a multidimensional, theoretical framework that integrates various aspects of the Southeast Asian refugee experience—providing coherent ways to recognize their bicultural strengths and struggles in school.

ASIAN PACIFIC AMERICAN DEMOGRAPHIC CHANGE

The growth and diversification of the Asian Pacific American population resulting from sustained immigration since 1965 and Southeast Asian refugee resettlement since 1975 has been phenomenal. Having nearly doubled in both the 1970s and 1980s, Asian Pacific Americans will continue to be the fastest growing population of color in the United States well into the twenty-first century (Ong & Hee, 1993; Gardner, Robey, & Smith, 1985). The Asian Pacific–American student population from preschool to graduate school has also grown dramatically during this period, driven by demographic changes and fueled by socioeconomic pressures and cultural priorities.

During the 1980s, the K–12 school-age Asian and Pacific Islander population grew by ninety percent nationally (Kiang & Lee, 1993). In many local school districts, the magnitude of Asian Pacific population growth has been even more dramatic. In Lowell, Massachusetts—home to the second largest Cambodian community in the country—the influx was so rapid that between thirty-five and fifty new Cambodian and Laotian children were entering the Lowell public schools *each week* during 1987 (Kiang, 1990). Across the country, the changing demographics of schools and society loom large for practitioners and policy makers who have been unable to meet the needs of Asian Pacific immigrant students, even at current levels.

Research on Asian Pacific–American students in either K–12 or higher education is quite limited. National studies typically neglect Asian Pacific Americans or aggregate data from diverse Asian nationalities under one umbrella category (Astin, 1988; Quality Education for Minorities Project, 1990). In spite of many critiques to the contrary, popular media images have portrayed Asian Pacific–American students as hard-working, overachieving "whiz kids" who outperform all competition for Westinghouse Science awards and national spelling bee championships (Suzuki, 1989a; 1977; Chun, 1980). Few studies have examined the experiences of Vietnamese, Cambodian, Laotian, or Hmong students, even though their communities, along with Pacific Islanders, face the greatest needs within the Asian Pacific American population (Kiang & Lee, 1993; Trueba, Cheng, & Ima, 1993; Kiang, 1993; Kiang, 1991b; Trueba, Jacobs, & Kirton, 1990; Chung, 1989; Nguyen & Halpern, 1989).

DEVELOPING A THEORETICAL FRAMEWORK

As Mai's situation illustrates, Southeast Asian refugee and immigrant students share a multiplicity of needs as well as a range of strengths that reflect various dimensions of their historical and cultural backgrounds, their individual identities, and their social realities. These background characteristics can be defined along four distinct dimensions (Kiang, 1992; 1991a):

• *as Southeast Asians* with distinct linguistic, cultural, and historical characteristics determined by growing up in their home countries and, to some extent, maintained by their continuing integration in their basic family and community structure in the United States;

• *as refugees* with survival skills and psychologies adapted to war, famine, flight and forced migration, loss of family members, secondary trauma from refugee camps, and resettlement;

• *as immigrants* in America adjusting to drastic changes in status, opportunity, living conditions, climate, and other aspects of daily life, especially in relation to culture and language;

• *as racial minorities* facing discrimination, disenfranchisement, racism, and violence as social, economic, and political realities in the United States.

As Southeast Asians, students' expectations, learning styles, and performance in school may reflect traditional values and educational practices of their homelands (Nguyen, 1984; Atkinson, Ponterotto, & Sanchez, 1984; Center for Applied Linguistics, 1981; Henkin & Nguyen, 1981; Bangsberg et al, 1967). Differences as well as similarities among each country and among regions within a single country in culture, language, history, religion, and geopolitical development are significant. For example, pursuit of higher education is especially important for Vietnamese and ethnic Chinese influenced by the standards of Confucian society (Henkin & Nguyen, 1981; Duong, 1958). Along this dimension, Southeast Asian students may experience problems related to cultural dislocation, but may also be able to draw from traditions and cultural values which enable them to achieve in school (Caplan, Whitmore, & Choy, 1989).

Having fled their home countries *as refugees,* Southeast Asian students reveal through life history narratives and their own writings common stories of war, rape, escape, and victimization, along with themes of guilt, survival, loneliness, family loyalty, and hope for the future (Welaratna, 1993; Nguyen & Halpern, 1989; Freeman, 1989). Wehrly (1988) defines their experience as one of *loss*—loss of family, friends, and social networks; loss of homeland, property, and culture; loss of identity, security, and self-esteem. Yet, they also have *strengths*—strengths of survival and sacrifice; strengths of shared support and loyalty; and strengths of values, especially with regard to education. Takami (1988) illustrates how the tragedy of the refugee experience may limit some in their pursuit of higher education, while motivating others to do so with even greater determination. While Southeast Asian refugee students may face a variety of mental health problems arising from their past experience of loss along this dimension, Wehrly suggests that their strengths, if recognized and engaged, can enable refugees to overcome their difficulties.

Over time, Southeast Asian refugees build new lives and undertake an adjustment process *as immigrants*. Little has been published about Southeast Asian students as immigrants with the exception of student writings for classes and school publications (Nguyen, 1989; Frakt, 1990; Nguyen, 1988). A common theme in these writings is "fitting in"—maintaining aspects of one's traditional identity while integrating comfortably into U.S. society. Other themes concern intergenerational conflict with one's parents and the importance of education to the family. According to Frakt (1990), "immigrant drive" may account for certain achievement patterns observed among Southeast Asians in school which parallel those of Jewish and Japanese immigrants. At the same time, immigrant family responsibilities and expectations may also intensify the problems and pressures faced by Southeast Asian students (Parmley, 1990).

Southeast Asians also face a distinct racial dynamic in U.S. society not experienced by European ethnic immigrant groups. *As racial minorities*, Southeast Asian students confront social conditions and institutional categories which situate them in the domain of Asian American minorities (Fernandez, 1988; Matin, Chan, & Tran, 1982; Skinner & Hendricks, 1979). Suzuki (1989b) notes that sociopsychological problems of Southeast Asian students may be increasing because of growing anti-Asian sentiment and racial violence on campuses throughout the country. At the same time, Nayematsu (1987) suggests that minority student support services enhance the persistence of Southeast Asian refugee students in school. Group mobilization and coalition building provide vehicles with which to gain greater access to resources and the potential for exerting political power (Chu, 1989).

Recognizing these four distinct background dimensions of Southeast Asian refugees provides a set of multiple lenses through which to understand their bicultural identities and realities. Considered individually, each dimension uncovers specific issues faced by Southeast Asian–American students and points to specific directions for intervention and further research. Considered together, they reveal the multidimensional complexities which characterize the extent of obstacles as well as the range of strengths that Southeast Asian students bring to their school experience.

The following sections draw on extensive qualitative research with Southeast Asian refugee college students and with Vietnamese–American secondary and elementary school students to illustrate ways in which this multidimensional theoretical framework has meaning and validity in relation to their voices and actual lived experiences (Kiang, Nguyen, & Sheehan, 1995; Kiang & Kaplan, 1994; Kiang, 1991a).

"I WILL COME BACK THERE"—THE SOUTHEAST ASIAN DIMENSION

In their native countries, some informants completed high school and even attended college, while others had little more than a third or fourth grade formal education. Differences in age, rural/urban origin, and family (class) status account for some of these variations in homeland educational level. In addition, disruptions resulting both from the war and from policy changes after 1975 limited the school-going opportunities of particular nationalities. For example, formal education in Cambodia virtually stopped after the Khmer Rouge took power in 1975. Cambodian informants in this study, despite coming from well-educated families, did not have opportunities to attend school during their preteen and adolescent years.

In Vietnam, a series of anti-Chinese government policies after 1975 closed many of the Chinese schools, thus preventing some of the ethnic Chinese Vietnamese informants from going beyond primary school. Donna,[2] for example, describes the impact of having her education in Chinese school in Vietnam stop at third grade. "That's why my Chinese is *ho gik yao hahn* [there is a limit to how good I can be]." In describing the difficulties of learning English when she arrived in the United States at age thirteen without having a strong foundation in Chinese, she code-switches and notes, "You can not learn a lot of things, you know when you're at age like ten, thirteen. So everything like in Chinese is *bun tong soy* [half empty bucket]. So, it's very difficult for me, too. I mean learn everything in the same time, and different languages." Donna's self-assessment is consistent with research on bilingualism and cognitive development, which suggests that children who continue to develop cognitively in their native language are better equipped to learn and develop cognitively in English than those whose native language learning is interrupted (Cummins, 1981, 1989).

Students who attended school in their home countries, however, feel that they experienced a stricter curriculum and school environment than in the United States. Hung, for example, completed ninth grade when he left Vietnam. He observes, "If they finish ninth grade [in Vietnam], they can graduate [in the United States.]. I mean the level is about twelfth grade [here]."

Mark attended Chinese schools until 1975, and escaped from Vietnam to China, and then to the United States at age thirteen with his family. He adds, "the requirement [there] is much more than the school system here . . . if you read a book, you almost have to memorize everything in the book."

The rote memorization style of learning is typical for many Southeast Asian students. Mai, who came in 1981 at age seventeen, clarifies:

In my high school years in Vietnam, we never been taught to say things like asking questions, like argue with the teacher. . . . So, when I go to school here, it's kind of hard for me to express my questions. So, whatever I don't understand, I just have to open the book. And if I don't understand [laughs], just don't understand.

Others refer to the same cycle—not asking questions, relying on the textbook for answers, and not understanding course material—to describe similar realities that they have accepted in the classroom.

Cultural differences affect not only the learning styles but also the relations of Southeast Asian students to their teachers. Sokal, who came from Cambodia at age fourteen with his family, remembers an incident from high school:

I was ESL student. The teacher, he ask me to sit and talk to him. I didn't look him in the eye. He said, "Are you listening to me," you know? "Are you listening to me?" Because I'm not looking him in the eye, and he doesn't understand the culture, you know, and there go the conflicts.

Chung (1994) cautions that cultural tradition is not the only explanation for Southeast Asian students averting their eyes from their teachers'. The language barrier and differential power relations are also factors. Nevertheless, Sokal still recalls the incident with some anger, feeling that his cultural norms were unrecognized or misinterpreted. While Southeast Asian students frequently describe experiences with culture shock and cultural differences in school, the adjustment process is often mistakenly viewed by both students and school personnel as unidirectional—with the burden on newcomer students. In contrast, Trueba, Jacobs, and Kirton (1990) argue that culture shock between students and teachers is a two-way, shared exchange. They note: "It is extremely important for teachers to realize that *they* are experiencing cultural shock when they try to function effectively with children who do not share their values and expectations" (1990, p. 135).

Traditionally high standards of discipline and order have also shaped the early learning experiences of students from Southeast Asia. Mark recalls:

If you do something wrong or you come to school late, or you try to sneak in, you have to stay after school and sit there straight like a bamboo stick. . . . Wait there for the teacher says you can go.

Seng, who left Cambodia alone and arrived in the United States at age eighteen, frames the expectation of classroom discipline within the larger social and cultural contexts of village life and teacher-student-parent relations:

We live in a small village, and the teacher live in this village and know who you are, who your parents are. What're you gonna do? The teacher knows everything about you. You cannot just cheat him, ya know? . . . When we go to school, it's like they are the parents, so we have to respect them.

Students often cite memories of life in Vietnam and Cambodia as reference points to contrast with life here. Seng, for example, observes, "Over here, right, everyone just concerned about their problem. They don't care about other people, just concerned about themselves, but in Cambodia, the people, they really care about each other." Tam, who came to the United States alone at age seventeen, agrees. "In Vietnam, people always care about each other.

But over here, only when things matter to them, then they care." Mark adds, "This country really rush. Everybody like, I fight for this, and he fight for that."

Recognizing the contrasts in both schooling and society between Southeast Asia and the United States, students also reveal desires to return to their homelands, at least to visit, if not to stay. Tam, for example, mentions her interest in going back to Southeast Asia to work in refugee camps after college. Mai lists several scenarios for life after graduation, including a plan "to go back to Vietnam and do something in Vietnam. . . . I want to go back badly." Ngoc, who came to the United States alone, returned to Vietnam during a summer break to visit her family after being separated for a decade. She says, "I miss my mom, so I went back. . . . I don't want to go back and live there, but I will come back there again."

Tam also refers to others in the Vietnamese community who, in spite of their refugee status and disagreements with Vietnamese government policy, as well as the lack of normalized state-to-state relations between Vietnam and the United States, have returned to Vietnam to visit. She notes:

Some people they live here with no education, no money and go to work two jobs or three jobs, and they didn't know how their life will go, they will live here or die here or will they see the people in Vietnam again. They really have no answer at all. They don't know anything, so now at least they can come to visit people. And they feel better.

Similarly, in spite of military shelling around her home city and continuing instability throughout the country, Seng's aunt returned to Cambodia to visit because "she love and she miss her country, her relatives so much."[3]

Though mention of their homelands reflects the students' background dimensions as refugees and immigrants as well as being Southeast Asians, it is clear that home countries serve as reference points for their past, present, and future. Childhood memories of the past—family unity, friends and neighbors who cared, the beauty of the land—provide standards with which to measure their present quality of life in the United States. Mark, for example, remembers, "when I came here, I saw all the trees the same, you know. Only one kind of tree. And I say, where did all those different trees [from Vietnam] go, you know? How come I don't see any other trees?"

Students who attended school in their home countries identify some assets of their traditional educational backgrounds such as discipline and rigor. Yet, they also confront cultural conflicts in U.S. classrooms, including expectations that they look teachers in the eye and challenge teachers with questions. This dimension, *as Southeast Asians,* is a core aspect of student bicultural identities and perspectives, regardless of their age of arrival in the United States. At the same time, it is linked to issues of refugee loss and immigrant cultural adjustment—other dimensions of their backgrounds and experiences.

"I'M A SURVIVOR"—THE REFUGEE DIMENSION

Students' experiences and status as refugees—reflected in both chilling and inspiring stories of survival—clearly shape their perspectives and identities. Khami-keaw, a Chinese Cambodian, first escaped to Laos with his family before coming to the United States at age seventeen. He remembers being separated from his siblings by the Khmer Rouge when he was nine years old and evacuated to a labor camp for five years. Working eighteen to twenty hours each day, Khami-keaw vividly describes the intolerable conditions that create refugees:

During the rainy season, everybody goes work in the farm. After you plant all the food and then . . . gathering all the crops. Then you worked as in the field filling the dam and you never stop . . . 365 days a year . . . I almost died a couple of times over there.

The decision to leave one's country is filled with ambivalence and uncertainty. Donna, a Chinese Vietnamese who was twelve when she escaped from Vietnam with her family, recalls leaving with feelings of resignation:

My parents, my brother, my mother taking care of it. I'm kind of young, so I know nothing about it. Actually, I don't even care where to go, 'cause it's all the same. It's not home. Not like home.

Enormous risks follow the decision to escape, as many Southeast Asian students can verify. Those who fled over land faced explosive mines, enemy patrols, wild animals in the jungle, and constant hunger. Sokal's escape story reads:[4]

After the Pol Pot's genocide, there was no reason to stay. There was no dream to dream after the nightmare but the hope to stay alive. So we decide to flee our homeland. We walked barefeet through precarious minefields and burned wheats, the rough edged wheats cut our feet to bleed. The cut was more painful than a razor blade. I was too small to endure the inconceivable pain and exhaustion from walking, from dawn to dusk, to reach the camp at Thailand border, so I cried. That is the only thing a child can do.

Refugees escaping by boat confronted comparable peril, including storms, rape and pillage by Thai pirates, and dehydration. During his escape, Mark also nearly died a couple of times:

When the big waves come, you always think that your boat will sink and you always think that you will be eaten by some kind of shark. And at that time we don't really have enough water. We actually cooked right with salt water, and after that we tried to eat it. We couldn't. It's too bitter. . . . People don't really know what to do. They just like pray, and everybody thought that they'd die in the middle of the ocean. . . .

I was about like ten, ten years old.... If the boat sink...my whole family's there.... We just die together.

Mark's escape story reveals not only the hardships involved in escaping by boat, but also the importance of family in the process. Some, like Mark, Sokal, and Donna, were protected as children and young teenagers escaping together with older members of their family.

Seng, however, escaped from Cambodia by hiding during the day and walking at night for three days across the border to Thailand without telling anyone, including his family, about his decision to leave:

If you want to escape from Cambodia, you don't want anybody to know about it. Like you have to escape one by one to be safe. If they know, they going to caught you, and then they going to send you to get killed.... Cambodian family, they have like, they are really really emotional, you know. They don't care how hard it is, as long as the family stay together. They don't care if they die or not, but, as long as the family stay together, that satisfy them. You know, when I escape, I didn't tell my Mom, I didn't tell anyone.

The emotional weight of Seng's decision to leave is compounded by the resulting family separation. Seng says:

When I left my family, I feel really bad, but I don't know what to do. But try to survive, you know. Like just keep thinking that someday like, someday I will see them if they still alive.

Seng's pain from family separation is shared by others of all ages. Hoa, a fourth grade bilingual student writes:

When I came to America I was so sad. And sometimes I cry by myself. Because I still thinking about my mother, and my grandmother. Sometimes I remember everything about my country, my neighborhood, and my house in Viet-Nam. So when I go to sleep at night I often dream about my country. Suddenly I wake up and I find tears on my cheek and it makes my hair wet. But I don't even care about that so, I remember my dream and I begin to cry again, for a few of minutes. In the morning I wash my face and I go to the dining room and I eat breakfast, and I tell my father about my dream.

Hai, who finished high school and two years of college in Vietnam before coming to the United States with his siblings, similarly reveals:

When I was first in the camp I had dreams about the trip. And when we were in America a couple of months I had dreams about my family. It's something very nice; it's so exciting to change your life; you feel good. But, then for a couple of months when you see the future, it's so dark. Your family is far away. You feel guilty, and when you sleep you dream some bad things.... I just remember a part of my dream. My parents treat me just like a strange person. And after, I think maybe I feel guilty and I cried. I woke up. It's never happened before. I never realized I had PTSD. Most people, they don't realize they have it.

Nightmares are typical symptoms of Post-Traumatic Stress Disorder or PTSD, as Hai recognizes. Mental health research with U.S. Vietnam veterans has shown conclusively that the experience of traumatic events in war can have short-term and long-term psychosocial consequences with varying degrees of severity (Kulka et al., 1990; Brende & Parson, 1985; Sonnenberg, Blank, & Talbott, 1985). In 1980, the American Psychiatric Association included PTSD as a diagnostic category in the Association's Diagnostic and Statistical Manual. Mental health researchers and clinicians also recognize the severity of PTSD in refugee communities, including refugee youth (Herman, 1992; Chung, 1994; Nidorf, 1985; Ascher, 1984), although the level of support services and culturally appropriate care is even less than the limited care offered to U.S. veterans (Kiang, 1991b).

PTSD is a major issue for some Southeast Asian students, particularly older Vietnamese students who survived longer periods of trauma and Cambodian students who endured the Khmer Rouge holocaust. Depression, guilt, anxiety, and anger are all manifestations of the continuing traumatic effects of their experiences. The mental health consequences faced by Southeast Asian refugees can seriously impact their performance in school. Minh, a Vietnamese informant, remembers:

Sometime you feel like, okay, you read the material, you understand. But when you sit in exam and that day you feel homesick, you feel something. I had that problem last January. It snowed heavily that day. I got homesick. . . . I took the exam and I didn't know what I did. . . . I flunked the exam.

Sokal explains further:

It used to be, you know, couldn't study. Go at night, sleep tossing and turning. Then you find a way to deal with it and get yourself straightened out . . .but it's still there, you know. People say, like Vietnam veterans say, you know, it's the same problem. You try to get rid of it . . .and it's like a walking time bomb. I used to be like that, waiting for somebody to bump into you, and then, you know, get into an argument or something. I used to get angry real quick, you know. Always, if you pass me [driving], I'm gonna, you know, [inaudible] my gas and slam into you, you know. I drive so bad. And you know, had many accidents. They want to revoke my license. Now I don't drive anymore. And it's pretty bad. I was younger, you know. Always get angry real quick . . . . Very hot temper. But not anymore. I learn a lot from my experiences, not to take it [out] on somebody else. Yeah, I used to get in the car, close the window, and start screaming, you know. It's like, do crazy things. Getting rid of your anger.

Sokal also admits, in terms of sharing these issues with others, that "I never talk with anybody, even my friends, we never discuss about what happened or this and that. We talk about present situation, you know. I never talk with anybody with that kind of matter."

Furthermore, initial research with the children of U.S. Vietnam combat veterans suggests that there are second-generation effects of PTSD. Pilot studies show, for example, a higher-than-average incidence of attention-deficit disorder and other learning disabilities. If generalizable, then the continuing social consequences of the Vietnam War may persist for a new generation of American-born children of Southeast Asian refugees as well.[5]

Beyond the internalized psychological cost of being a refugee, there are also implications for social relations. Tam, for example, worries that "because I am a refugee and I receive help from the government and the people have to pay tax, and I feel like a handicapped person." The social stigma of being a refugee has made Tam feel reluctant to ask for assistance of any kind, even from tutors and advisors at school, because "I don't know if they really want to help me or I come to beg them to do things." Coming as a refugee and being grateful to the United States for her freedom, Mai also recognizes problems in her relations to the larger society. She says:

I always think that people who control the system, they always right. I always have to listen to them . . . like instructor tells me to do things, then I have to do it without complaining, without being question why he told me to do this.

Chanda, who lost her family in Cambodia and came to the United States at age twenty, adds, "the society have the prejudice and discrimination, yeah. It really hard, too, because I always treated as refugee from Third World country." Hai wonders: "Are refugees the enemy of the people in this nation? Is the wave of refugees coming the reasons of losing jobs and higher taxes? Or because of people selfishness, the olders fight against the newcomers on their homeland?"

Hai is disillusioned because "when we were in the [refugee] camp and we learned about the culture and the people in America, they said every one in America is the same." According to Tollefson (1989), both the formal and hidden curriculum of refugee camp schooling encourage refugees to adopt submissive behavior and idealized images of U.S. society. Many Southeast Asians share stories of prejudice and discrimination in which their multidimensional status as refugees, immigrants, and racial minorities intersect. The irony of these experiences, when viewed along the dimension *as refugees,* is their expectation of peace in coming to the "freedom country."

Schools in Southeast Asia were disrupted both by war and by the social chaos of revolution. Mai writes, "I hate the war which killed my people and collapsed my Vietnam and buried my childhood memory. During the war I had to move from city to city with my family in order to survive." Sokal adds:

Somehow you never had time to think, you know, you never had a childhood life, so you never dreamed what you want to be when you grow up, you know, that kind of question that children dream of. And you always had more time, more important things to think about, survival.

In refugee camps, too, schooling was limited at best, and perhaps distorted due to the assimilationist intent of the curriculum. In the United States, mental health issues resulting from trauma and family separation further confound the difficulties confronted by Southeast Asian refugee students in school.

Yet, while the problems are clear, the refugee experience also forges resilience and determination. Minh signifies:

I'm a survivor. I mean, I don't have to do things I want to do or are interested to do. But I have to do things I have to do. . . . You have everything, your family, everything supports you. . . . But I don't. I'm a survivor.

Hai, recognizing his own PTSD, adds, "sometimes I thought . . . just a couple of times . . . I'm crazy. But I'm strong. My spirit is strong enough to fight." From that strength develops a powerful sense of purpose to pursue their education. Seng observes:

I think I am a strong person, you know. I have gone through a lot of things during Khmer Rouge; the day I escaped from Cambodia; I lived in the camp. Over there I faced so many things. . . . I really want to help my family and my own people . . . the experience I'd gone through before and my family in Cambodia, all those things is just in my mind. It always pushes me to work hard, to get a good education, to get more money and try to survive. Another thing I want to go back to see my people, to see my homeland, to see my friends around in Cambodia. All of those things push me.

Sokal agrees:

I look through my past, you know. I say, well, I've been through this and I've seen many things. I've been through a lot of stuff that, you know, I thought I never come out of it alive. And then, you know, here's my father who brought me here . . . he want you to get through education and he struggle to get here, and, you know, you don't want to disappoint your parents. It really motivates you, you know. Psychologically, that's what I live by.

Instances of strength and motivation forged by Southeast Asian students' experiences as refugees are also witnessed in Suarez-Orozco's powerful psychosocial study (1989) of Central American refugee high school students. Suarez-Orozco's research initially grew out of classroom studies he was conducting on Mexican-American students with whom the growing numbers of Central American students shared a common language but distinct perspectives and educational needs reflecting their backgrounds *as refugees*. Escaping war, torture, and repression in their home countries, tens of thousands of Central American youth fled to the United States during the 1980s.

Suarez-Orozco (1989) suggests that many Central American refugee and immigrant students are driven to achieve in school because of survivor guilt and family responsibility. He argues that achievement motivation theories emphasizing individualized efficacy and independence as the motivating forces for student achievement are culture-bound, and fail to recognize his students' background dimensions either *as Central Americans* or *as refugees*:

Leaving one's family behind is an improbable route for these youths to follow because the very motivational dynamics that drove them to study and work so hard are rooted in a strong sense of obligation and duty to relatives. We have seen how a harsh sense of guilt surfaced among many informants because they were sent out of the Central American nightmare when others, parents and siblings, had to remain behind; that they now had the opportunity to study in the affluent society when most of their parents had had to leave school to join the labor force at an early age; that they may conceivably enter a college or professional training program in the new land, when their siblings' opportunities to do the equivalent in Central America are almost nonexistent (p. 128).

His analysis complements the perspectives shared by Southeast Asian refugee students. Trauma and family separation as well as obligation and determination to survive characterize the experiences of Southeast Asian students along the dimension *as refugees*.

Furthermore, given their living, collective memory of war, loss, and dislocation, Southeast Asian refugee students also share deep desires for peace and healing. Following a race riot in his high school, Ky recalls: "[The riot] brought back a lot of bad memories about the past. . . . The whole experience that I have been through. And I said, this is really sad."

After the riot, Dung asserts, "Fighting is bad, because my country very very hard fight. . . . Because I am Vietnamese, if I have trouble, I make it better." Ha adds, "We need to study for my life, for my future. And we don't want to fight." These qualities are much needed in urban schools and communities where violence and the war at home demand urgent intervention and prevention (Kiang & Kaplan, 1994; Kiang, 1991c).

"I STILL LEAVE MY HAIR LONG"—THE IMMIGRANT DIMENSION

Building new lives in this country and making the transition from refugees to immigrants is the primary focus of attention for many Southeast Asian Americans in school. Adjustment issues concerning lifestyle, weather, language, family responsibilities, and changing identity arise frequently in student interviews and writings. A central theme along this dimension is the experience of isolation and culture shock. A Chinese Vietnamese student eloquently writes:

Since the day I arrived in the United States, the word "stranger" never leaves my mind. I always find myself as a stranger here, even though I have been in many places, met many people. I feel frustrated sometimes because my neighbors or people in the community did not welcome me here or they looked at me as if I did not belong here. I still always wonder why do they treat me and other immigrants in such a way? Weren't they themselves immigrants or descendants of immigrants? In brief, the discrimination is officially banned, but one still find, in American society, discrimination exists in some places such as classrooms and many other public places as well. The longer I stay here, the more I feel isolated.

As described earlier, memories, cultural norms, and ideals of life in Vietnam, Laos, and Cambodia continue to have meaning for Southeast Asian refugee students, especially as reference points with which to contrast their sociocultural realities in this country. Some, for example, find it difficult to adjust to changes in the pace and style of life. Quynh, who came from Vietnam and is married with three children while attending college full-time, observes:

Here, life is complicated. Everything. . . . You have to work and work. You have to think about health insurance. In my country it's not like that. If you are rich, you can go to a private hospital. If you are not rich, the government can take care of you. You don't need to pay anything. Here I worry a lot more.

Daily life for immigrant households is filled with problems which require the attention of those family members who are most bilingual and bicultural, regardless of age. Students become interpreters and mediators between their families and U.S. society. A Chinese Cambodian student describes his duties as: "translate problems and reading English, writing, . . .go to hospital, pay the bill, writing letter, making phone calls, communicating with outside, and also, I worked to support my family, help pay rent."

In this context, immigrant students quickly develop important strengths of discipline, maturity, and reliability. A Chinese Vietnamese student reports: "We children in America are like decision maker in family." Sokal explains:

I handle that kind of situation every day at home. Taking care of my sister. When there's a meeting [at her school], you know, they ask me to go. It's like your mother can't do it, you know. She doesn't understand English.

The pressure may become overwhelming, however. Mai recalls:

I was too young to be responsible for this, I worried at every decision I made, I felt tired and depressed after work, the job I had after school hours. That's my senior year in high school. I knew it was too much for me but I had no choice.

The difficulties of immigrant family life also affect students' schoolwork. Sokal acknowledges:

I can't study at home. I have room to study but when I get home, something, you know, your sister tell you about this happened, your mother says, well, you have to do this, all the oil is gone, you know, the boiler is not working. There's so many things going wrong, and you say, well, I got to do this, I got to do that, and I can't study.

The central difficulty for students along this dimension, however, is being excluded from school discourse because of limited English proficiency. A Vietnamese high school student recalls, "When I came here, I don't feel free to speak and I always think that people don't want to hear me." Sokal states:

When you talk, people kind of look at you and say, you've got a funny pronunciation, you know, funny accent. . . . You don't want to raise your hand. You know the answer, what the answer is, but you don't want to say it.

Students experience isolation socially as well as academically. Tam observes: "I don't feel free to speak in American class, and I don't have a lot of American friends. I don't know their history or maybe the culture or anything. We don't talk together a lot."

Nevertheless, some recognize their native language skills as assets and their bilingual, bicultural skills as resources for other immigrants and the larger society. A Chinese Vietnamese woman writes:

What I want most to do for a career is to be a translator for the Chinese and Vietnamese community. Having gone through the handicap of not knowing what to do, where to go myself, not speaking a word of English, I feel compassionate for non-English speaking new immigrants. If I can make their lives a little easier, I will be satisfied.

Others connect their individual struggles to speak up in school to larger issues of voice for their communities (Nieto, 1992; Darder, 1991; Walsh, 1991). Linh states, "before I very silenced, afraid to talk to anybody. But now when I want to say something, I say it. . . . I want to have the right to talk, speak, or vote." Mai agrees: "You have to be strong and you have the voice, then you have the power and then you can help other people to realize what it is to have a community, to have a voice."

INTEGRATING VOICE AND GENDER: WOMEN'S CHANGING ROLES

Chanda views developing a voice in relation to changing gender roles, noting, "Here, women can develop their voice. They can participate, involve more. . . . The more you learn, the more you understand and you're aware of what's going on."

Immigrant women face a socioeconomic reality that places them in school and work, where they develop new views of their individual capabilities and social potential. Coming to the United States, in part, represents an opening of opportunities that would not have been available to them if their traditional social roles were maintained. Minh asserts: "In Vietnam, women's role is just housewife, staying home, do housework. And when they got here they change because the environment here is different. They have to go out and study and get a job." Seng adds:

Women change faster than men . . . [men] don't want to change anything. They like the way it is. But women, they want to change because they want the equality, they want the freedom, they want to be independent.

Amidst these contradictory experiences of exclusion and engagement, profound questions about identity emerge. Chanda sighs:

I'm happier here in a way because I can look for a better future. But in spirit, no. In Cambodia, I would feel shoulder to shoulder with the people. Even if I were a farmer, I would be proud; I would be qualified. Here, I feel so bad spiritually.

A Chinese Vietnamese student echoes:

After I had spent eight years in America, all I experienced is a very negative thing which I felt that I don't belong to any place. . . . I'm just a person who is being put in another society with no option and being pushed to assimilate quickly with American culture in order to fit in.

Alternatively, Mai suggests the possibility of constructing a new ethnic American identity:

I cannot say I'm Vietnamese, but I'm saying I'm Vietnamese American. Because I keep some and I, because I'm exposed to this society, to this custom, so I'm not being completely Vietnamese. I'm not being completely American. . . . But I still leave my hair long [laughs].[6]

Issues of immigrant acculturation and ethnic identity formation are especially relevant, though contentious at times, between generations within the family. Lien, for example, describes some of the cultural conflicts arising between herself, her mother, and her younger sister:

Sometimes I'm totally stuck in the middle. And I don't know how to deal with that problem because they are two different generations. . . . My sister, she doesn't spend a lot of time in Vietnam, I mean, talking about morals and values. . . . Sometimes, they have arguments, so, my Mom said, "You have to listen to me because I'm older and I have a lot of experience." Sometimes it's right. But sometimes it doesn't fit with the environment.

Many students are conscious of changes taking place in relation to their parents. Mai, for example, notes that, "Dealing with my father, I used to be quiet, not saying things back to him. . . . So now I change, well now I argue with him, but before I just listen."

While becoming more mature and outspoken through her Vietnamese-American identity, Mai also notes, "I think of my life and what I have gone through, maybe you can say a little bit I'm conservative, like look at tradition more and values." Chanda, who has also become increasingly acculturated to American society during her years at college, explains this contradictory process more fully:

When I first came, I just want everything just imitate American way. Everything Western way is just great, civilized! But when I grow older, I think how important my culture, the heritage, as I grow older I realize that how much I miss, I lose, and feel so sad, feel like why all this time I deny it? I deny it, I just think even being a Cambodian or anything part of Cambodian is just come from a Third World country is just so bad! And now it's just different. Now I feel like nothing should be ashamed of it. I should keep it and maintain it because it's something I can identify with, something that I not just hope that I maintain those traditional culture or customs, language for myself, but for my children, for the Cambodian population here. It's so important since the refugees, especially the Cambodians, are not treated as equals, are not treated as part of the mainstream. No matter what, we, why deny our own and want something that never never accept me? So, before I never think that Cambodian is good, the language. But now I suddenly just think it is so important and I try to learn more. Even write in Cambodian. I never think even, I never wore a traditional Cambodian dress, I just hate it! It's so too feminine to me. But now, you know, I love it. I even imagine to see if I have a wedding I would wear it. It's just beautiful! [laughs] So, yeah, the more I get older, the more I learn to appreciate my culture, everything.

While Mai's and Chanda's senses of becoming more traditional seem to contradict their senses of becoming more comfortable in American society, their perspectives are consistent with research by Portes and Bach (1985), which suggests that as acculturation takes place among Cuban, Puerto Rican, and Mexican immigrants through their familiarization with the American social system and through increased competence in the English language, their critical understanding of discrimination and prejudice in society increases along with their awareness of cultural identity and minority group consciousness. This challenges the melting-pot model of U.S. society, which assumes that immigrant acculturation accompanies a loss or weakening of ethnic identity along a linear path toward full assimilation. Such a path has never been possible for refugees and immigrants who are also non-white.

"I NEED A COMMUNITY TO GET SUPPORT"—THE DIMENSION AS RACIAL MINORITIES

Added to the difficulties of school, work, and family life, Southeast Asian immigrant and refugee students also face the realities of being urban minorities in a racist society. During the 1980s and 1990s, anti-Asian violence has escalated throughout the country (Aguilar-San Juan, 1994; U.S. Commission on Civil Rights, 1992). Racial violence and harassment against Asian Pacific Americans in schools have also caused alarm in recent years (U.S. Commission on Civil Rights, 1992; Kagiwada, 1989; Morse, 1989). Suzuki (1989b) suggests that social-psychological problems of Asian Pacific American students may be increasing because of the climate of growing anti-Asian sentiment.

In an urban high school, Vietnamese-American students confirm that they witness or experience racial conflict and harassment every day (Kiang & Kaplan, 1994). One student protests, "I feel like I get stepped on every day in that school." Individual black, white, and Hispanic students daily disregard the Vietnamese students' ethnic, linguistic, and cultural identities, and instead assign them a racial identity as "Chinese" and "Chinks." A student recounts: "When we pass by them, they give you some kind of like a dirty look. . . . They say, "Look at that Chinese girl . . ." And then they call like, 'Chinks, go back to where you belong.'"

In elementary schools, too (Kiang, Nguyen, & Sheehan, 1995), Vietnamese-American fourth graders similarly complain. "A big teenager fight with me on the bus and swear at me"; and "I didn't do anything but they did that to me. . . . Maybe they thought I was Chinese."

Many college students also recall occasions of verbal harassment and even physical violence. Donna writes:

School was like a hell to me because I do not speak English. Everyone make fun of me, calling me names, oppressed me. Especially in the school bus, they pull my hair, hit me, and I do not know how to say do not pull my hair or anything. No one help me because I am the only yellow skin in the bus.

Recognition of minority status emerges amidst isolation, institutional categorization, and ongoing experiences of discrimination. Mai writes: "I really did not thought much that I was an Asian until I lived in America." Mai's initial awareness of racism comes from a job on campus:

They try to ignore me, whenever I say hi to them, so it really frustrating, like I'm not being treated as human. . . . How come they act like that to me? I told myself maybe that my fault, that I didn't do a good job. But then I think it over. I didn't do anything wrong. . . . I feel really bad. I still angry. . . . I never forget this thing.

She later describes her developing minority group consciousness:

The experience I face in American society as a whole, the experience of facing racism . . . because I am a minority, I need a community to get support. I want it to be strong and deal with whatever happen in the society . . . but the only thing that you can do is you have to fight. The more you get higher, then the more you have to fight to fit in.

Mai's minority group identification and analysis of power relations are shared by others. Linh also recognizes the importance of having collective community support for minority group members:

We have to be in groups because we are minority, so we have to be together in order to survive . . . because we are a minority we must have the community so it's easy to another student when they first arrive here. Give them advice or when they have a problem. Like me when I had a lot of problems in high school I had no one ask, no one help me.

For Southeast–Asian American students, jobs are a central concern because they typically work as many hours each week as they go to school. In the work setting, many face inequities which affect their material and psychological well-being. Phat comments:

The reason they hire minority students is because they're looking for some workers who are cheaper labor and trying to fulfill the affirmative action regulations. . . . On my job, they don't need the second languages I speak. All they're looking for is cheaper labor to minimize the costs of the company.

Though Phat's assessment, at first glance, may seem cynical, his view is strongly supported by the socioeconomic reality in which he and his peers as refugees, immigrants, and minorities are located in the low-wage sector of the local service economy—hotels and restaurants, janitorial services, data entry, and clerical work. In many cases, they also experience discrimination on the job from employers who assign them extra work without extra compensation and from customers who direct racial slurs against them. The demands of work further reduce both the quantity and quality of time available for school, and take their toll on the self-esteem of Southeast Asian students.

Like their escape stories, many students have discrimination stories to share. Linda, a Chinese Vietnamese, recalls:

It is long story. I was hired in a hospital. . . . I did exactly the same work other people did, but I found out I was paid $2 less than other people. The other bad thing was that my supervisor calculated my hours less than I worked . . . in my department I was only Chinese girl. . . . I hated that job.

Chanda also remembers:

I work in a cleaning company in a nursing home. They treated me very badly, the boss. They pay me less than other people and some people that were hired at that time, in a later period, they got higher wage than I did. The way they treated me like in a very cruel behavior . . . sometimes I want to kill them. . . . I cannot live in a society that put you down because you are an ethnic group. And without education, you are nothing. So that's why, you know, I think no matter how hard it is, I have to struggle in school. I have to have education so people would not treat me that bad.

For some like Chanda, their experiences of being exploited as minorities in the workforce motivate them to continue their education. Others like Mai and Linh recognize the need for minority group identification and community support as a way to help themselves and their peers from being isolated and victimized by racial discrimination. After hearing others' discrimination stories, Minh concludes:

They tried to harass you and prove that they have power and that you are a dumb gook. That's what my supervisor did to me. . . . That's the attitude that a lot of people treat you that way. So that's why I say we have to tell each other these stories.

INTEGRATING THE DIMENSIONS

A multidimensional theoretical framework offers a valuable approach with which to analyze the complex layers of problems facing Southeast Asian refugee students in school. Issues and barriers such as conflicting learning styles, family loss, PTSD, limited English proficiency, family responsibilities, exclusion, alienation, discrimination, and racism significantly hinder their achievement and quality of life for students in both the academic and social domains of school.

However, the multidimensional framework also serves to identify vital sources of strength that enable Southeast Asian refugee students to cope with their difficulties. These internal resources include: homeland reference points, critical thinking skills, well-tested survival strategies, resilience, maturity, discipline, motivation to succeed based on family duty, deep desires for peace and healing, bilingual and bicultural skills, recognition of the importance of voice, dynamic views of identity and changing gender roles, and collective minority group awareness. Schools cannot afford to let these strengths go untapped and unrecognized.

The validity of this type of multidimensional approach can be further tested with other non-white, immigrant, and refugee populations such as Salvadoran or Haitian students in U.S. schools. Other background factors, including refugee wave, gender, and family context (Nidorf, 1985) are also important to consider in working with Southeast Asian–American students.

In the lives of the students, however, these distinct dimensions *as Southeast Asians, as refugees, as immigrants,* and *as racial minorities* are integrated, as illustrated by Mai's story about her family's car being firebombed. In a typical written narrative, Chanda weaves these various dimensions together and profoundly shares the meaning of her lived experience and multidimensional identity. She signifies:

The more I absorb the environment I live in, the more I have a better sense of real life, I continue to see things that divide me from American society. But I could not recognize what it is and why. Everyday living just puts a lot of pressure on me, the anger and struggle I am facing are never overcome. It is crying inside me . . . . I want to be accepted, recognized and authorized not just in paper but in action. I came from a family of five, I am the only girl in the family. My parents and one of my brothers died in the Cambodian civil war in 1975. I have one brother left who I just heard from that he is in a Thailand refugee camp. After the Khmer Rouge took place, my comfortable city life was destroyed. I had very little schooling, just enough to read and write my native language. I was forced to leave my hometown to an out of date civilization. There in an adolescent development stage I received nothing but a very hard condition of life. I became illiterate, did not know what day, month, or year or anything that had to do with the inside or outside world. I could not bear life on the plantation, I became very sick and was in a stage of dying several times. Life over there was very hard but one thing that I want to tell you proudly is that although I lived in a condition of poverty, I had the privilege of being a citizen among my own people. There was no prejudice against me and I did not even know prejudice exists. What I want to point out is that this is a value of a person when he or she has a native country . . . . I have to admit that I did not have to fight hard against the war of poverty [in America] as I did at home. But, indeed, I have fought very hard against the war of discrimination, prejudice, and their being so ignorant about other races.

Chanda's multilayered narrative construction reflects her crafting of an integrated, multidimensional identity, filled with pain, pride, and contradiction. Yearning for the past while living for the future, Chanda, Mai, and many other Southeast Asian Americans are here in our present. Their strengths and struggles in school and society have much meaning, if we recognize who they are.

NOTES

1. Support for this work, by the Institute for Asian American Studies and the William Joiner Center for the Study of War and Social Consequences at the University of Massachusetts, Boston, is gratefully acknowledged.

2. Pseudonyms are used for all informants. Quotations are excerpted from interview transcripts.

3. Research by Jaime Rodriguez, Erwin Parson, and the Full Circle Trauma Recovery Project of the William Joiner Center for the Study of War and Social Consequences suggests that returning to the battlefield facilitates the psychoemotional healing process for some U.S. Vietnam veterans by replacing their memories of war and trauma with fresh images of a country and people at peace. Research on post-traumatic stress disorder and the mental health needs of Southeast Asian refugees has not yet addressed the psychoemotional impact of refugees returning to their home countries voluntarily to visit. Although U.S. veterans and Southeast Asian refugees do not share equivalent experiences of trauma, it is possible that returning to one's homeland tempers the guilt and grief of forced exile. The sense of loss associated with leaving one's family, country, and culture is, perhaps, alleviated if one can return, even as a visitor. Anecdotal evidence such as the observation by Tam suggests that this may be true for some. This is a promising, albeit complex and politically difficult, area of refugee mental health research to develop if conditions in both the United States and Southeast Asia allow. Further discussion of PTSD and refugee mental health is presented in the next section, titled "The Dimension as Refugees."

4. Like the interview quotes, excerpts from student writing are presented verbatim, including errors in spelling, word selection, and grammar.

5. For more information on these pilot studies, contact The William Joiner Center for Study of War and Social Consequences, University of Massachusetts, Boston, MA 02125–3393.

6. Women traditionally in Vietnam wear long hair as a symbol of beauty and femininity.

REFERENCES

Aguilar-San Juan, K. (ed.). (1994). *The state of Asian America*. Boston, MA: South End Press.

Ascher, C. (1984). "The social and psychological adjustment of Southeast Asian refugees." *ERICICUE Digest* (April).

Astin, A. W. (1988). *Four critical years*. San Francisco, CA: Jossey-Bass.

Atkinson, D. R., J. G. Ponterotto, & A. R. Sanchez. (1984). "Attitudes of Vietnamese and Anglo-American students toward counseling." *Journal of College Student Personnel*, 25(5), pp. 448–452.

Bangsberg, H. F. et al. (1967). *Public universities of the Republic of Vietnam*. Wisconsin State University, Stevens Point.

Brende, J. O. & E. Parson. (1985). *Vietnam veterans: The road to recovery*. New York, NY: Signet.

Caplan, N., J. K. Whitmore, & M. H. Choy. (1989). *The boat people and achievement in America*. Ann Arbor, MI: University of Michigan Press.

Center for Applied Linguistics. (1981). "Indochinese students in U.S. schools: A guide for administrators." In *Language in Education* (42). Washington, DC: ERIC Clearinghouse on Language and Linguistics.

Chu, T. (1989). "The role of the youth in building a community overseas." *The Bridge*, 6(4) (December), pp. 9–11.

Chun, K. (1980). "The myth of Asian American success and its educational ramifications." *IRCD Bulletin*, Teachers College, 5(1, 2), pp. 1–12.

Chung, C. H. (1994). *Vietnamese students: Changing patterns, changing needs*. San Francisco: Many Cultures Publishing.

Cummins, J. (1989). *Empowering minority students*. Sacramento, CA: California Association for Bilingual Education.

———. (1981). "The role of primary language development in promoting educational success for language minority students," in California State Department of Education (ed.), *Schooling and language minority students: A theoretical framework*. Los Angeles: Evaluation, Dissemination and Assessment Center, California State University.

Darder, A. (1991). *Culture and power in the classroom*. New York, NY: Bergin & Garvey.

Duong, B. (1958). "The Confucian tradition in the history of Vietnamese education." Ph.D. dissertation, School of Education, Harvard University.

Fernandez, M. S. (1988). "Issues in counseling Southeast-Asian students." *Journal of Multicultural Counseling and Development, 16* (October), pp. 157–166.

Frakt, D. (1990). "The Vietnamese American college student." Senior Honors Thesis, History Department, University of California at Irvine.

Freeman, J. M. (1989). *Hearts of sorrow*. Palo Alto, CA: Stanford University Press.

Gardner, R. W., B. Robey, & P. C. Smith. (1985). "Asian Americans: Growth, change and diversity." *Population Bulletin, 40*(4).

Henkin, A. B. & L. T. Nguyen. (1981). *Between two cultures: The Vietnamese in America*. Saratoga, CA: R & E Publishers.

Herman, J. L. (1992). *Trauma and recovery*. New York, NY: Basic Books.

Kagiwada, G. (1989). "The killing of Thong Hy Huynh: Implications of a Rashomon perspective," in Gail Nomura et al. (eds.), *Frontiers of Asian American studies*. Pullman, WA: Washington State University Press, pp. 253–265.

Kiang, P. N. (1993). "Stratification of public higher education," in L. A. Revilla, G. M. Nomura, S. Wong, and S. Hune (eds.), *Bearing dreams, shaping visions*. Pullman, WA: Washington State University Press, pp. 233–245.

———. (1992). "Issues of curriculum and community for first-generation Asian Americans in College," in L. S. Zwerling and H. B. London (eds.), *First-generation students: Confronting the cultural issues*. New directions for community colleges, No. 80. San Francisco, CA: Jossey-Bass, pp. 97–112.

———. (1991a). *New Roots and voices: The education of Southeast Asian students at an urban public university*. Ed.D. dissertation, Harvard Graduate School of Education.

———. (1991b). "About face: Recognizing Asian/Pacific American Vietnam veterans in Asian American studies." *Amerasia Journal, 17*(3), pp. 22–40.

———. (1991c). "Social studies for the Pacific century." *Social Education, 55*(7) (November/December), pp. 458–462.

———. (1990). *The challenge of changing demographics: Southeast Asian parent empowerment in Lowell, Massachusetts*. Monograph No. 1. Boston: Massachusetts Association for Bilingual Education.

Kiang, P. N., & J. Kaplan. (1994). "Where do we stand?: Views of racial conflict by Vietnamese American high school students in a black-and-white context." *Urban Review, 26*(2), pp. 95–119.

Kiang, P. N., & V. W. Lee. (1993). "Exclusion or contribution: K–12 education policy." *The State of Asian Pacific America.* Los Angeles, CA: LEAP Asian Pacific American Public Policy Institute and UCLA Asian American Studies Center, pp. 25–48.

Kiang, P.N., N. L. Nguygen, & R. L. Sheehan. (1995). "Don't ignore it: Documenting racial harassment in a fourth-grade Vietnamese bilingual classroom." *Equity and Excellence in Education,* 28(1), pp. 31–35.

Kulka, R. A. et al. (1990). *Trauma and the Vietnam War generation: Report of findings from the National Vietnam Veterans readjustment study.* New York, NY: Brunner/Mazel.

Matin, G. H., K. N. Chan and T. H. Tran. (1992). "The Indochinese in Wisconsin." *The Wisconsin Counselor,* 6(1) (Fall).

Morse, D. (1989). "Prejudicial studies." *Northeast— The Hartford Courant* (November).

Nayematsu, C. S. (1987). "An investigation of the cognitive and non-cognitive variables affecting Asian American students' academic progress at a midwestern university." M.A. thesis, University of Minnesota.

Nguyen, A. Q. (1988). "The Yale Vietnamese community." Unpublished paper.

Nguyen, H. L. & J. M. Halpern (eds.). (1989). *The Far East comes near: Autobiographical accounts of Southeast Asian students in America.* Amherst, MA: University of Massachusetts Press.

Nguyen, T. (1989). "Vietnamese identity: Are you Vietnamese or Vietnamese American?" *Pacific Ties,* University of California at Los Angeles (November), pp. 16–17.

Nguyen, T. P. (1984). "Positive self-concept in the Vietnamese bilingual child." *Bilingual Journal* (Spring), pp. 9–14.

Nidorf, J. F. (1985). "Mental health and refugee youths: A model for diagnostic training," in T. C. Owan (ed.), *Southeast Asian mental health: Treatment, prevention, services, and research.* Washington, DC: National Institute of Mental Health, pp. 391–429.

Nieto, S. (1992). *Affirming diversity.* New York, NY: Longman.

Ong, P., & S. J. Hee. (1993). "The growth of the Asian Pacific American population." *The state of Asian Pacific America.* Los Angeles, CA: LEAP Asian Pacific American Public Policy Institute and UCLA Asian American Studies Center, pp. 11–23.

Parmley, S. (1990). "The 'model minority' myth." *Boston Globe* (August 20), pp. 1, 8–9.

Portes, A. & R. Bach. (1985). *Latin journey.* Baltimore, MD: Johns Hopkins University Press.

Quality Education for Minorities Project. (1990). *Education that works: An action plan for the education of minorities.* Cambridge, MA: MIT.

Skinner, K. A. & G. L. Hendricks. (1979). "The shaping of ethnic self-identity among Indochinese refugees." *Journal of Ethnic Studies,* 7(3), pp. 25–41.

Sonnenberg, S. M., A. S. Blank & J. A. Talbott (eds.). (1985). *The trauma of war: Stress and recovery in Viet Nam veterans.* Washington, D.C.: American Psychiatry Press.

Suarez-Orozco, M. M. (1989). *Central American refugees and U.S. high schools.* Stanford, CA: Stanford University Press.

Suzuki, B. H. (1989a). "Asian Americans as the 'model minority.'" *Change* (November/December), pp. 13–19.

———. (1989b). "Higher education issues in the Asian American community." Unpublished paper.

———. (1977). "Education and socialization of Asian Americans: A revisionist analysis of the 'model minority' thesis." *Amerasia Journal, 4*(2), pp. 23–51.

Takami, D. (September 1988). "Growing pains: Southeast Asian refugee youth." *Rice,* pp. 50–54.

Tollefson, J. W. (1989). *Alien winds: The re-education of America's Indochinese refugees.* New York, NY: Praeger.

Trueba, H. T., L. Cheng, & K. Ima. (1993). *Myth or reality: Adaptive strategies of Asian Americans in California.* London, England: Falmer Press.

Trueba, H. T., L. Jacobs, & E. Kirton. (1990). *Cultural conflict and adaptation: The case of Hmong children in American society.* Philadelphia, PA: Falmer Press.

U.S. Commission on Civil Rights. (1992). *Civil rights issues facing Asian Americans in the 1990s.* Washington, D.C.

Walsh, C. E. (1991). *Pedagogy and the struggle for voice: Issues in language, power, and schooling for Puerto Ricans.* New York, NY: Bergin and Garvey.

Wehrly, B. (1988). "Cultural diversity from an international perspective." *Journal of Multicultural Counseling and Development, 16* (January), pp. 3–15.

Welaratna, U. (1993). *Beyond the killing fields.* Palo Alto, CA: Stanford University Press.

Language Policy and Social Implications for Addressing the Bicultural Immigrant Experience in the United States

Alberto M. Ochoa

Immigrants and refugees will continue to come, giving rise to energetic communities, infusing new blood in the local labor markets, filling positions at different levels of the economy, and adding to the diversity of sounds, sights, and tastes in our cities. The history of America has been, to a large extent, the history of its immigrants—their progress reflecting and simultaneously giving impulse to the nation's expansion. Although problems and struggles are inevitable along the way, in the long run the diverse talents and energies of the newcomers will reinforce the vitality of American society and the richness of its culture (Portes & Rumbaut, 1990, p. 246).

Immigrant bashing is a popular activity in assigning blame for the nation's economic problems. When stagnation is evident in the national economy and unemployment exceeds seven percent, a pervasive fear that one's job is on the line often emerges. Anxiety triggers frustration and blame; resentment towards immigrants, documented and undocumented, becomes an ugly side of racism, nativism, and xenophobia. Such fear and xenophobia is reflected in our nation's language policy. At best it tolerates linguistic and cultural differences, with the condition that those who speak a language other than English need to assimilate as quickly as possible to the language of dominance—the English language.

This chapter will examine four issues. First, a typology will be provided for understanding the relationship between language policy and the social and educational implications for immigrant communities. Second, an analysis of language policy in the United States will be provided that addresses the evolution of language rights and educational tensions that have emerged in response to the rights of immigrant communities in the schools of our nation. Third, it will address ten factors that contribute to the promotion of racism, nativism, and xenophobia when bicultural persons choose to maintain their primary language. Last, policy recommendations will be provided to address the sociopolitical, economic, and educational rights of immigrant communities in the United States. Immigrant communities consist of American citizens who continue to practice their cultural traditions and speak the language of their national origin, permanent resident aliens, refugees, and undocumented persons.

LANGUAGE POLICY TYPOLOGY

An analysis of immigrant youth success in the schools of our nation initially points to students who are semilingual and underachieving (Portes & Rumbaut, 1990). For the most part, these students attend schools whose language policy is directed at assimilating these students to English language use in order to provide them with equal educational opportunity. Embedded in this policy are values that work to assure that schools socially reproduce a class structure. This is evident by language policy designed to assimilate immigrants to the dominant American values through educational practices that have a low cognitively demanding curriculum, and without regard to the incorporation of their language and culture into the curricula of the school (Skuttnab-Kangas, 1981). In our schools ethnically diverse students are referred to as being "disadvantaged," "economically deprived," and having "linguistic deficits."

An international perspective of language policy is useful in analyzing educational services to immigrant communities in the United States. A policy of forced assimilation can be understood through conflict theory. This theory examines the relationship between those in control of the dominant cultural group and the subordinate cultural groups in society in terms of how they do or do not support cultural and structural integration (Skuttnab-Kangas, 1981; Feinberg & Soltis, 1992).

Figure 1 illustrates a model of language policy, applicable to the United States and the international community, by using the categories of language policy, language outcome, educational intervention under a given policy, and the dominant society's position on cultural and structural integration. Cultural integration calls for the recognition, acceptance, and incorporation of subordinate cultural communities in all aspects of society's institutions. Structural integration calls for access to the goods and services and to the institutional privileges of the dominant and mainstream society. In addition, structural incorporation calls for social security, economic and occupational life, political participation, and opportunities for social mobility (Paulston, 1975). Within this model, five language policy scenarios can be identified.

The first scenario is the monolingual language policy. This policy calls for the immigrant student to acquire English proficiency as quickly as possible without any type of educational support. This intervention is referred to as

Figure 1
Language Policy: Typology

SCENARIO	Language Policy	Linguistic Outcome	Educational Intervention	Dominant Culture Support for Structural and Cultural Incorporation	
				STRUCTURAL	*CULTURAL*
US PERSPECTIVE	MONOLINGUAL	MONOLINGUAL ENGLISH (Semilingualism)	SINK OR SWIM Subtractive Immersion	Non-Supportive and limited Integration	Not Valued Forced Assimilation
	BILINGUAL	MONOLINGUAL ENGLISH (Limited Bilingualism)	TRANSITIONAL Bilingualism	Non-Supportive with minimal Integration	Not Valued, with Toleration & Assimilation
GLOBAL PERSPECTIVE	MONOLINGUAL	BILINGUAL	Additive Immersion in another language other than the language of the economy L2	SUPPORT with dominant cultural group providing access	YES with support for multiculturalism
	BILINGUAL	BILINGUAL	Maintenance Bilingualism biliteracy in L1 & L2	SUPPORT for equal integration	YES cultural pluralism
	BILINGUAL	MULTILINGUAL	Maintenance Bilingualism multi-literacy in L1 & L2 & L3	SUPPORT for direct access and economic Integration	YES socio-political pluralism

the "sink or swim" approach. This policy is strongly supported by the English Only movement in our nation. The social outcome of this policy is forced assimilation, for the cultural background of the immigrant is not valued or accepted, if one is to benefit from the goods and services of society. This policy provides no educational intervention to address the linguistic and academic development of immigrant youth. Furthermore, no structural access is possible given the low academic attainment and career options available to these students under this subtractive immersion language policy (Espinosa & Ochoa, 1992).

The second scenario is the subtractive bilingual language policy. This policy goal is to tolerate language and cultural differences, with the goal of assimilating the student to the dominant language of the economy as quickly as possible through support of some kind of bilingual instruction. Generally, this approach is known as "transitional bilingualism." With respect to cultural integration, this policy tolerates cultural diversity, but within the domain of the dominant cultural values. Structural incorporation is denied by deficit-based academic interventions that prevent access to higher education (Espinosa & Ochoa, 1992).

The third scenario is the additive bilingual language policy. This policy values the acquisition of a second language through immersion in a language other than English, with the goal of developing full literacy (speaking, reading, and writing) in a second language and the language of the dominant economy. Students enter school speaking only the dominant language of the economy, and desire to acquire a second language. A cognitively demanding achievement curriculum is provided through programmatic bilingual instruction that yields access to higher education. Cultural integration is promoted through the support of multiculturalism and structural incorporation is supported by the dominant cultural group through providing access into the salient institutions of society. Generally, this policy is driven by a dominant culture which desires that its children have access to and understanding of the international economic community.

The fourth scenario also calls for additive bilingualism. This policy is best known as "maintenance bilingualism." This policy, from the initial entry into the schooling process, promotes the acquisition of full literacy in two languages, with the first being the language of the student and the second the language of the dominant economy in the society. This policy supports and values the language of the immigrant student. As with additive bilingualism, a cognitively demanding achievement curriculum is provided through programmatic bilingual instruction that yields access to higher education. Cultural integration is valued and promoted, while structural incorporation into all of the institutions of society is the desired goal. Few schools in the United States support this policy.

The fifth policy is one that calls for multilingualism and cultural pluralism. This policy promotes the full development of literacy skills in at least three languages, and full recognition of multicultural values and structural incorporation into all institutions of society. This policy supports sociopolitical cultural pluralism and the right to direct access and economic integration. The language communities have the same access to educational benefits, economic opportunities, and political representation as any other language community in the society.

Scenarios four and five suggest a participatory democracy that is guided by the right to equal encouragement and equal status. In the United States, the language policy that guides our institutions is at best "transitional bilingualism." This policy tolerates language diversity, while negating structural access to the economic and political institutions of society. A brief overview of this position follows with an examination of statutes and regulations that have evolved through the civil rights movement of the 1960s and 1970s. Such proscriptions currently promote a language policy that is transitional and assimilationist in nature and is defined in multiple political ways by the policy stakeholders of our nation.

ANALYSIS OF LANGUAGE POLICY IN THE UNITED STATES

Historically, from the nineteenth century to the present, America's democratic ideology has purportedly sought a means of providing equal opportunity for everyone. Within this perspective, education has often been viewed as the means of assuring that all members of society can begin at the same starting line regardless of parental occupation or social class (Spring, 1978). However, for immigrant students whose dominant language is other than English, their right to equal educational opportunity is a recent phenomenon that is embedded in the struggle for civil rights and social justice.

As a nation struggling to provide equal educational opportunity for all students, one can trace the initial operationalization of this ideal to six specific historical milestones:

- The 14th Amendment of the U.S. Constitution, 1868.
- *Plessy v. Ferguson* Supreme Court Decision of 1896.
- *Brown v. Board of Education* Supreme Court Decision of 1954.
- Civil Rights Act of 1964.
- Department of Health, Education and Welfare, May 25, 1970 Memorandum to all of the school districts in the nation.
- *Lau v. Nichols* Supreme Court Decision of 1974.

The concept of equal educational opportunity for linguistically diverse persons has evolved from a series of judicial, legislative, and administrative rulings that can be traced to the U.S. Constitution. These rulings provide the legal bases for school districts to address the needs of linguistically diverse immigrant (LDI) students.

The initial impetus for the equal educational opportunity concept can be found in the 14th Amendment of the U.S. Constitution. The 14th Amendment was adopted in 1868. It was one of three Civil War amendments drafted by Congress to ensure the permanence of the Civil Rights Act of 1866, by placing it beyond the reach of presidential, congressional, or Supreme Court interference (Winston, 1980). More specifically, the three amendments guaranteed the following:

• The 13th Amendment abolished slavery in the United States.

• The 14th Amendment declared that all persons born or naturalized in the United States and subject to the jurisdiction thereof, are citizens of the United States and of the State wherein they reside. No State shall make or enforce any law which shall abridge the privileges or immunities of citizens of the United States; nor shall any State deprive any person of life, liberty, or property without due process of law; nor deny to any person within its jurisdiction the equal protection of the laws.

• The 15th Amendment established the right to vote for all citizens regardless of "race, color, or previous condition of servitude."

In addition, the 14th Amendment (1868) provides four directives: (1) protects the privileges and immunities of all citizens; (2) provides equal protection under the law; (3) gives Congress the power to enforce by legislation; and (4) establishes the principle of equal opportunity.

However, between 1868 and 1896, the courts of the nation struggled to define the application of the "equal protection" clause of the 14th Amendment, while southern states enacted the Black Codes that restricted the newly gained freedom of ex-slaves. It was not until 1896 that the Supreme Court issued a decision in *Plessy v. Ferguson* (163 U.S. 537, 1896). This decision advanced the concept of equal opportunity as meaning "separate but equal." *Plessy* was a challenge by a black man to a Louisiana statute which required blacks and whites to sit in separate cars on trains. The statute was attacked on the grounds that it conflicted with the 14th Amendment's equal protection of the laws and due process provisions. The Court, however, interpreted the equal protection clause as requiring the enforcement of absolute equality of the races before the law, not as requiring the abolition of distinctions based upon color or to enforce social, as distinguished from political, equality.

Thus, thirty-one years after slavery was abolished, the Supreme Court upheld the constitutionality of the segregation of the races and established the "separate but equal" doctrine with respect to the concept of equal opportunity. Two separate societies—one black, one white—were sanctioned by the Supreme Court. The "separate but equal doctrine" emerged in "Jim Crow" laws across the South. Laws were enacted that required the separation of people of color and whites in almost every realm of life, in schools, housing, jobs, public accommodations, cemeteries, hospitals, drinking fountains, and labor unions. In 1931 and 1947, Latinos in California challenged the "separate but equal doctrine" through the court cases in *Alvarez v. Lemon Grove School District* (Superior Court of the State of California, Writ of Mandate No. 66625, March 30, 1931), and in *Mendez v. Westminster School District* (64 F. Supp. 544, 1946). Both cases documented that children of Latino background were segregated solely on the basis of their national origin and language. By 1940, the issue of what constitutes segregation of the races was quite clear. The courts in a number of cases declared that any person of color other than white belonged to the colored race (Tesconi & Hurwitz, 1974).

It was not until the *Brown v. Board of Education of Topeka, Kansas* court case of 1954 (347 U.G.S. 483) that the Supreme Court of our nation, using the 14th Amendment, overruled all its earlier "separate but equal" decisions, concluding that in the field of education the "separate but equal" doctrine had no place. Also in the case of *Hernandez v. Texas* (347 U.S. 475, 1954) the Court held that Latinos/Hispanics constituted an identifiable class for the purpose of the 14th Amendment. Hence, the *Brown v. Board of Education* decision: (1) struck down the "separate but equal" doctrine; (2) declared the separation of black and white students to be unconstitutional; (3) ordered desegregation of schools with "deliberate speed"; and (4) established the principle of equal educational opportunity.

Ten years elapsed before the U.S. Congress passed into legislation the Civil Rights Act of 1964, in response to *Brown v. Board of Education.* Title VI of the Civil Rights Act of 1964 (42 U.S.C. 2000c, d) declared:

No person in the United States shall, on the ground of race, color, or national origin, be excluded from participation in, be denied the benefits of, or be subjected to discrimination under any program or activity receiving federal financial assistance (P.L. 88–352, 78 Stat. 252).

In addition, the provisions of Section 601 of the Civil Rights Act of 1964 called for the U.S. federal government to: (1) forbid discrimination on account of race, color, or national origin (language) in any federally funded activity; (2) authorize the Department of HEW to apply compliance procedures and to review and withhold funds; (3) authorize the Department of Justice to sue in federal court to secure the desegregation of public facilities; and (4) establish the principle of equal opportunity for linguistically diverse immigrant (LDI) students.

Six more years passed before the U.S. Department of Education sent a memorandum to school districts with more than five percent national origin minority children. The HEW May 25, 1970 Memorandum (42 U.S.C. 2000d Office for Civil Rights Notice 35 Fed. Reg. 11595) specified how Title VI of the Civil Rights Act of 1964 applied to LDI students. The memorandum stated the intent of affirmative steps to be taken by school districts (Department HEW):

Where inability to speak and understand the English language excludes national origin minority group children from effective participation in the educational program offered by a school district, the district must take affirmative steps to rectify the language deficiency in order to open its instructional program to these students (1970, pp. 1–2).

Any ability grouping or tracking system employed by the school system to deal with the special language skill needs of national origin minority group children must be designed to meet such language skill needs as soon as possible and must not operate as an educational dead-end or permanent track (1970, p. 2).

The memorandum affirmed the application of the Civil Rights Act of 1964 to language minority children and identified three main areas of concern: (1) unequal access to participation in school programs because of language, (2) segregation by tracking, ability grouping, and assignment to special education; and (3) the exclusion of parents from school information. It instructed the U.S. Office for Civil Rights to implement review and compliance procedures, and established the principle of equal educational opportunity for language minority children.

The last legal milestone is the *Lau v. Nichols* Supreme Court decision of 1974. The evolution of the Supreme Court case of *Lau v. Nichols* began on March 25, 1970 when thirteen non-English-speaking Chinese American students filed suit in the Federal District Court in San Francisco against the San Francisco Board of Education (SFUSD) on behalf of nearly 3,000 Chinese-speaking students. In their complaint, the non-English-speaking Chinese-American students argued for second language instruction and content instruction in the basic skill areas in the target language of the students. The SFUSD argued that its sole responsibility to any child was equal access to the resources provided to all children on the same basis (SFUSD, 1975).

In 1970, the Federal Court agreed with the school district and denied the non-English-speaking children any relief. In 1972, the case was appealed in the U.S. Court of Appeals for the Ninth Circuit Court. Again, the Appellate Court expressed sympathy for the plight of the students but concluded that rights to equal educational opportunities had been satisfied through the equal access perspective. On January 21, 1974, the Supreme Court issued its unanimous decision reversing the Appellate Court opinion. Relying on Title VI of the Civil Rights Act of 1964, the Supreme Court ruled that the failure of any school system to provide English language instruction to its non-English-speaking students constitutes a denial of the "meaningful opportunity to participate in the equal treatment of unequals." Refuting directly the position and language of the lower courts, the Supreme Court declared (*Lau v. Nichols*):

There is no equality of treatment merely by providing students with the same facilities, textbooks, teachers, and curriculum; for students who do not understand English are effectively foreclosed from any meaningful education (1975, p. 566).

The unanimous decision by a court emphasizes loudly and clearly that the court in *Lau* was not concerned with the intentions or motivations of the school district. Regardless of how much good faith a school district might be exercising in trying to meet the problem, the only relevant factor is whether the child receives a "meaningful" and "comprehensible" education and "effective participation in the educational program." Thus, under the *Lau v. Nichols* decision, the highest court of our nation (1) determined a denial of equal educational opportunity under the Civil Rights Act (CRA) of 1964; (2) authorized the enforcement of the CRA of 1964; (3) affirmed the validity of the HEW May 25, 1970 Memorandum; and (4) affirmed the authority of the government to require affirmative remedial efforts to give special attention to linguistically diverse immigrant students.

In response to the *Lau* decision, the U.S. Office for Civil Rights issued in July 1975 a set of guidelines for schools to follow in order to attain *Lau* compliance. The guidelines became known as the "Task Force Findings Specifying Remedies Available for Eliminating Past Educational Practices Ruled Unlawful Under Lau v. Nichols." From July 1975 through 1981, the guidelines served as interpretive federal guidelines by which the Office for Civil Rights conducted compliance reviews and served to determine educational minimal expectations for districts, should they desire to develop and implement guidelines that are equal to or better than the *Lau* remedies.

Since 1974 some major legal and educational issues have been raised with respect to the educational rights of linguistically diverse and immigrant students. A brief overview of these issues will be discussed. Thirteen educational tensions have emerged since 1974 as school districts throughout the nation began to address the spirit of the *Lau v. Nichols* Supreme Court decision. These tensions deal with the legal responsibility of educational institutions to provide equal educational opportunity to linguistically diverse immigrants and ethnolinguistic students, as well as with the resistance of educational institutions to provide even the minimal educational services that are meaningful to students.

The first tension covers *State responsibility to linguistically diverse immigrant students*. Congress through the passage of the Equal Educational Opportunity Act (E.E.O.A.) of 1974 included provisions under Section 1703 prohibiting a state from denying equal educational opportunity. This statute (E.E.O.A, Section 1703 f) recognizes the state's role in assuring equal educational opportunity for LDI students. The statute reads:

No state shall deny equal educational opportunity to an individual on account of his or her race, color, sex, or national origin, by the failure by an educational agency to take appropriate action to overcome language barriers that impede equal participation by its students in its instructional programs (88 Stat. p. 515).

The second tension in question is *school district responsibility to provide effective instructional programs for LDI students.* In the U.S. District Court of New York, in the case of *Rios v. Read* in 1977 (480 F. Supp. 14 [E.D.N.Y.] 1978), the court discussed the school district's responsibilities for the adequacy of instructional programs for immigrant students. The court indicated that unless the district's bilingual program was effective, a *Lau* violation would be triggered the same as if no program were offered. Furthermore, the court ruled that "affirmative steps" required under *Lau v. Nichols* refers to an educational program that emphasizes the importance of bilingual education in the academic and personal growth of the "language deficient child." The court in its finding stated (*Rios v. Read*, 1977):

It is not enough simply to provide a program for language disadvantaged children or even to staff the program with bilingual teachers; rather, the critical question is whether the program is designed to assure as much as is reasonably possible the language deficient child's growth in the English language. An inadequate program is as harmful to a child who does not speak English as no program at all (p. 15).

The third tension relates to a *school district's responsibility to employ certificated personnel* who can address the linguistic and academic needs of immigrant students. In the U.S. District Court, Eastern District of New York decisions of August 22, 1977 and January 10, 1978, and in the case of *Elis Cintron et al. v. Brentwood Union Free School District et al.*, the court ordered the district to develop and implement instructional programs for LDI students. While the district was never found in noncompliance with Title VI of the Civil Rights Act, the district was facing decreased enrollment with an increase of LDI students. The district was faced with the issue of what criteria to use to retain certificated personnel—senority/tenure or educational necessity of its students. In its finding, the court based its decision on the educational necessity of its students, and requested the district to expand its best efforts in hiring sufficiently qualified and experienced personnel to staff the bilingual education programs in the district. The court also declared (Cintron v. Brentwood, 1978): "The goal is instruction by competent bilingual teachers in the subject matter of the curriculum while at the same time teaching non-English speaking children the English language" (p. 64).

The opinions issued by the California Attorney General on January 23, 1976 (Opinion No. CV 74–250) and on February 15, 1978 (Opinion No. CV 76–37) also support the responsibility of school districts for the educational needs of LDI students. In his first opinion, the Attorney General ruled that a school district with a bilingual education program may retain junior employees who have the competency to teach bilingually and terminate senior employees lacking such competency, pursuant to the Education Code, Section 13447. In his second opinion, the Attorney General reaffirmed his opinion of 1976. The main issue addressed in both *Cintron v. Brentwood* and the California Attorney General's opinions is the responsibility of districts to employ competent and skilled certificated personnel who can implement effective programs to meet the linguistic and academic needs of its schools/communities.

The fourth area of tension concerns the *use of the student's native language for academic instruction.* A number of court decisions, resting upon federal statutes implementing Title VI of the Civil Rights Act of 1964, the Equal Educational Opportunity Act of 1974, as well as the Lau Task Force Remedies, have required school districts to use the student's native language as part of the instructional program provided to LDI students. The findings of the following court cases support bilingual instruction for LDI students.

- *United States v. Texas*, U.S. Court of Appeals, Fifth Circuit, 342 F. Supp. 24 (Ed.D. Tex., 1971).

- *Serna v. Portales Municipal Schools*, U.S. Court of Appeals, Tenth Circuit, 499 F. 2nd. 1147 (10th Cir. 1974).

- *Aspira v. Board of Education of New York City*, U.S. Court of Appeals, New York, Consent Decree, 72 Cir. 4002 (S.D.N.Y., August 29, 1974).

- *Morales v. Shannon*, U.S. Court of Appeals, Fifth Circuit, 423 U.S. 1034 (1976).

- *Rios v. Read*, 480 F. Supp. 14 (E.D.N.Y., 1978).

- *U.S. v. State of Texas*, U.S. District Court for the District of Texas, Tyler Division, Civil Action No. 5281 (January 9, 1981).

- *Keyes v. Denver School District*, 576 F. Supp. 1503 (D Colorado, 1983).

In the *Keyes v. Denver* (1983) case, parents and educators filed suit against the Denver public school system to remedy the lack of appropriate education for LDI children. The court in its findings called for the Denver public school system to not only use a bilingual approach to both recruit teachers (having the primary language, culture, and methodology skills to educate limited English–proficient students), but also to monitor the success of LDI students once they exited a bilingual program. In addition, the district was required to evaluate the quality of services provided to LDI students to enable them to compete academically with native English speaking students. Thus, the courts have required that school districts take affirmative action in the form of instructional programs to improve the quality of services provided to LDI students.

The fifth tension focuses on the *responsibility for fiscal allocation and resources* to provide instructional services to LDI students. Many school districts faced with fiscal constraints due to the changing characteristics of their school communities—declining student enrollment, a decrease in state education aid, rising opposition from local taxpayers who resist growing school budgets, and collective bargaining—have sought relief from state and federal statutes requiring services to linguistically diverse and immigrant students. With the passage of Proposition 13 in California in 1978, the U.S. Office for Civil Rights issued the following response to the California Superintendent of Schools (Tatel, 1978):

Clearly school districts must continue to provide bilingual education programs to all children eligible under the Lau Guidelines to receive such services. Therefore, bilingual teachers must be made available in sufficient numbers to allow the school district to meet its obligations under Lau. While we understand fully the economic crunch facing California school districts, the absence of funds cannot justify a failure to comply with Title VI (p. 2).

In its request for districts' instructional services under the *Lau* decision, the U.S. Office for Civil Rights saw the solution to appropriate services as the reallocation of A.D.A. (Average Daily Attendance) funds generated by linguistically diverse students, over a period of one to five years, in a manner that will impact positively on the implementation of programs for these students. Thus, under the *Lau v. Nichols* decision, the reallocation of existing fiscal and program resources is an implied practice.

The sixth tension is the *challenge of the legal status of the Lau Task Force Remedies*. As early as 1978 a number of school districts and educational associations in the nation questioned the U.S. Office for Civil Rights (OCR) in its enforcement of the Lau Task Force Remedies. While the U.S. OCR presented the Lau Remedies of July 1975 as guidelines to be followed for meeting *Lau* compliance, districts challenged these guidelines. It should be noted that the U.S. OCR noncompliance letters to school districts did specify to the districts that they had the option not to follow the Lau Remedies. The only condition given is that the district provide educational services equal to or better than those proposed in the Lau Remedies.

In 1978, in the court case of *Northwest Arctic School District et al. v. Joseph A. Califano et al.* (1978), the issue of the Lau Remedies was raised by the State of Alaska. The state argued that the Lau Remedies lacked the "force of law" and would not develop a Lau Compliance plan. The U.S. Department of HEW argued the rights of LDI students to equal educational opportunity under Title VI of the Civil Rights Act of 1964. In the settlement agreement, the State of Alaska agreed to comply with the *Lau* decision, and the U.S. Department of HEW agreed to publish the Lau Task Force Remedies in the Federal Register. On August 5, 1980, the Department of Education published the Proposed Title VI Bilingual Education (Lau) Rules. A seventy-five-day public comment period for citizen input was afforded through six public hearings across the nation. However, with a change in government on November 1980, the Reagan administration, under its policy to reduce federal regulations, announced on February 2, 1981, the withdrawal of the proposed bilingual education policies. Secretary of Education Terrel H. Bell, in a press release, stated (U.S. Office of Education, 1981):

I take this action for many reasons. The policies are harsh, inflexible, burdensome, unworkable, and incredible costly. The rules are fiercely opposed by many, supported by few. All these are sufficient reasons for withdrawing the proposed bilingual policies. There is no quicker way to kill a civil rights law than to enforce it with heavy handed misdirection and I am sworn to uphold the law, not to kill it (p. 2).

Because the proposed Title VI Bilingual Education (Lau) Rules were not published, since 1981 the U.S. Department of Education has proposed a more flexible role in evaluating school districts' plans to eliminate Title VI Civil Rights Act (CRA) violations resulting from the "exclusion of students whose English is limited" policy.

The seventh tension addresses the push to *replace the Lau Task Force Remedies with a more flexible policy*. With the withdrawal of the Title VI Notice of Proposed Rulemaking in August 5, 1980, Secretary Bell emphasized that school districts be given latitude in devising and implementing special programs of instruction to meet the needs of LDI students. This new policy approach by the U.S. Department of Education led the U.S. Office for Civil Rights to use a three-part test of school districts' compliance with the Title VI of the CRA of 1964 requirements. This three-part test to determine a school district's obligation in educating LDI students is based on the court case of *Castañeda v. Pickard* (648 F. 2nd. 989 [5th Circuit], 1981).

The first requirement under *Castañeda* is for school districts to demonstrate that LDI students are being provided with programs based on sound educational theory and principles. The court's second inquiry would be whether the program practices actually used by the school system are being implemented effectively with adequate resources. A third and final area of inquiry is triggered only upon a positive finding in the first two areas. It calls for determining whether the school district has persisted in maintaining the same approach over time when it is evident that it is failing. Although the *Castañeda* court case makes it clear that there is not an affirmative obligation to implement a bilingual program as such, the educational deficits suffered by delaying substantive instruction to LDI students cannot be ignored. The court stated (*Castañeda v. Pickard*, 1981):

We understand 1703(f) to impose on educational agencies not only an obligation to overcome the direct obstacle to learning which the language barrier itself poses, but also a duty to provide limited English speaking ability students with assistance in other areas of the curriculum where their equal participation may be impaired because of deficits incurred during participation in an agency's language remediation program (p. 1011).

The eighth tension addresses *services to undocumented children.* In 1975, the Texas Education Code was amended to bar the use of state funds for the education of undocumented children. Local school districts could either bar undocumented students entirely or admit them to public school upon payment of a tuition charge. The Tyler Independent School District implemented the Education Code by requiring undocumented children to pay a tuition charge of $1,000 per year, thus effectively barring them from the school system.

A suit was filed on behalf of the undocumented children claiming that their exclusion from public school violated the Supremacy Clause, the Equal Protection Clause, and the Due Process Clause of the United States Constitution. The Supremacy Clause precludes state laws that interfere with the accomplishment of federal objectives. The United States District Court agreed that state efforts to impose what amounted to punishment upon the undocumented conflicted with a comprehensive federal scheme for immigration and naturalization. Therefore, it held that the state law was invalid. The Court also held that the Texas School Code exclusion violated equal protection because the discrimination embodied in the law was not supported by a rational basis. Texas then took the case before the Supreme Court. On June 15, 1982, the United States Supreme Court in the case of *Plyer v. Doe* (50 Law Week 4650) held that undocumented children cannot be denied a free public education because such a denial would violate their constitutional rights of equal protection. Because *Plyer* is a decision of the United States Supreme Court, it is binding on all school districts in all states. The Court in *Plyer v. Doe* stated that the denial of education to some isolated group of children poses an affront to the Equal Protection Clause of the 14th Amendment. Under *Plyer v. Doe,* a school district cannot distinguish between citizens and non-citizens, but can require proof of residency in the community. Court cases that have addressed this issue include: (1) *Martinez v. Bynum,* 461 U.S. 321 (1983); (2) *Horton v. Marshall Public Schools,* 769 F. 2nd 1323 (8th Cir. 1985); and (3) *Byrd v. Livington School District,* 674 F. Supp. 225 (E.D. Texas 1987). And in the wake of the passage of Proposition 187 in California, which excludes undocumented children from public school attendence, a number of federal court cases have challenged the constitutionality of such State legislation.

The ninth tension focuses on *State failure to provide LDI students with equal educational opportunity.* In the State of Texas, a suit was filed in June 1975 at the request of the G.I. Forum and the League of United Latin American Citizens. In this suit, the plaintiffs claimed that Mexican-American students were being denied equal educational opportunities by the State of Texas as required by federal statutes. The plaintiffs also included charges of violations under the equal protection clause of the 14th Amendment and Section 1703 5(f) and 1703(b) of the Equal Educational Opportunities Act of 1974.

After reviewing the evidence and testimony presented, in the case of *U.S. v. State of Texas et al.,* U.S. District Court, Eastern District of Texas, Tyler Division, the court's finding under Civil Action No. 5281, signed in January

9, 1981, declared the State of Texas had demonstrated pervasive, system-wide discrimination against Mexican American children in the field of education. The court (*U.S. v. State of Texas*, 1981)

found that Mexican Americans in Texas have been subjected to de jure discrimination by the defendants, the State of Texas and the Texas Education Agency, in violation of the Equal Protection Clause of the Fourteenth Amendment. Accordingly, the learning difficulties of Mexican American students attributable to defendants' actions must be redressed, and the remaining vestiges of past discrimination must be eradicated (p. 428).

As part of its ruling, the court requested that the State of Texas develop a comprehensive plan for K–12 that would provide equal educational opportunity and the provision of bilingual instruction to all Mexican American students who were English-proficient limited and attended Texas public schools. While the *U.S. v. State of Texas* court decision applies only to Texas and the Mexican-American student, the legal basis of the decision is consistent with the principle of equal educational opportunity for linguistically diverse and immigrant students.

The tenth tension questions the *responsibility of a state in supervising school districts to ensure educational services*. Guidance on this issue is found in the case of Idaho Migrant Council v. Board of Education (647 F. 2nd. 69 [9th Cicuit] 1981), brought by LEP students against the Idaho Department of Education, State Board of Education, and Superintendent of Public Instruction for failing to ensure the equal educational opportunities of LEP students. In this case, the appellate court said that the Equal Educational Opportunity Act of 1974, and Title VI of the Civil Rights Act of 1964, requires state education agencies to supervise local school districts to ensure that needs of students with limited English proficiency are addressed.

The court remanded the case to the district court to determine whether federal requirements were being met. The court determined the obligation of state education agencies, based on their contractual agreement with the U.S. government, to comply with requirements outlined in the Equal Education Opportunity Act and other federal and state statutes. In other court cases, such as in *Debra P. v. Turlington* (644 F. 2nd. 397 [5th Circuit], 1981), using the Equal Educational Opportunity Act, the State of Florida was held responsible to enforce federal mandates. In *Debra*, the State of Florida could neither impose nor permit a testing scheme that unfairly impacted upon minority students. Using Title VI of the Civil Rights Act of 1964, another court found the California State Education Agency (SEA) responsible to remedy discriminatory testing practices by local officials in *Larry P. v. Riles* (495 F. Supp. 926 [N.D., Ca.], 1979).

Thus, as a matter of federal law, every SEA must take responsibility for ensuring civil rights compliance by local officials. A state department of education must monitor and require corrective action when violations are found. In a consent decree between the State of Florida and META (Case No. 90–1913 CIV [S.D. Fla.], 1990), the state of Florida was required to follow the spirit of the law and guaranteed the equal access of linguistically diverse immigrant students to state and federal categorical programs.

The eleventh tension calls for *monetary damages if knowingly they violate the civil rights of students.* The Constitution and laws, both federal and state, define the constitutional and civil rights of the students. Under the court case of *Wood v. Strickland* (420 U.S., 308, J. 43 L. Ed., 2nd. 214, 1975), the Supreme Court held that school officials who violate the civil rights of students and SEA officials who fail to prevent violations by local educational officials can be personally liable for monetary damages. Thus, school officials who know or should know that they are violating students' constitutional rights are personally liable.

The twelfth tension concerns the *special education needs of linguistically diverse students.* While LDI students have the right to bilingual special education services, a significant discrepancy exists between policy and practice. The rights of LDI and limited English–proficient students that have a handicapping condition are protected by federal laws, namely, the Education of the Handicapped Act (20 U.S.C. 1401 et seq.), Section 504 of the Rehabilitation Act of 1973 and Education of the Handicapped Act Admendments of 1990 (U.S.C., Sections 1400–1485), and the Individuals with Disabilities Education Act (29 U.S.C. 794). These laws secure the rights of LDI students to receive proper assessment, treatment, staffing, parent participation, due process, and evaluation of services. The following court cases established appropriate special education testing and programs for LDI students: (1) *Covarrubias v. San Diego Unified*, No. 70–394T (S.D. Cal, February 1971); (2) *Larry P. v. Riles*, 502 F 2d 963 (9th Cir. 1974); (3) *Jose P. v. Amback*, 3 EHLR 551 (E.D.N.Y. 1979); and (4) *Y.S. v. School District of Philadelphia*, C.A. 85–6924 (E.D.P.A. 1986).

The thirteenth tension questions what law to follow when *federal and state policies are incompatible.* School districts often take the position that their state law does not require that special programs be provided to LDI or linguistically diverse students. Thus, federal policy should not be followed. When incompatibility between state and federal regulations exists for meeting the linguistic and academic needs of immigrant students, the following guideline is offered to address that problem (Hiller, 1979):

Where federal law governing the duties of school districts to limited English speakers confers additional rights and imposes additional obligations upon the school districts, the federal law should be followed. However, where compliance with State law also fulfills the federal obligations, adherence to State law will be satisfactory. Only where there is a positive conflict between federal and state law, and only where the effect of adhering to a particular State law mandate compromises or hinders the federal law, should the State law be eschewed (pp. 4–5).

In summation, before 1954, "the separate but equal" doctrine governed our nation. Since this period our nation has begun to implement the democratic principles of "equal opportunity and justice for all." The overview of the thirteen areas of legal tension serve to document the resistance of our educational and political institutions to provide linguistically diverse and immigrant students with the right to their language and culture. Behind the resistance to provide comprehensible, meaningful and culturally-based instruction to bicultural students are sociocultural conditions which contribute to racism, nativism, and xenophobia when bicultural communities or persons choose to resist assimilation to the dominant culture and maintain their own culture and language. The recent passage of Proposition 187 in California provides a vivid example of the current wave of intolerance at work.

FACTORS THAT CONTRIBUTE TO RACISM, NATIVISM, AND XENOPHOBIA

The research on prejudice and racism identifies sociocultural factors that contribute to racism, nativism, and xenophobia (Allport, 1979; Triandis, 1988; Yans-McLaughlin, 1990). A brief description of these factors can shed some light on the fears that the dominant culture exhibits toward bilingual-bicultural education and cultural and structural integration.

Increasing Heterogeneity of the Society

As the cultural and linguistic diversity of society increases and differences of life-styles become more apparent, the dominant culture begins to internalize that its values and behaviors are being questioned. This threat gives rise to social distinctions and conditions of distrust. The clash of ideologies and cultural differences creates a condition of conflict and preferred social characteristics that are used to dictate preferred behavior that gives rise to prejudice and discrimination (Allport, 1979; Giroux, 1992). According to the 1990 U.S. Census, five states in our nation have the majority of linguistically and culturally diverse immigrants, namely, California, New York, Florida, Texas, and New Jersey, with California having approximately forty-four percent of all new immigrants. In these five states heterogeneity will be of greatest concern. In California the workforce in the next decade is predicted to be eighty percent Latino and Asian, and is replacing a white workforce (California School Board Association, 1992). The federal response to the influx of linguistically diverse immigrants in the 1980s was the passage of the Immigration Reform and Control Act (1986). This legislation established criteria as to who is acceptable to become a legal resident and who should be deported. Furthermore, school districts in the border regions of the nation in the 1990s have been raided by the immigration agents to reduce the number of immigrant children to be educated. A person of color only needs to drive through the various border patrol monitoring stations on the highways of America to experience racial and cultural prejudice. Heterogeneity in a society that values Anglo-conformity will no doubt experience cultural and social conflict as a result of the changing labor workforce that will demand social justice.

Vertical Mobility

When culturally and linguistically diverse persons begin to have access to social mobility, prejudice and discrimination serve to regulate access to one's social status. Allport (1979) states that "It is not a person's present status in society that is important. It is rather the shifting of his/her status upward or downward that regulates prejudice" (p. 223). Social mobility becomes an important variable that affects access to positions of influence and power. Portes and Rumbaut (1990) speak to the issue of immigrants' occupational and economic adaptation as a means to "making it in America" (p. 57). While linguistically and culturally diverse immigrant arrivals since 1980 reflect a wide diversity of occupational skills (including self-employment) through hard work, persistence, and material survival, many succeed and become educated. As immigrants become educated they begin to have access to positions at the top of the social pyramid through their self-employment ventures. This not only serves as an indicator of economic self-reliance, but also as a potential means of upward vertical mobility. Yet, the dominant society counteracts the access to vertical mobility of bicultural immigrants by frequently discriminating against them in the labor market and excluding them from employment or by providing access only to the least attractive jobs (Portes & Rumbaut, 1990). What begins as economic survival, in order to make it in society, becomes groups (that are discriminated against) pooling their resources, forming credit associations and cooperative organizations to provide for mutual support. Thus, the economic self-reliance of bicultural immigrants against racism provides them with access to social mobility.

Effects of Rapid Social Changes on the Job Market

As our economy is transformed through new technologies, rapid social change accelerates prejudice during times of crisis. This is evident in times of economic problems when the feelings of nativism take the form of discrimination toward immigrants. When our economy is unproductive, the media seeks to blame the undocumented immigrant who is said to be taking the jobs of Americans. This behavior occurs when people perceive social and economic disruptions in their lives (Allport, 1979; Portes & Borocoz, 1989). Headlines in newspapers often reflect the sentiment of one that read "Illegal Immigration Hurts State" (Marelius, 1993).

Americans historically have had conflicting feelings about bicultural immigrants. On the one hand they are proud of their immigrant heritage, and on the other they feel threatened by linguistically and cultural diverse immigrants. Marelius, in an article in the *San Diego Union Tribune* dated August 19, 1993, states, "the xenophobic aspects of this ambivalent feeling are coming to fore; particularly fueled by the recession" (p. 1). Furthermore, one finds a correlation between public attitudes and the condition of the state's economy. Tolerance is high during an robust economy, while hateful feelings permeate during an economic recession. Often, the linguistically diverse immigrant becomes the scapegoat for explaining economic problems. The political response is to militarize the 2,000-mile common border with Mexico and build a "Berlin Wall" at the border of our nation to prevent immigrants from entering our democracy, rather than addressing the failure of our educational and social infrastructure to respond to the economic shifts and technological changes of our economy and economic interdependence with other nations.

Ignorance and Barriers to Communication

Knowledge of other cultures derived through free communication is a rule correlated with lessened hostility and prejudice. When the opposite is present, ignorance contributes to rumor, suspicion, and stereotype. This becomes pronounced when the dominant culture perceives a bicultural person as being different culturally and linguistically, and as a threat to their social reality (Allport, 1979). Prejudice, xenophobia, and discrimination are most visible in the way languages other than English are valued in the United States. Language marks personal differences. When social norms require language conformity (English) and promote a selection process that favors those that "look American" and "sound American," social prejudice and racism governs human behavior (Katz & Taylor, 1992). Evidence of this behavior is frequently found in our daily newspapers. For example, the *Wall Street Journal* of November 7, 1989 reported that a Filipino nurse filed suit against the hospital where she worked, charging the hospital with discrimination for limiting her right to speak her language during her working hours and also during her break. The research on this theme (Allport, 1979; Katz & Taylor, 1992; Pettigrew, 1989) suggests that knowledge of linguistically and culturally diverse immigrant communities derived through free communication and social contact is highly correlated with lessened hostility and prejudice.

Size and Density of the Cultural Group

Growing density of an ethnic or linguistic group triggers manifest and latent prejudice. As the dominant culture perceives a culturally different community as growing in a sizable number, such growth is menacing and conflicting. In the early 1990s, immigrants entered the nation at a rate of 1,130,000 per year (U.S. Census Bureau, 1992) and forty-one percent of these were non-European immigrants. Historically our nation has welcomed bicultural immigrants, yet today this practice is being questioned and seen as a difficult policy to continue, for they are becoming a sizable group that detracts resources from our economy. McCarthy (1983) and Yans-McLaughlin (1990) assert that we need to decide to let current and future immigrants make it on their own—a decision which may have little effect on most immigrants but could increase the potential for an underclass among the most needy—or we decide to facilitate the adjustment process by providing the necessary services and increasing our taxes. To decide on the latter, they point to the risk of fostering resentment and conflict among the native-born poor who question why, in the time of economic trouble, biculturally and linguistically diverse immigrants are getting special help. Additionally, as immigrant communities increase in size and density, prejudice takes the form of zoning practices that serve as a policy for social segregation by language, culture, life-style, and income. This leads to many ethnically diverse communities becoming a community within a community. Segregation becomes the norm, and low educational attainment and earnings between linguistically diverse immigrant communities and the white community becomes the expected way of life (Allport, 1979; Orfield, 1988; Yans-McLaughlin 1990).

Direct Competition and Realistic Conflict

As subordinate cultural group members take on the jobs least desired in a community and become residents of the community, the threat of taking away the "good jobs" of the community increases. Their willingness to work long hours for minimal wages and under poor conditions become attributes of suspicion and realistic conflict. The dominant culture counteracts by initiating rumors that linguistically diverse immigrants do not want to learn English, abuse the health services of the community, don't pay taxes, increase crime in the community, and do not desire to assimilate. According to Allport (1979) and Portes and Rumbaut (1990), prejudice contaminates the issue of social justice, equal opportunity, and the core of the real problem—racism.

There are at least two ways to increase direct competition. The first is via the salaried professional/managerial route. The second is through the hard work, skills, motivation, knowledge, and resources that bicultural immigrants bring to the workplace. Initially, they encounter racism because of their language and lack of a job track record. Yet through time and understanding of the economy they become equally competitive. Racism in response to direct competition can take the form of discriminatory political governmental policies, conditions placed upon the labor market, the use of criteria for employment that excludes equal access to jobs, preferential hiring, and wage differentials.

Exploitative Advantage

The person or institution that controls the means of production dictates the wages that linguistically diverse and immigrant persons will receive as they struggle to find work in order to eat and survive in a new social environment. Exploitative advantage is seen when immigrant farm workers accept work for low wages and in the worst conditions. Because of their legal status, they are at the legal and economic mercy of the grower. This factor underscores the perception that, in order to achieve economic or social gains, prejudice is often propagated by those in power and in control of resources (Allport, 1979; Mc-Carthy, 1983). Seventy percent of the nation's culturally and linguistically diverse immigrants come from Asia and Latin America. These immigrants for the most part are young, energetic, have limited proficiency in English, and are eager to find work. Because a large number of linguistically diverse immigrants, especially the first generation, are concentrated in low-skill, low-wage jobs in the service and manufacturing sector, their presence is used to depress wages. This action is rationalized as an efficient way to use cheap labor in order to keep the nation's low-wage industries from going out of business or moving to another country (McCarthy, 1983). Government sanctions these behaviors as necessary to keep the economy on track and competitive. Furthermore, these newly arrived immigrants are accused of being intensive users of such public services as health care, welfare, and job training and are seen as a social burden instead of productive, hard-working, and contributing members of our communities. Racism becomes pronounced with the stated notion that our present immigration policy raises important questions about the kind of "capital stock" (McCarthy, 1983, p. 8) that is best suited for our labor force that is increasingly composed of immigrants and their offspring.

Social Regulation of Aggression

When social tensions exist and there is a need for a safety-valve, societies informally encourage the open expression of hostility toward certain groups. In the case of bicultural communities, immigrant bashing is a safety valve for communities, government, and industry to redirect social attention of the failure of social and economic policy (Allport, 1979). Starr (1993) writes on the blaming of the linguistically diverse immigrant for the conditions of the economy,

the state's current malaise cannot be blamed on the young busboy, far from home, washing dishes late into the night in an upscale restaurant on the Westside. Indeed, in the vast majority of instances, recent [immigrants] are doing the work that others—even those on welfare—will not do, yet needs to be done" (p. M6).

Why then in an open, democratic society that promotes liberty and justice is the government arming its borders against persons struggling to improve their lives? Yanking students from classrooms? Working to pass legislation that requires people of color to carry an identification card to prove residency? Racism is present in the paranoia that blames others for problems that government and citizens cannot confront directly, yet exploits the same people that work in low-paying jobs in factories and agricultural fields.

Cultural Devices to Ensure Loyalty

Cultural devices to ensure loyalty constitute part of a social mechanism that is used to pressure ethnically and linguistically diverse people to assimilate and become good Americans. This phenomenon focuses on the use of prejudice as a device to pressure linguistically diverse persons to feel shame and guilt about practicing their traditions and openly using their home language. To be a good American is to reject one's primary language and accept the language of the dominant culture. In the case of a maintenance bilingual policy, such policy is often discussed as un-American and working against the solidarity of the society. Furthermore, this point of view is shared by many Americans that view bilingual language policy as a misdirected public policy that has been created by the federal government, at the interest of special interest groups (Allport, 1979; Crawford, 1992). These views are part of a culturally monolithic system that rejects biculturalism and fears others who uphold their identity and culture. Racism is promoted by the proponents who view biculturalism, bilingualism, and multiculturalism as dangerous, conflicting, and as the ungluing of the melting pot as a form of disunity. Only those that speak the English language and espouse Anglo-conformity values and political loyalty to the United States are considered truly American.

Differences in the Ideology of Cultural Pluralism and Assimilation

In the United States two primary language ideologies exist, the "English Only" (assimilationist) and the "English Plus" (cultural pluralism) (Crawford, 1992). The assimilationists take the position that educating children in the language and traditions of the ethnic group, different from preferred American culture, is dysfunctional and works against the fabric of American values. The cultural pluralists take the opposite perspective, that in a democracy the right to one's language and culture is a fundamental constitutional right and social principle. "Each culture has distinctive contributions to make, and while divergent customs and languages seem strange, they are stimulating, instructive, and beneficial to society" (Allport, 1979, p. 239). Crawford (1992) and Pettigrew (1989) speak of the assimilationist perspective as serving the interests of the dominant society. The assimilationist equates equality with access to the resources of society by becoming Americanized and rejecting one's cultural self-determination. The pluralist equates cultural pluralism as a system of government that accepts and values cultural diversity and structural incorporation to social access and means of production. Thus, racism is promoted by the notion that if an immigrant values his/her identity and insists on rights to cultural pluralism, he/she is viewed as rejecting democracy and working to divide the country into cultural chaos.

These sociocultural factors serve to illustrate the hegemonic modes of resistance which exist toward linguistically and ethnically diverse bicultural communities in the United States. While society has taken significant steps in establishing the principles of equal opportunity, equal access, and equal benefits, the practice of these principles are at best assimilationist in application. Cultural and linguistic diversity has only begun to be tolerated given a national policy of social and cultural assimilation that denies structural access to the institutions of our democratic society. Thus, the need for socially oriented policy that provides for social-political, economic, and educational access to immigrant communities is imperative if we are to survive as a participatory democracy.

POLICY ADDRESSING CULTURAL AND STRUCTURAL ACCESS

Both in absolute number and in proportion, linguistically and ethnically diverse communities will continue to increase in our nation. More than a hundred nations have sent immigrants to the United States. In the school context, in 1976, it was estimated that there were 2,520,000 limited English–speaking immigrant students in the United States. Projections for the year 2000 point to an increase to 3,400,000—a growth rate of fifteen percent per decade. Furthermore, in the California economy it is predicted that more than eighty percent of the labor force growth in the next decade will be Latinos and Asians who will need to be prepared for the future workforce (U.S. Census Bureau, 1991).

Our society faces a complexity of social, economic, and political problems related to equity in its attempt to operationalize the basic principles of the Constitution and the belief system that calls for liberty and justice for all. In order to provide economic and cultural access to ethnically and linguistically diverse communities, educational institutions must operationalize policies that empower bicultural communities. Such policies must be part of the guiding principles of any school, higher educational system, and social institution that is committed to social justice, equal opportunity, equal access, and equal benefits. The claim of providing equal educational opportunity requires that action in the form of policy and practices be in place to democratize public education.

What conditions are necessary for social and language policy in the United States to respect and nurture the development of linguistically and ethnically diverse immigrants? Three conditions at least are necessary: (1) government

promotes an additive multicultural policy that views linguistically and ethnically diverse immigrants as having equal rights (equality of results); (2) policy
on equal rights supports multilingualism and social integration in the achievement of social justice; and (3) institutional support for assuring equal rights to
linguistically and ethnically diverse immigrants is arranged and operationalized (equality of process).

Equality of result (macrojustice) and equality of process (microjustice) are
necessary conditions for the support of an additive multicultural policy and to
prevent economic exploitation, the denial of social rights, and the oppression
of the human condition. Macrojustice through equality of result provides the
rationale for resources to be used to overcome social injustices due to socioeconomic, linguistic, cultural, and handicapping (physical) differences, while
microjustice through equality of process assures the accountability of the available resources to directly empower the human condition. Among the policies
that must be considered and acted upon are the following:

- A maintenance bilingual language policy must be in place if all students are to have
  cultural and structural access. This means that schools should provide all children,
  and specifically immigrant children, with the right to retain their own culture and
  language and become biliterate.

- Social and educational policy must value and support the emerging lifestyles of immigrant communities and prepare bicultural youth to cope with the world of work
  and the society of the twenty-first century.

- Social and educational institutions must advance the development of multicultural
  values and multilingual competence to prepare youth and communities to cope with
  the social tensions and communication needs of our culturally diverse society.

- Social and educational institutions must recognize and support cultural and linguistic
  uniqueness in the development of youth to be socially literate and responsible for
  the maintenance of democratic principles.

- The organizational structure of schools and institutions of higher education must
  incorporate trained, competent and credentialed bicultural personnel that guide
  youth to achieve academically and to attain the necessary skills to enter careers and/
  or higher education.

- Educational institutions must implement strategic planning and reallocation of resources as a process of social planning. The quality of schooling provided to immigrant and native-born students is largely driven by the capacity of the local
  communities. The limitation of human and fiscal resources often results from a lack
  of aggressive reallocation of resources and failure to have strategic planning to address staffing and programming needs of all students.

- Immigrant students must have opportunities to succeed through a core curricula that
  serves to develop their full potential rather than new categorical programs that promote compensatory and remedial education.

- Educational institutions must view the bicultural experiences of the immigrant child not as deficits, but as experiences to be valued and used to develop concepts, literacy skills, and critical thinking.

- Schools must use diagnostic and assessment approaches as empowering tools for identifying the strengths and cognitive needs of students in order to enrich their cognitive skills and to develop their intellect.
- It is important that teachers recognize and use different learning modalities that enable bicultural students to learn through different approaches and learning styles.
- Schools must provide different types of curricular programs, while maintaining the high standards and expectations, and a bilingual/multicultural core curricula to address the diverse academic and linguistic development of students.
- School districts must incorporate and connect parents to the education of their children and school community through status equalization approaches that value and use the talents of parents.
- The public sector must prepare and incorporate immigrant communities into the informational work force in order to provide for productive human capital and active participants in the world economy.

In the face of egalitarian ideology, persisting educational practices, economic, and political inequalities among different ethnically and linguistically diverse segments of society suggest the need to reexamine language, educational, and social policy (Kozol, 1992). We face the commitment to reexamine the values of social justice and democratic schooling, and their implications for the social, economic, political, and educational institutions of our society. This reexamination of values must encourage a renaissance of social justice in this country as we press forward to actualize equality, freedom, and democratic principles. Our search for answers and solutions to the problems facing our culturally and linguistically diverse society has profound implications within and across all societal sectors, both structurally and ideologically (Giroux, 1992; McDonnel & Hill, 1993; Triandis, 1988).

REFERENCES

Allport, G. (1979). *The nature of prejudice*. Reading, MA: Addison-Wesley.
Alvarez v. Lemon Grove School District, Superior Court of the State of California, Writ of Mandate No. 66625, March 30, 1931.
Aspira v. Board of Education of New York City, U.S. Court of Appeals, New York, Consent Decree, 72 Cir. 4002 (S.D.N.Y., August 29, 1974).
Brown v. Board of Education of Topeka, Kansas, 347 U.G.S. 483, (1954).
California School Board Association. (1992). *Federal immigration policy and its impact on the public schools*. Sacramento, CA.
Castañeda v. Pickard, 648 F. 2nd. 989 (5th Circuit, 1981).
Cintron, E., et al. v. Brentwood Union Free School District et al., 455 F Supp. 57 (1978).
Crawford, J. (ed.). (1992). *Language loyalties*. Chicago, IL: The University of Chicago Press.

252   Culture and Difference

Debra P. v. Turlington, 644 F. 2nd. 397 (5th Circuit, 1981).

Department of HEW, May 25, 1970 Memorandum, 35 Fed. Reg. 11595, (1970).

Education of the Handicapped Act, 20 U.S.C. 1401 et seq.

Espinosa, R. & A. Ochoa. (1992). *The attainment of California youth*. San Diego, CA: SDSU Policy Studies Department.

Equal Educational Opportunity Act of 1974, 20 U.S.C. 1703 (f).

Feinberg, W. & J. F. Soltis. (1992). *School and society*. New York, NY: Teachers College Press.

Giroux, H. A. (1992). "Educational leadership and the crisis of democratic government." *Educational Researcher* (May).

Hernandez v. Texas, 347 U.S. 475 (1954).

Hiller, R. J. (1979). "The rights of language minority students under federal and state laws: Real or imagined conflict?" Paper developed for the Bilingual-Bicultural Office, California State Department of Education, 1979.

Idaho Migrant Council v. Board of Education, 647 F. 2nd. 69 (9th Circuit, 1981).

Individuals with Disabilities Education Act, 29 U.S.C. 794.

Katz, P. A. & D. A. Taylor. (1992). *Eliminating racism: Profiles in controversy*. New York, NY: Plenum Press.

Keyes v. Denver School District, 576 F. Supp. 1503 (Colorado, 1983).

Kozol, J. (1992). *Savage Inequalities*. New York, NY: Harper Perennia.

Larry P. v. Riles, 495 F. Supp. 926 (N.D., Ca. 1979).

Lau v. Nichols, 414 U.S. 563 (1974).

Marelius, J. (1993). "Illegal immigration hurts state." *San Diego Union Tribune* (August 19).

McCarthy, K. F. (1983). *Immigration and California: Issues for the 1980s*. Santa Monica, CA: RAND, publication no. P-6846.

McDonnel, M. L. & T. P. Hill. (1993). *Newcomers in American schools: Meeting the educational needs of immigrant youth*. Santa Monica, CA: RAND.

Mendez v. Westminster School District, 64 F. Supp. 544 (1946); 161 F. 2d. 744 (1947).

Morales v. Shannon, U.S. Court of Appeals, Fifth Circuit, 423 U.S. 1034 (1976).

Northwest Artic School District et al. v. Joseph A. Califano et al. United States District Court for the District of Alaska, No. A-77–216 Civil, September 29, 1978.

Orfield, G. (1988). The growth and concentration of Hispanic enrollment and the future of American education. Presented at National Council of La Raza Conference, Albuquerque, NM, July.

Paulston, C. B. (1975). *Ethnic relations and bilingual education: accounting for contradictory data*. Working papers on bilingualism, No. 6. Ontario, Canada: The Ontario Institute for Studies in Education.

Pettigrew, T. F. (1989). *Modern racism: American black-white relations since the 1960s*. Cambridge, MA: Harvard University Press.

Plessy v. Ferguson, 163 U.S. 537 (1896).

Plyer v. Doe, 50 Law Week 4650 (1982).

Portes, A. & R. G. Rumbaut. (1990). *Immigrant America: A portrait*. Berkeley, CA: University of California Press.

Portes, A. & J. Borocoz. (1989). "Contemporary immigration: Theoretical perspectives on its determinants and modes of incorporation." *International Migration Review, 23* (Fall), pp. 606–630.

Rios v. Read, 480 F. Supp. 14 (E.D.N.Y. 1978).

San Francisco Unified School District. (1975). *Abstract of the Master Plan for Bilingual-Bicultural Education.* Citizens Task Force for Bilingual Education, January 21.

Serna v. Portales Municipal Schools, U.S. Court of Appeals, Tenth Circuit, 499 F. 2nd. 1147 (10th Cir. 1974).

Skuttnab-Kangas, T. (1981). *Bilingualism or not: The education of minorities.* Clevedon, Avon (England): Multilingual Matters.

Spring, J. (1978). *American education.* New York, NY: Longman, Inc.

Starr, K. (1993). "California reverts to its scapegoating ways." *Los Angeles Times* (September 26), pp. M3, M6.

Supreme Court of the State of California, County of San Diego, Petition for Writ of Mandate No. 66625. Roberto Alvarez, a minor, by Juan M. Gonzales, guardian ad. litem. Petitioner versus Lemon Grove School District (February 13, 1931).

Tatel, D. S. (July 1978). *Memorandum.* Director of the U.S. Office for Civil Rights to Dr. Wilson Riles, Superintendent of Schools of California.

Tesconi, C. A., Jr., & E. Hurwitz, Jr. (1974). *Education for whom?* New York, NY: Dodd, Mead and Company.

Title VI of the Civil Rights Act of 1964, 42 U.S.C. 2000c,d.

Triandis, H. C. (1988). "The future of pluralism revisited," in P. A. Katz and D. A. Taylor (eds.), *Eliminating Racism.* New York, NY: Plenum Press.

Rehabilitation Act of 1973 and Education of the Handicapped Act Admendments of 1990 (U.S.C., Sections 1400–1485).

United States v. Texas, U.S. Court of Appeals, Fifth Circuit, 342 F. Supp. 24 (Ed.D. Tex., 1971).

U.S. Census Bureau. (1991). *Current population reports.* Series P-20, No. 455. Washington DC: U.S. Government Printing Office.

U.S. Census Bureau. (1992). *Urban institute, INS statistical yearbook.* U.S.C., Sections 1400–1485; Education of the Handicapped Act Amendments of 1990.

U.S. Office of Education. (February 2, 1981). Press release from Secretary of Education, Dr. Terrel H. Bell.

U.S. v. State of Texas, U.S. District Court, Eastern District of Texas, Tyler Division, Civil Action No. 5281, Pursuant to the Provisions of Rule 52, F.R. CIV. P., January 9, 1981.

Winston, J. A. (1980). *Legal overview of school desegregation, constitutional equal protection theories and federal anti-discriminatory statutes.* Division of Educational Equity, Office of General Counsel, U.S. Department of Education.

Wood v. Strickland, 420 U.S., 308, J. 43 L. Ed., 2nd. 214, 1975.

Yans-McLaughlin, V. (1990). *Immigration reconsidered.* New York, NY: Oxford University Press.

Index

About the Contributors

MAKUNGU M. AKINYELA is an ordained minister in the African Methodist Episcopal Church and received his theological training at the School of Theology in Claremont, California. He is completing his doctoral studies at Emory University in Atlanta, Georgia in Black Theology and Social Change. He is the Coordinator of the Ujamma Family Life Project of the Malcolm X Center for Self-determination in Decatus, Georgia. He is the author of *Conscious Parenting for African American Excellence.*

LOURDES ARGUELLES is Professor of Education at the Claremont Graduate School (Claremont, California) and a psychotherapist working primarily with gays and lesbians of color and people with HIV/AIDS.

ANTONIA DARDER is Associate Professor of Education at the Claremont Graduate School, and is the author of *Culture and Power in the Classroom: A Critical Foundation for Bicultural Education* (Bergin & Garvey, 1991).

DAVID R. DIAZ earned his M.A. in City and Regional Planning at the University of California, Berkeley, and his Ph.D. in the Urban Planning Program at the University of California, Los Angeles. He has held previous positions in private and public sectors and the political arena.

GARRETT DUNCAN is an adjunct faculty member and administrative associate in the Office of Teacher Education, the Claremont Graduate School. He writes and lectures on cultural psychology, critical educational theory, and linguisitics. Previously, Garrett has taught in public middle and high schools in Pomona (southern California), where he was selected, by the Pomona High

School student body, Teacher of the Year (1992). Among his other honors, Garrett has been named a Christa McAuliffe Fellow (1989) and National Science Teacher Fellow (1990), and designated a Distinguished Alumnus of California State Polytechnic University of Pomona (1990).

ALICIA GASPAR DE ALBA is an Assistant Professor at the University of California, Los Angeles in Chicano/a Studies. She is the author of a collection of short fiction, *The Mystery of Survival and Other Stories*, which received the Premio Aztlan for 1994. Gaspar de Alba's literary work focuses on borders of identity, sexuality, and language.

DEENA J. GONZÁLEZ is an Associate Professor and Chair of Chicano Studies at Pomona College in Clarement, California. She is the author of the forthcoming book *Refusing the Favor: The Spanish-Mexican Women of Santa Fe*. Gonzalez's scholarship focuses on the theorizing of Chicana identity and Chicana feminisms.

PETER NIEN-CHU KIANG is Assistant Professor in the Graduate College of Education and American Studies Program at the University of Massachusetts/Boston, where he teaches graduate courses in multicultural education and social studies curriculum design and undergraduate courses in Asian American Studies. He is engaged in a wide range of curriculum, teaching, and policy issues related to immigrants and people of color in both K–12 and higher education. His articles include "Southeast Asian Parent Empowerment: The Challenge of Changing Demographics," which received first prize in the 1990 monograph competition of the Massachusetts Association for Bilingual Education. He is also principal author of the *Asian American Studies Curriculum Resource Guide, Massachusetts K–12*, a collaborative publication of the University of Massachusetts and the Massachusetts Asian American Educators Association.

CHORSWANG NGIN received her B.A. in sociology and Asian studies from Wellesley College, Massachusetts, and her Ph.D. in anthropology at California State University, Los Angeles. She has written on Asian and Asian-American cultures and communities. More recently, her research has been on the theoretical issues of racism, migration, and Asian Americans in California.

ALBERTO M. OCHOA is a Professor in the Department of Policy Studies in Language and Cross-Cultural Education at San Diego State University. Since 1975 he has directed training centers in the areas of bilingual education, desegregation, teacher education, and parent leadership. These centers have received national and state recognition for their educational change focus and staff capacity building models. In the last six years Dr. Ochoa has written and co-authored over fifteen publications on bilingual education, national origin desegregation, student achievement trends, staff development, and educational equity.

ANNE RIVERO is a licensed clinical social worker with Kaiser Permanente in Los Angeles, California. Her clinical work has focused on gay/lesbian identity issues, post-traumatic stress, and sexual abuse victimization.

LUIS J. RODRIGUEZ is a poet, writer, and publisher living in Chicago. Mr. Rodriguez has written two collections of poetry: *Poems across the pavement* and *The concrete river*, and a prose memoir, *Always running, La Vida Loca: Gang days in L.A.* His poems have been published in numerous journals, including *Chiron Review*, the *Los Angeles Times*, *ONTHEBUS*, and *Poetry East*. Mr. Rodriguez is also the publisher of Tía Chucha Press. The recipient of a fellowship from the Lannan Foundation, he has also recieved the Poetry Center Book Award from San Francisco State University and the PEN West/ Josephine Miles award. In addition to his duties with Tía Chucha Press, Mr. Rodriguez conducts poetry workshops in homeless centers in Chicago.

RODOLFO D. TORRES recieved his B.A. in comparative culture from the University of California, Irvine, his M.A. in public policy, and his Ph.D. in an interdisciplinary program in education, policy studies, and political economy from The Claremont Graduate School, Claremont, California. He is an Associate Professor of Public Policy and Administration and Chicano and Latino Studies at California State University, Long Beach. His research centers on the political economy and policy dimensions of racism and inequality, and the global restructuring and changing boundaries of urban life in "postindustrial" society and "postmodern" culture.

VICTOR VALLE is Professor of Journlism at California Polytechnic University, San Luis Obispo. He has written numerous articles on Latino politics and culture, including the Pulitzer Prize-winning series "Southern California's Latino Population" for the *Los Angeles Times*.

DAPHNE C. WIGGINS is a Ph.D. candidate in the Graduate Insitute of Liberal Arts, Emory University, Atlanta, Georgia. Her dissertation is entitled "The Socio-Cultural Determinants of Church Attendance Among African American Women." She is the recipient of the Patricia Roberts Harris Fellowship and a fellow of The Fund For Theological Education. She is also an ordained American Baptist clergywoman, and served as Associate Chaplain at Brown University prior to pursuing doctoral studies.

KENT WONG is Director of the UCLA Center for Labor Research and Education. He teaches Labor Studies and Ethnic Studies at UCLA, and directs an interdisciplinary program in Labor Studies. Mr. Wong worked for six years as staff attorney for the Service Employees International Union, Local #660, representing 40,000 Los Angeles County workers. Mr. Wong is a founder and the National President of the Asian Pacific American Labor Alliance, the first nationwide Asian-American labor organization within the AFL-CIO. He regularly writes articles for various journals and newspapers, and has written chapters on Asian-American labor for several books.